AFFLUENCE AND ANXIETY, AMERICA SINCE 1945

Cover Photo: George W. Gardner

AFFLUENCE and ANXIETY

AMERICA SINCE 1945

Second Edition

CARL N. DEGLER

Stanford University

Carl N. Degler, Editor
American History Series

Scott, Foresman and Company   Glenview, Illinois
Dallas, Texas   Oakland, N.J.   Palo Alto, Cal.   Tucker, Ga.   Brighton, England

To the memory of my mother

Library of Congress Cataloging in Publication Data

Degler, Carl N.
Affluence and anxiety.

(Scott, Foresman American history series)
Includes bibliographies and index.
1. United States — History — 1945–   2. United
States — Foreign relations — 1945–   I. Title.   II. Series.
E839.D44 1975   973.92   75-8591
ISBN: 0-673-07956-2

Affluence and Anxiety: America Since 1945 *is a revision of* Affluence
and Anxiety: 1945/Present.

FOREWORD

This book is one in a series that encompasses the history of the United States from the early days of the Republic to the present. The individual volumes cover specific chronological periods and may be used either separately or in combination. Both this book and the series as a whole are intended to be different from the material covered in the usual survey text.

Customarily a textbook is largely filled with a chronological account of the "essential" facts of the past. Facts and chronology are, it is true, the building stones of historical knowledge, and familiarity with both is essential, but they do not provide the structure of the past by themselves. Rather it is the framework of an era that students must grasp if they are to retain and make sense out of the myriad facts that any book — text or other — throws in their path. By framework, however, we are not suggesting a skeleton or outline, but the unity or essential thrust of the period — in short, its meaning.

Emphasis falls throughout upon explanation of the past. Why did events turn out as they did? What significance did these developments have for subsequent American history? What importance do they have for the present? How does the American experience compare with that of other countries in similar circumstances? How and why did American attitudes and values alter during the period in question?

The organization and some of the less important facts that are to be found in more conventional textbooks are absent from these pages. It is the conviction of the author and the editor of the series that understanding the relationship among events is more important than just memorizing customarily agreed-upon facts. Therefore, some facts have been omitted simply because they do not contribute to an understanding of the structure of the period.

This book has been written for American college students; that is, readers who have some acquaintance with the history of the United States. While the usual effort has been made to clarify and define obscure or unfamiliar terms and persons, a certain basic familiarity with the subject has been taken for granted. No students who have passed successfully through an American high school need worry about their ability to comprehend what appears within these covers, but it is hoped that their understanding of the direction and the causes behind the movements of American history will be enhanced by reading this book.

Carl N. Degler

PREFACE TO THE SECOND EDITION

For a historian to attempt to write a short interpretive history of the last thirty years is a risky business at best, even after he has had the opportunity to revise some of the misjudgments he made previously. Eight years after the First Edition of *Affluence and Anxiety* there are still not many monographs or specialized studies of the years since World War II. Moreover, the events are still so fresh in mind that they cannot easily be placed in perspective. Indeed, the fact that the author actually lived through the period makes it difficult for him to achieve the detachment that traditionally strengthens historians as they seek to recreate the essential past out of the infinite number of available facts. And if writing recent history is risky, attempting to discern meaning is doubly so; yet this book attempts to do just that. Like other volumes in the Scott, Foresman American History Series, *Affluence and Anxiety* seeks to provide some understanding of the period it covers—in this instance, the years since 1945—by organizing the myriad events of those years around a few central themes. The themes in this case are the great prosperity within the United States and the threat of world war from without.

Since this book is intended primarily, though hopefully not exclusively, for college students, much of the history it contains is as unknown to its readers directly as events of the nineteenth century. For that reason essential factual information has been provided in some detail. At the same time, it is equally important that the reader not be innundated with facts and events. Consequently, the book provides an understanding of the direction and thrust of the period, rather than a recital of people and events.

In addition to viewing the events of the period as manifestations of affluence and anxiety, the book takes two approaches that are worth emphasizing here at the outset. One of the revolutionary changes occurring after 1945 was the involvement of the United States with the rest of the world as never before in its history. As a result, this book allots as large a place to foreign affairs as to domestic history. Chapters on international affairs alternate with those on domestic matters. No longer is it possible to tuck away foreign affairs into a chapter at the end, as is often done in books on earlier periods of American history. In this book the Asian revolution of the 1940s is properly as much a part of United States history as the election of Harry Truman.

The second approach that characterizes this book is the effort made in Chapter Six to view recent American cultural, intellectual, and social history as expressions of the two great influences of the years since 1945. Not everything in the wide spectrum of cultural achievement could be included, but hopefully enough has been to allow the reader to gain not only an adequate factual knowledge of the social and cultural developments but also an integrated understanding of their relationship to political and economic history.

For those who have used the First Edition of *Affluence and Anxiety,* it might be useful to point out the principal changes made in the Second Edition. First, the whole text has been gone over carefully, and many changes have been made to bring the book up to date and into conformity with the most recent scholarship, as well as to remove infelicities of style and presentation. Most significantly, the revisionist view of the origins of the Cold War (Chapter One) and of the Cuban missile crisis (Chapter Four) is now considered. Much of the text concerning the Negro Revolution and the Johnson administrations has been rewritten and expanded. A new chapter on the ending of the Johnson years and on the two Nixon administrations has been added to make the book as timely as possible. Chapter Six, the Culture of Affluence and Anxiety, has been entirely rewritten and sections on youth and the counterculture added.

In making these changes the advice and suggestions of a number of people have been valuable. While I cannot identify personally those whose critiques were anonymous, I can thank Peter G. Boyle, Samuel B. Hand, and Michael R. Beschloss for taking the trouble to point out errors in the First Edition, which I trust are now corrected. The Second Edition also profits from advice from my Stanford colleague Barton J. Bernstein on my handling of the origins of the Cold War and from the generally incisive comments of David Ebbitt. Diane Culhane, my editor at Scott, Foresman, has been thorough and thoughtful in suggesting editorial changes in the interest of clarity and precision. Obviously all errors of fact and judgment that persist despite this advice are my responsibility. Vicki Cooper has earned my gratitude for her accurate and swift typing of the revision, as has the Institute of American History at Stanford for its financial aid while I was preparing the revision.

Carl N. Degler

CONTENTS

AFFLUENCE AND ANXIETY, AMERICA SINCE 1945

CHAPTER ONE

ADJUSTING TO A NEW ERA

I N THE YEARS immediately after the Second World War Americans were taken doubly by surprise. Having been highly successful in their global war effort, they confidently believed that the question of peace or war had been settled for the foreseeable future. Had they not worked hard at home and fought bravely abroad to secure peace? Had they not committed themselves unprecedentedly and with almost complete unanimity to a new international organization designed to maintain that peace? Americans were no less certain about their domestic future, though here their optimism gave place to foreboding. They could not shake off the memory of the long, dispiriting Depression from which the nation had emerged only upon the onset of war. Most Americans, of both high and low station, were sure that the prosperity of the war years would not survive the slower economic pace of peace. Accordingly, they braced themselves for another depression.

As events turned out, they were wrong on both counts. In international affairs the nation was almost immediately plunged into a protracted period of agonizing decision making amid constant danger of war, while on the domestic front the prosperity born and nurtured in the hothouse of war took firm root and flourished. Never before in American history had the country been free of a major depression for as long as three decades. For these reasons the thirty years after World War II were, in truth, a period of affluence and anxiety.

The Breakup of the Grand Alliance

The Death of F.D.R. On April 12, 1945, as the Allied armies were knifing into the very vitals of what Hitler had called his "thousand-year Reich," Franklin Roosevelt died of a cerebral hemorrhage in his summer White House at Warm Springs, Georgia. For weeks his friends and intimates had been worried by the devastating physical effects of the severe burdens under which he was laboring, but his death surprised as well as saddened the entire Allied world. It not only saddened but stunned Harry S. Truman, who now assumed the suddenly vacated office.

Four days after he was catapulted into office, the new President wrote a revealing letter to his mother and sister, telling them of his first few hours as President and of the demanding tasks that now confronted him. He had gotten an inkling that something was wrong in the afternoon of April 12, for as he entered the office of his old friend Speaker Sam Rayburn he was told that Steve Early, the President's confidential secretary, wanted to talk with him. Early told him to come to the White House "as quickly and as *quietly*" as possible. Truman literally ran all the way to his office in the Senate to tell his staff that he had been summoned to the White House and that no one was to be told about it. At the White House he was ushered quickly upstairs to Mrs. Roosevelt's study, where she put her arm around his shoulder and said, "Harry, the President is dead." Truman was staggered as never before in his life. "I had hurried to the White House to see the President," he wrote, "and when I arrived, I found I was the President." His most trying task, he went on, was addressing Congress three days later. It went off well, he thought, even though he still felt "almost as scared as I was Thursday when Mrs. R. told me what had happened. Maybe it will come out all right."

Churchill, Truman, and Stalin at Potsdam. *Photo: Courtesy of Imperial War Museum, London*

Seeds of Suspicion. Truman came to the intricate problems of international relations uninformed and unprepared. Since his inauguration as Vice-President over two months earlier, he had seen Roosevelt only twice in private, and at neither of these times nor in Cabinet meetings, Truman later recalled, had he been informed or consulted about the weighty foreign policy decisions then being taken or contemplated.

Already the Grand Alliance which had won the war against Hitler was entering upon its dissolution. For several weeks before the death of F.D.R., Prime Minister Winston S. Churchill had been warning Roosevelt of the differences between the Soviet and Western conceptions of the Polish settlement agreed to at Yalta. As early as March, for example, Churchill was convinced that Stalin would not honor the agreement made at Yalta to permit all political factions to be represented in the new Polish government. Although Roosevelt opposed Churchill's suggestion that a strong protest be lodged with Stalin, on April 1 F.D.R. firmly informed the Russian dictator that the Yalta agreement on Poland could not be ignored by the Soviets. Roosevelt was firm in this instance, but basically he was determined, as he once said, to get along with the U.S.S.R. in the postwar period regardless of the difficulties. He was convinced that an enduring peace depended upon Western and Soviet amity, though he ignored advice given as early as 1944 that the United States share with the Russians the secret work then being done on the development of the atomic bomb. Churchill was more narrowly nationalistic and European in his diplomacy; he thought in terms of spheres of influence and power politics. Consequently he appeared more realistic than F.D.R., who, like the President he had served under during World War I, emphasized international organization and trusted in the liberal belief that most nations wanted peace and order in the world. Roosevelt was convinced that he could cajole and charm the Russian dictator out of his xenophobic suspicions and that the basic interests of the West and the Soviet Union were the same, or at least reconcilable. Since Roosevelt did not outlive the war, it is impossible to know whether he would have changed his mind about the best way to insure peace in the postwar years.

More important than speculations about Roosevelt's attitudes after 1945 is the question whether a different American policy from that which was pursued could have avoided the Cold War, which followed hard upon the cessation of the war against Hitler. In recent years a number of scholars—called "revisionists"—have argued that the causes of the Cold War lay more in the actions of the United States than in those of the Soviet Union. Among the more important revisionists are William Appleman Williams, Joyce and Gabriel Kolko, Walter LaFeber, Lloyd Gardner, and Barton J. Bernstein. Certainly it is true, as we shall see, that even before the war ended some American leaders were fearful of the new power of the Soviet Union and deeply distrustful of its Communist ideology. It is equally certain that some acts of the United States provided a basis for Russian anxieties about the intentions of the United States. The revisionists, however, go further to contend that American hostility toward or pressure upon the Soviet Union stemmed from the need of a capitalist America to keep open the markets of Europe and the world for its industrial and agricultural production. To William Appleman Williams, the seminal writer among the revisionists, this "open door" motivation for American involvement abroad was operative long before the Cold War. Other revisionists, like the Kolkos, go beyond the open door argument, asserting that American policy sought the suppression of socialistic or radical movements in Europe as well. While there can be no doubt that economic considerations played a part in the thinking of American officials in 1945 and after, as they had earlier, the role of economic concerns in shaping foreign policy after 1945 was clearly secondary to considerations of world order—from the American standpoint—and a retention of the predominance in international affairs that victory in the war had brought.

If the economic explanations for the origins of the Cold War have not been widely accepted, a different point made by revisionists certainly does need to be heeded. American policy in these years was primarily self-interested, not altruistic. The differences between the United States and the Soviet Union after the war were several and sometimes profound, but they were not usually those of altruism on the American side and selfishness on the Russian. Rather they were differences between two powerful countries with opposing ideologies and economies, and with quite different internal and external histories and relationships with Europe and Asia. Both were confronted with working out their respective roles in the world after a common victory that left each with unprecedented power and influence.

Although some revisionist historians feel the Soviet occupation and domination of eastern and central Europe was at the expense of the people in that region, others stress the defensive character of the Russian domination. What the revisionists overlook or deny is that Russian power threatened the independence of western Europe as well. Yet, Communist ideology aside for the moment, the great fact of the postwar world was that Russian military power had tipped the traditional balance of power in Europe, thereby threatening the continent and the world. It was, after all, Hitler's threat to western Europe and the balance of power that had brought the United States into Europe in 1941.

On the other hand, both American and western European leaders, we can recognize today, seem to have exaggerated the degree and threat of Soviet military power. Russian land forces in 1945 and 1946 were, to be sure, large in comparison with the armed forces of western Europe. But the Russian economy after four years of occupation and war was probably too weak to have sustained an invasion of the West or a war. What is recognized today was not perceived at the time: Western leaders were mesmerized by what they took to be the Red Army's power to dominate and perhaps control western Europe.

In addition, the new President was more like Churchill than F.D.R. in his perception of the Soviet Union. Unlike Roosevelt, Truman during the war had not thought there was much difference between Hitler and Stalin other than that the latter was on the American side. Churchill's suspicions of the Russian's intentions after the war did little to alter the new President's views. An early as June 1945 Churchill wrote Truman that he had "profound misgivings" because the American armies were being withdrawn westward before the Russian advance. This practice, Churchill complained, allowed "Soviet power into the heart of western Europe and the descent of an iron curtain between us and everything to the eastward." And when Truman in his dealings with the Russians encountered instances of obstinance or suspicion, his patience and flexibility proved limited. Truman's well-known sharp responses to the Russians may well have arisen, too, from his lack of self-confidence—a state of mind that never afflicted his predecessor—in a job that at first clearly overawed the new President.

The First Signs of Rift. Even before F.D.R. died, Stalin had shown his displeasure over the refusal of the United States and Great Britain to accede to his demands for a pro-Russian Poland. Well aware of the importance Roosevelt attached to the United Nations as a part of the peace settlement, Stalin announced that Foreign Minister V. M. Molotov would be unable to attend the signing of the United Nations Charter in San Francisco in June 1945. Only after strong urging by the United States, and in deference to Roosevelt's memory, did Stalin finally agree to Molotov's attendance at the signing, but the petulant gesture had been made. The Americans, too, at this early stage demonstrated a lack of sensitivity toward their wartime ally. On May 8, the day after the Germans surrendered, the Truman administration ordered all lend-lease shipments to the U.S.S.R. terminated because the war was now over. The Russians were genuinely shocked; as recently as January 1945 Molotov had talked to American officials about the need for large-scale aid from the United States to restore his devastated country. Truman, concerned over the obviously deteriorating relations between the United States and Russia, at the end of May dispatched Harry Hopkins as special envoy to Moscow to talk with Stalin. As a result lend-lease shipments were temporarily reinstated, but the unfriendly gesture—though unintended as such—had been made. Historic Russian suspicions of outsiders, always near the surface, as well as Communist suspicions of capitalist states, were aroused.

Suspicion, however, was not a Russian monopoly. Specific Soviet actions aside, American leaders were anxious about Russian intentions and ambitions in Europe even before the war ended. As early as April and May 1945, Secretary of the Navy James F. Forrestal and Ambassador to the U.S.S.R. Averell Harriman were writing memoranda filled with misgivings and concern about the intrusion of a powerful Russia into the heart of Europe. Even Secretary of War Henry L. Stimson, who was inclined to grant the Russians the benefit of the doubt in the interest of working with them for a durable peace, was shocked by the repressive nature of Soviet rule as he saw it in action behind the Russian lines at Potsdam in July. He wondered whether any accommodation was possible with a regime so antithetical to Western democracy.

Indeed, it was at the Potsdam meeting of heads of government that the quite different conceptions of the future of Germany held by the Soviets and the West came out into the open—differences that would still not be resolved a generation later. Prior to the conference the Russians had granted to the new Soviet-dominated Poland a slice of eastern Germany to make up for the territory the U.S.S.R. had taken over from Poland in 1939. At Potsdam Stalin insisted that this new German-Polish border along the Oder-Neisse rivers be accepted by the United States and Great Britain, declaring that no Germans remained in the territory. Neither the British representatives nor Truman would accept this patent falsehood, and they argued that the principle of self-determination of peoples could not be so casually overthrown. The most the Western powers would concede was that the Oder-Neisse line could be temporarily accepted, with the final determination of the border to be left to the peace conference with Germany. They did acknowledge as final the claim of the U.S.S.R to portions of East Prussia.

The interminable arguments over reparations also boiled down to a conflict over the future of Germany. At Yalta Stalin had extracted agreement from the Western Allies that, in view of the devastation wrought by the German armies, the U.S.S.R. was entitled to reparations. At Potsdam Stalin spoke up for a definite figure; he asked for $10 billion worth of German capital equipment. Well aware that the Russians were already taking whatever they could use at home from their occupation zone of Germany, the Western Allies were reluctant to commit themselves to the denuding of the rest of Germany, too. For days the three parties wrangled over reparations, with the Russians holding out for an absolute figure and the Americans insisting that a percentage of *surplus* equipment—i.e., equipment not needed for a peacetime German economy—should be made available for reparations. The Soviets obviously feared that if a percentage figure were used, the actual amount of reparations would depend upon how much German equipment was declared as surplus. The Americans and British, for their part, feared that, considering the battered state of the German economy, an absolute figure would reduce German economic capacity to such a low point that the United States and Great Britain would have to pour money into the country if Germany were ever to revive economically. The impasse was broken at the very end of the conference by the Russians' agreement to accept 10 per cent of the surplus German industrial equipment from all of the western zones and another 15 per cent in exchange for goods from the Russian zone. Considering Stalin's suggestions at Yalta that 80 per cent of German industry be given as reparations, the final agreement was a real concession on his part.*

One further conclusion of the Potsdam meeting was that Germany should remain a political and economic unit, though temporarily divided into Russian, American, British, and French zones. A similar temporary division of Berlin was also made, though the city was located over a hundred miles inside the Soviet zone of Germany. The decision to seek a unified Germany was a triumph for the two extracontinental powers (Britain and the United States), which had the least to fear from a revived Germany. France, though unrepresented at Potsdam, was as dissatisfied with the prospect of a united Germany as the U.S.S.R. For the first few years after the war the French resisted any steps which seemed to further the Potsdam decision to unify Germany, even going so far as to veto the printing of common postage stamps for all four zones.

It was evident from Potsdam that the Soviets expected the Germans to underwrite the rehabilitation of the U.S.S.R.; the revival of the German economy was neither desired nor assisted by the Russians. The Americans and the British, on the other hand, by their insistence that reparations be taken only from surplus equipment, demonstrated that their principal concern was the rapid restoration of German economic life. These two opposing attitudes toward German recovery were but one manifestation of two quite different conceptions of Germany's place in Europe. In the conflict between these conceptions, as we shall see, lay the seeds of the Cold War.

* It has been estimated that the Russians took about $12 billion in reparations from the eastern zone of Germany. To this total should be added a few factories in the western zones which were turned over to the Russians pursuant to the Potsdam agreement. All reparations to the Soviets from the western zones were halted permanently in the spring of 1946.

The differences over the future of Germany, however, were only signs of a much broader divergence of interest between Russia and the West. There was the immense ideological difference between Communism as a totalitarian political system and the free societies of western Europe and the United States. At times in the minds of American leaders and certainly in the minds of the American public this difference was understandably paramount. But there was also a historical difference stemming from the special experience of Russia, irrespective of its Communist ideology. Throughout its history Russia, for all its great size, had been the object of foreign invaders; its long, open borders, devoid of natural defenses, were easily penetrated. From the east during the Middle Ages, for example, it had been overrun by the Mongols and occupied for two centuries; in more modern times it had been invaded from the west by Poland, Sweden, Napoleonic France, Imperial Germany, Poland again, and then Hitler's Germany. To the czars, as to Stalin later, the great Russian defense had been space—retreat into the vastness of Russia itself during war and annexation or domination of surrounding territories when peace came. Thus, for all its vulnerability to outside attack, Russia had been an expanding state ever since the sixteenth century. Through the centuries its expansion into Europe had been held in check by equally powerful states—Poland, Austria, and Germany. With the destruction of German power in central Europe in 1945 Russian power flowed easily and, from Stalin's point of view, naturally into the vacuum. To the West, however, the thrust of Russia into the heart of Europe could appear only as a threat, not simply because of Russia's frankly hostile Communist ideology, but also because this thrust upset the historic balance of power on the continent and threatened to disrupt, if not close, the traditional trade patterns of western Europe and the United States. After all, Germany's overthrowing of that balance in 1939 had forged the Grand Alliance in the first place. As we shall see, it was the increasing signs of Russian—and Communist—expansion during 1946 and 1947, when no state in Europe was capable of resisting it, that kept a reluctant United States in Europe to restore the balance. Ironically, it was what we today recognize as Russia's military weakness that often exacerbated suspicions between the two nations. In order to conceal his weakness Stalin often assumed a truculent attitude in dealing with the West. That weakness also caused him to deny easy access to his country from the West, thereby further arousing suspicion.

Further Strains on the Grand Alliance. This sense of weakness in the midst of unrivaled opportunities to expand Russian authority may have been an important reason behind the many insistent demands and objections made by the Russians in 1945 and most of 1946. At the meetings of the U.N. and of the Council of Foreign Ministers (set up at Potsdam for the discussion of unfinished business), the differences between the Western Allies and the Soviet Union caused constant recrimination and ever growing hostility. Russian demands were pointed and extravagant in the light of what the Western powers were prepared to concede. One day Russia would demand a say in the operation of the industry of the Ruhr region of Germany; another day, control over former Italian colonies in North Africa; a third day, a part in the governing of conquered Japan.

By the beginning of 1946 Truman's patience with Russian tactics and demands was fast running out. In January, for example, he wrote privately that he thought the Russians intended to invade Turkey and take over the straits. "I am tired of babying the Soviets," he declared. "Unless Russia is faced with an iron fist and strong language another war is in the making." With the President in such a frame of mind, the Soviet refusal to honor the agreement to evacuate neighboring Iran could only seem ominous to him. During the war the Soviet Union and Great Britain, in order to keep the Germans from taking over the rich oil fields there, had divided the country between them with the understanding that the troops of both parties would be withdrawn within six months after hostilities ended. March 2, 1946, was the end of the six months, but the Russian troops, instead of leaving (British troops had left on March 1), were actually working to set up a puppet regime in the north Iranian province of Azerbaijan. The United States vigorously protested this expansion of Soviet power in violation of a recognized international agreement; Iran itself appealed to the U.N. The aroused opposition of world opinion finally forced the Soviets to withdraw their troops in late May.

Even before the Iranian matter was concluded, Truman had made public his concern about Russian intentions. He sat on the platform at Fulton, Missouri, while former Prime Minister Winston Churchill deplored the "iron curtain" which he said had "descended across the continent . . . [from] Stettin in the Baltic to Trieste in the Adriatic. Behind that line lie all the capitals of the ancient states of central and eastern Europe"—under the increasing control of the Soviet Union. Churchill gave accurate voice to the worries of American leaders when he said, "Nobody knows what Soviet Russia and its Communist international organization intends to do in the immediate future, or what are the limits, if any, to their expansive and proselytizing tendencies." He called for a close alliance of the English-speaking peoples to combat Soviet expansionism.

Additional concern about Russian expansionism was aroused two months after the Iranian matter was concluded, when Russian pressure was felt by another Middle Eastern country bordering the Soviet Union. Turkey was asked to grant naval bases to its giant neighbor and to share with Russia its control over the Dardanelles. Small pieces of Turkish territory were also claimed. The Soviet Union appeared to be reasserting the old czarist ambition to control the exit from the Black Sea; to many Western observers, historical Russian expansionism was on the march once again.

That same month Americans were thoroughly aroused when two American transport planes were shot down over Communist Yugoslavia by Yugoslavian fighter planes. Secretary of State James F. Byrnes sent Marshall Tito, the dictator of Yugoslavia, an ultimatum to return the captured airmen or face an appeal to the U.N. Tito complied. (In 1948 Yugoslavia broke with Russia, though remaining Communist in ideology. Ever since American relations with Yugoslavia have been friendly.)

During the summer and fall in the United Nations the representatives of the Soviet Union turned down the American plan for international control of nuclear energy, largely because the plan would have required the Russians to acquiesce in the American monopoly at a time when, as later events were to demonstrate, Soviet scientists were feverishly working to perfect their own nuclear weapons. But once again it seemed to American eyes as if a generous gesture—that is, voluntarily giving up exclusive control over the tremendous power of nuclear fission—had been rebuffed by the secretive, uncooperative Soviet state. As one

New Left scholar wrote in 1974, "The dispute over atomic energy was both a cause and a consequence of the Cold War."

The German question, despite seemingly endless meetings of the Council of Foreign Ministers, remained unsettled and a constant source of Soviet-American mistrust. By the fall of 1946 Secretary of State James F. Byrnes, apparently convinced that the Soviet Union did not desire a settlement of the German question at all, moved to resolve the matter without the U.S.S.R. In a speech delivered before a group of German leaders in Stuttgart in September, he informed the Germans that it was the Russians who were preventing the emergence of a viable and united Germany. Then, in effect, he abandoned the drive for a united Germany by accepting its division in fact. Soon after, upon Byrnes' invitation, the British merged their zone with the American one; the French, still anxious over the implications of revived German power, did not join the merger until 1949. But already, by the close of 1946, it was evident that a divided Germany was the potentially explosive result of the inability of the West and the East to agree as to the place of Germany in postwar Europe.

The Beginning of the Cold War. Some historians have seen in Secretary Byrnes' speech at Stuttgart the beginning of what columnist Walter Lippmann named the Cold War—that state of hostility between the superpowers which remained precariously poised just short of actual military engagement. With the Stuttgart speech and the decision to merge the western zones, a new era opened. From now on conquered Germany would be increasingly wooed by the West in the contest with the Soviets. Less than two years after the fall of Berlin, the Grand Alliance was not only ruptured, but the former Allies seemed to be on the verge of war.

In looking back on that first year and a half of uneasy peace, it is hard to isolate the precise origins of the rising tensions and hostility. In the eyes of the Western powers the pretensions of the Russians seemed excessive; the very audacity of Stalin's numerous demands alarmed Western leaders who were not used to thinking of the Soviet Union as a European power and frankly feared its domination over Europe. They naturally preferred a free hand in the settlement of European affairs, while Stalin thought Russia was entitled to a major share in the affairs of his neighbors in the light of Russia's enormous effort in the war. Furthermore, the West was deeply distrustful of Communist ideology and its potentiality for what Churchill called proselytizing and what a later day would call subversion. During that year and a half the Russians demanded control of the Dardanelles, colonies in North Africa, territory from Turkey, the Italian city of Trieste for Communist Yugoslavia, oil concessions if not territory in Iran, huge reparations from western Germany, active participation in the industrial Ruhr region of western Germany, a large loan from the United States, and a share in the occupation of Japan. But it is also important to recognize that almost none of these demands bore the fruits the Soviets wanted. The U.S.S.R., it is true, did obtain reparations from eastern Germany, though precious little from the western part, and about $100 million from Italy and one third of the defunct Germany navy; but all the other demands were resisted successfully by the Western powers. Yet the very inability of the one-time Allies against Germany to look upon Europe and Russia's place in it with the same eyes made the Cold War a reality. Suspicion fed upon suspicion, as the next few years would show.

The postwar adjustment abroad, then, was a cold war ever threatening to become hot. It was the primary source of American anxiety for the next fifteen years.

Readjustment at Home

Harry S. Truman. As the great wartime alliance disintegrated and the problems of reconversion at home mounted, the man who headed the government of the United States seemed singularly ill-prepared for his momentous tasks. Born in 1884 in western Missouri, Harry Truman grew up on a farm and, except for a few months in law school, received no education beyond high school. A serious, even studious lad, he read much when a boy, if only because the glasses he wore seemed to preclude more active pastimes. As a young man he worked in a bank, ran the family farm for ten years, and upon the outbreak of war in 1917 entered the army as a captain in the artillery. After the war Truman tried his hand at running a haberdashery with an army buddy, only to have what promised to be a flourishing business go under in the little crash of 1921. For most of the 1920s and early 1930s he was active in local politics in Jackson County, Missouri, where he supported the Kansas City political machine of Tom Pendergast. In 1934, with the permission of Pendergast, he ran successfully for the United States Senate. Truman was never well-to-do, and as late as 1940 he was too poor to save his mother's home from foreclosure. As a senator Truman made a national reputation for himself by his diligent, honest, and important work during the war as head of a senatorial committee investigating the fulfillment of war contracts. Largely on the strength of the reputation he earned in that capacity, he received the nomination for Vice-President in 1944.

Personally, as he himself once said, "I look just like any other fifty people you meet in the street." Yet there was something more than ordinariness about him, as he was soon to demonstrate in the White House. Despite his limited background, he exhibited while President a remarkable talent for making quick, unambiguous, and generally sound decisions. His forthright, even naive outspokenness won him respect among his subordinates; his honesty and dignified sense of duty evoked the admiration of those who at first may have felt he was too unimpressive for the most awesome office in America. He could, it is true, be unduly irascible in public, and he was sometimes intensely loyal to those who were unworthy of such sentiment. Thus when he was Vice-President he insisted upon attending the funeral of his corrupt former boss, Pendergast, despite the objections of his advisers, because he thought Pendergast had been a good friend.

His simple dignity and sense of humility in the big job at first won him the support of most Americans, who are always ready to sympathize with a man struggling to do his best against great difficulties. In the long run, however, he still had to prove himself. When, in the early months of his administration, the knotty problems he was called upon to unravel did not yield to easy solution, wits soon began poking fun at his inadequacies. "I wonder what Truman would do if he were alive?" was one of many jokes at his expense.

Although Truman retained the Roosevelt Cabinet for a while, he soon found his own men to take up the principal posts. The two most influential voices in his administration were those of James F. Byrnes of South Carolina, who became Secretary of State in June 1945, and Fred M. Vinson of Kentucky, who assumed the duties of Secretary of the Treasury that same summer. Henry A. Wallace, a holdover from the Roosevelt Cabinet, was compelled to resign as Secretary of Commerce in September 1946 after he publicly criticized the foreign policy of the administration at the very time that Secretary Byrnes was in Europe carrying on particularly frustrating negotiations with the Russians. Wallace's sympathy for the Soviet Union would find further expression when he was the presidential candidate of the Progressive party.

The Problems of Demobilization and Reconversion. Upon the surrender of the Japanese, the dismantling of the military might of the United States proceeded rapidly. On September 18, 1945, the President told the country that men were being returned to civilian life at the rate of 650 an hour, every hour of the day, every day of the week. By the first month of 1946, he promised, the rate would be up to 35,000 discharges a day. Although the rate did reach that level, Americans were still not satisfied. Early in January 1946 American soldiers rioted and demonstrated in Japan, France, India, Korea, and Germany, demanding an even faster return home. Relatives at home were also putting pressure upon Congress and the White House toward the same end. Straining transportation and discharge facilities to the utmost, the government had released almost 7 million men and women from the armed forces by April 1946. At the end of that year the armed forces had been cut by more than 80 per cent from wartime strength.

The economic problems posed by the ending of the greatest war effort in American history were enormous. Factories that had been producing for the war now needed suddenly to be converted to peacetime production. The imminent cancellation of a large part of the $100 billion of annual wartime government expenditures presaged serious effects upon the economy. Within a month after Japan's surrender, $35 billion of war contracts were cancelled and armament production was cut back 60 per cent. At war's end 10 million civilian workers were employed in war work and another 12 million members of the labor force were in the armed services. As demobilization proceeded and war plants closed, millions of workers poured into the labor market seeking jobs. Within ten days of the Japanese capitulation, 2.7 million men and women were released from armament and other war production. In the light of these circumstances, it was quite realistic in the fall of 1945 to expect 10 to 12 million unemployed by the end of 1946. Indeed, as late as the end of 1946, 58 per cent of some 15,000 businessmen questioned confidentially by *Fortune* magazine said that they thought a depression with large-scale unemployment would surely occur within a decade.

Yet at the same time that it looked as if the threat of depression were most pressing, other factors suggested that a runaway inflation was also possible. As a result of the war-born prosperity, property values, both urban and rural, had climbed over 40 per cent since 1939, and stock market prices were 80 per cent above the level of 1942. Such inflated values inevitably encouraged speculation and pushed up prices. Moreover, spending power, which had accumulated in the hands of consumers long unable to spend their money because of wartime shortages and controls, was tremendous. Liquid assets of individuals and corporations in 1944 totaled almost $200 billion; in 1920 at the end of the First World War, the figure had been only $45 billion. These inflationary pressures also acted, of course, as antidepression forces.

Another force acting to prevent a depression was the high level of government expenditures. In 1945 professional economists had confidently assumed that the annual federal budget after the war would not go above $25 billion. But in point of fact it never fell nearly that low. Indeed, it seldom went below $45 billion, and by the end of the 1950s the budgets were almost double that figure. For these reasons, despite the expectations of businessmen and economists alike, no postwar depression occurred.

The Eruption of Labor Unrest. During the war labor unions, which had taken a voluntary no-strike pledge for the duration of the conflict, generally lived up to their agreement, despite a 30 per cent rise in prices. Upon the conclusion of the war in Europe, however, workers became increasingly restless and the number of strikes began to shoot upward. Once the war with Japan was over, the pressure for wage increases could no longer be contained. In the fall of 1945 a wave of strikes broke over the nation. Usually the demand was for a 30 per cent wage increase, by which workers sought to maintain wartime levels of income now that overtime pay was no longer likely. The rash of strikes spread alarmingly. In September over 4 million man-days were lost in strikes as compared with fewer than 1.5 million in April. In October the record of the previous month was more than doubled. The high point was reached in February 1946, when some 23 million man-days were lost because of strikes.

The President, though he conceded the justice of many of the demands for higher wages, was worried that the interruption of production would delay, if not endanger, a smooth transition to a peacetime economy. He exhorted both management and labor to seek peaceful solutions to their differences, but such appeals did nothing to halt the strikes or to induce employers to grant wage increases without strikes. Equally unsuccessful was the labor-management conference which the President hopefully called in November to discuss the insistent demands for wage increases.

Actually the President sometimes seemed to encourage labor unrest. In a radio address to the nation at the end of October, for example, he pointed out that, with the reduction in overtime pay, purchasing power might shrink by as much as $20 billion. As a consequence, he said, whenever company profits seemed to permit, higher wages were necessary in order "to sustain adequate purchasing power and to raise the national income." On the other hand, in the same speech he told employers that they must not expect any price increases because inflation was also an ever present danger. The President, like the economy itself, seemed to be caught between the devil of inflation and the deep blue sea of depression.

The wave of strikes continued through most of 1946, with the number of workers out that year reaching 4.6 million, as compared with slightly fewer than 3.5 million in 1945. (Yet this postwar labor unrest was slighter than that after the First World War. The year 1919, the comparable postwar year after the First World War, witnessed over 4 million on strike, out of a considerably smaller total work force.) Although the number of workers on strike diminished in 1947, the continuing rise in prices in subsequent years encouraged strikes. No sooner would an industry gain a wage increase than inflation would induce the unions to go out on strike again in an effort to keep up with prices. This pattern continued into the early fifties as inflation became the persistent tendency of the economy.

Returning to Economic Normalcy. As workers went out on strike in order to keep up with the rising cost of living, the government began to drop the economic controls it had imposed during the war. The number of ration points on butter was reduced in July 1946. In August gasoline rationing was ended, and the death toll on the highways that month jumped 26 per cent over that for the same month in 1944. Shortly thereafter new automobiles were taken off the ration list. In rapid fashion the other extreme wartime restrictions on the economy were removed, though price and wage controls remained. The nation was fast returning to its old ways. As after the First World War, what the people seemed to want was "normalcy."

One other sign of the desire for normalcy was the public clamor for tax relief. To win the war the government had spent $380 billion between 1940 and the close of 1945, about 40 per cent of which had been raised by taxes, a proportion unequaled in the history of American war financing. The administration, uncertain whether inflation or deflation would be the major problem of the postwar era, hesitated to alter the tax structure, but Congress and the nation were determined to cut taxes; to them the only question was how large the cut should be. When Secretary of the Treasury Vinson, responding to the public wish, recommended a small cut to Congress (it would have amounted to about $5 billion in 1946), he was greeted with open arms, for he was the first Secretary of the Treasury to propose a tax cut since the halcyon days of Andrew Mellon almost two decades earlier. The bill Congress wrote cut much deeper into revenues than Vinson had recommended. The Revenue Act of 1945, which the President signed in November, reduced individual and corporation taxes by $9 billion and, in an effort to stimulate business, repealed the wartime excess profits tax. All told, an estimated 12 million taxpayers were removed from the tax rolls by the cut. It was not yet six months since the end of the war with Japan; normalcy was coming up fast.

Prices and Unions. Two big unresolved issues harrassed the nation through most of 1946. One was prices and their control, and the other was the power of labor unions.

With the war over, price controls seemed to many much less justified than during the emergency. And it was true that, with the incentive of war patriotism removed, many Americans refused to abide by government regulations on prices. The fight in Congress and in the press over price controls was certainly encouraged by political partisanship—but it was more than that. It was, in reality, a continuation of the debate begun in 1932 over the extent of the government's role in the economy. One group, largely composed of liberals, New Dealers, the administration, and northern, urban Democrats in Congress, insisted upon a continuation of government price controls in order to hold down prices for consumers until supply could catch up with demand. Their opponents, mainly businessmen and Republicans in and outside Congress, contended that unless the incentive of price rises was restored—i.e., unless government controls were removed—supply would never be sufficiently stimulated to equal demand. The latter group, in short, wanted to leave the matter to private business and the market.

The history of the period gave some support to both sides. When in the summer of 1946 the President, by vetoing a price control law that was full of loopholes, allowed price controls to lapse entirely, prices rose 16 per cent within two weeks, just as he had predicted. On the other hand, when controls were reinstated on meat, cattle raisers and packers kept beef off the market and the nation's consumers once more found it impossible to obtain a piece of good meat legally at a butcher shop. Illegal operations flourished; one survey showed that in the fall of 1946 more than 66 per cent of all meat sold was purchased from black-market butchers. By late 1946 price controls were so strongly objected to and so ineffectually supported that, when the election returns in November showed a Republican victory, the administration abandoned virtually all controls over wages and prices.

The ending of controls, however, did not result immediately in either the elimination of shortages or the stabilization of prices. Shortages continued in a whole range of products, from butter and bacon to lumber and coal, from X-ray tubes, white shirts, and chewing gum to beer, washing machines, and toasters. The wartime earnings and savings of the American people, now suddenly released, gobbled up goods as they poured forth from the factories and sales-rooms. Almost a year later, in September 1947, prices were still breaking records, with butter selling for a dollar a pound and eggs for a dollar a dozen, at a time when wages were half those of the seventies.

Rising prices did encourage a high rate of business activity. Department-store sales in 1946 were 263 per cent above the 1936–1938 average, and obvious luxuries like phonograph records were being sold like penny candy; some 7 million Decca records alone were sold in the first quarter of 1946. Reports even circulated that prosperous farmers in Nebraska and Oklahoma were buying light airplanes to travel to their widely separated farms. Employment was also up. America was in the midst of a postwar boom of prodigious proportions. What surprised everybody was that it did not end in a grand bust.

The second pressing issue of 1946 was the power of organized labor. Labor unions had grown greatly under the encouragement of New Deal legislation and wartime demand for workers. But the power of national unions to disrupt the economy seriously did not become evident until several postwar strikes had taken place. During strikes in the steel, automobile, coal, and shipping industries, all citizens, in one way or another, felt the great power labor could exert. (Actually most of the strikes were settled quickly with an 18.5 cent wage increase, following the pattern set by the General Motors strike in the winter of 1945–1946.) These big national strikes were provoking congressional concern.

Congress was already considering a labor control bill introduced by Repre-sentative Francis Case of South Dakota when the President, in early 1946, was compelled to deal with a national railroad stoppage. Some weeks before, in an effort to prevent the strike, Truman had ordered the government to assume operation of the railroads, but on May 23 the workers went out on strike anyway as planned. With all the railroads halted, the country was faced with the prospect of economic breakdown. Truman, choosing to see the strike as a blow against the government because of the nominal control it had been exercising over the roads, told the nation that "the crisis of Pearl Harbor was the result of action by a foreign enemy. The crisis tonight is caused by a group of men within our own country, who place their private interests above the welfare of the nation." The next day, in an atmosphere of mounting apprehension, he appeared before a joint session of Congress to ask for legislation that would permit him to draft all railroad workers into the Army. But even while he was speaking, the show of government power brought the strike to an end. Even so, the House quickly passed Truman's labor draft by the overwhelming vote of 306 to 13. The Senate would not go along because the conservative, highly respected Republican Senator Robert A. Taft would have nothing to do with a measure which "offends not only the Constitution, but every basic principle for which the American Republic was established. Strikes cannot be prohibited without interfering with the basic freedom essential to our form of government."

Soon thereafter, when Congress passed the Case labor bill, Truman vetoed it on the grounds that its way of controlling nationwide strikes was basically antilabor and therefore conducive to further strife. His veto was sustained by the House. Yet the growing demand for some federal controls over labor unions did not die. It became a major issue in the 1946 congressional elections, and more successful efforts to curb union power would be mounted in the next Congress.

Looking Backward and Forward. Despite the boom, the country could not yet forget the Depression, as the Employment Act of February 1946 made evident. Originally planned during the war years as a measure that would have committed the federal government to maintain full employment, the bill was pared down considerably as it passed through Congress. Provisions for mandatory government expenditures in times of depression were removed. Instead, a council of economic advisers was created to inform the President on economic matters, and the President was required to submit to Congress an annual report on the state of the economy. Despite its lack of antidepression machinery, the measure revealed the revolution that had taken place in American political and social thought since the days of Herbert Hoover. It was now officially recognized that the government bore responsibility for checking on, if not maintaining, employment rates. Never again would action to counter massive unemployment be viewed as beyond the legitimate power of the federal government. In that sense the Employment Act of 1946 was the last of the Depression-born New Deal measures. Thereafter economic reform measures would be sparked by the recognition that affluence was characteristic of the American economy. This new approach would be most evident in the antipoverty measures of the Kennedy and Johnson administrations, when the principal justification was that an affluent society could not countenance poverty among a minority of its citizens.

In marked contrast to the backward-glancing Employment Act was the Atomic Energy Act of the same year. It looked to the future—an anxious future dark with the fearsome mushroom cloud. After much debate in Congress, the law placed control and development of nuclear energy exclusively in the hands of a civilian Atomic Energy Commission. For the first time in the history of the technological revolution that had begun over two centuries earlier, an American government assumed full responsibility for the regulation of a scientific innovation. The act also lodged in the President alone the power to decide on the use of nuclear weapons in war.

The Election of 1946. If Harry Truman and his administration, in carrying through the principles of the New Deal, thought of themselves as dealing with the concerns of the people, the first postwar congressional election showed how mistaken they were. In November 1946 a Republican Congress was returned for the first time since the election of 1928. The Republicans, capitalizing on the pervasive dissatisfaction with rising prices and strikes and the anxieties aroused by the Cold War, campaigned with the simple and effective slogan "Had enough?" The response of the voters was to award the Republicans majorities of fifty-seven in the House and six in the Senate. Democratic losses were not only substantial, but some of the old stalwarts of the New Deal, like Senator Joseph Guffey of Pennsylvania, went down in defeat. Furthermore, forty-five of the 128 House members who had voted to sustain Truman's veto of the antilabor Case bill failed to retain their seats. Despondent Democratic Senator William Fulbright even publicly suggested that Truman resign in favor of a Republican so that the country would be spared the handicap of a divided government.

Truman Versus the Eightieth Congress

Congressional Republicans. The new Congress that convened in January 1947 rightly interpreted its election as a mandate to enact a substantial tax cut, to free business from government interference, and to pass legislation regulating labor unions. The social outlook of the Republican party and its leaders in Congress was decidedly conservative. Many of its members had been waiting a long time to be in a position to reverse the social and economic trends set in motion by Franklin Roosevelt's New Deal. The intellectual as well as the political leader of the Republicans in Congress was Robert A. Taft, the senior senator from Ohio. The son of a former President, Taft had twice been brushed aside by his party in presidential nominating conventions, but he was still hopeful. Although in the context of the post-New Deal years Taft was generally denominated a conservative, a more accurate description would have been nineteenth-century liberal or individualist. His single-handed killing of Truman's very popular move to draft striking railroad workers stemmed from his firm belief that the individual should be free from governmental regimentation. He did, however, support federal housing legislation and federal aid to education on the grounds that a free society needs to care for the environment and education of its children. (Many years later President Eisenhower, often regarded as a more liberal Republican than Taft, admitted that he was not prepared to support such uses of federal power.) Taft's independence was also evident in the blunt and impolitic statements he made, such as his advice in 1946 that those complaining of high food prices should "eat less." As chairman of the Senate Labor Committee, Taft was responsible for writing the labor legislation the country seemed to be waiting for.

The Taft-Hartley Act. Interest in a labor control bill was strong from the outset of the Eightieth Congress. On the very first day seventeen labor bills were dropped into the House hopper. Indeed, as the passage of the Smith-Connelly War Labor Disputes Act in 1943 and the Case bill in 1946 showed, congressional sentiment for greater control over labor had been growing for some time. Moreover, the President himself, despite his favorable attitude toward labor and his veto of the Case bill, encouraged Congress in his State of the Union message to consider some kind of labor-management legislation.

The labor bill that Fred Hartley of New Jersey introduced and that was passed in the House by an overwhelming vote was extremely restrictive of labor unions, and the Democrats were incensed at the speed with which it was rushed through. The Senate, under the guidance of the careful and principled Taft, was more deliberate, and its bill became, in effect, the final version. Working closely with southern Democrats, many of whom agreed with him on the need for curbs on labor unions, Taft succeeded in writing a bill that could withstand a presidential veto and yet do the job its authors set for it.

As finally enacted, the Labor-Management Relations Act of 1947 listed a number of unfair labor practices of unions, much as the Wagner Act of 1935 had listed unfair labor practices of employers. Indeed, it was evident from the act that one of the authors' intentions was to counterbalance the advantages that labor had secured under the New Deal. Hence the act outlawed secondary boycotts (boycotts against an employer by a nonstriking union to help a striking union), the closed shop (one which hired only union members), the checkoff (the collection of union dues by employers from pay envelopes), certain kinds of jurisdictional strikes, and featherbedding (pay without performance of commensurate work). To cope with strikes that threatened a national emergency, the President was empowered, regardless of the Norris-LaGuardia Anti-Injunction Act of 1932, to seek a court injunction and to proclaim a "cooling-off" period of up to eighty days. If the dispute was not settled at the end of that period, the last offer of the employer had to be presented to a vote of the union members before the strike could be resumed.

In this last-offer provision and in the requirement that all union leaders legally attest that they were not Communists, the act revealed its authors' distrust of labor leaders. "The vote for the Taft-Hartley bill," Representative Hartley wrote later, "was not a vote against unions. It was a vote against the tactics of the *leaders* of union labor" and a "vote for the rank and file within the labor movement." The distrust many businessmen felt for the New Deal's prolabor Wagner Act was also reflected in the provision creating the office of the General Counsel, separate from the National Labor Relations Board itself. In this way the Taft-Hartley Act gave credence to the charge of many employers that the board under the Wagner Act acted as both prosecutor and judge.

In general it might be said that whereas the Wagner Act had placed the power of government behind the organizing of labor, the Taft-Hartley Act now shifted the emphasis to concern and protection for the workers who did not want to join unions. Only in that sense was the act anti-union, for it did nothing to change the Wagner Act's basic assumption that labor unions and collective bargaining were desirable. The supporters of the bill, Hartley wrote, saw it as "the first step toward an official discouragement" of a trend which had "permitted and encouraged" labor "to grow into a monster supergovernment."

Leaders of labor and liberals in general opposed the bill during its passage through Congress, calling it a "slave labor" bill. In view of the large majorities that passed the bill originally, Truman had reason to fear that his veto might be overridden. Nonetheless, he sent the measure back to Congress with a stinging veto message, concluding that "the bill is a clear threat to the successful working of our democratic society." The House and then the Senate quickly passed the bill over his veto.

Despite the unremitting opposition of labor unions and Democratic presidential candidates and Presidents ever since, the Taft-Hartley Act has remained on the books without substantial change. The act seems to be in accord with what the American people wanted to see after a decade of prolabor legislation under the New Deal. The Taft-Hartley Act is unique in being the only piece of legislation in thirty years that seriously altered a policy instituted by the New Deal.

The Drive for Tax Relief. Even before the conservative Republican Congress got around to labor legislation, it turned eagerly to tax reduction. H.R. 1, the first bill in the House that session, provided for a flat 20 per cent cut for all taxpayers with net incomes below $302,400. Liberal Democrats as well as administration leaders scornfully denounced such a windfall for the big taxpayer. The bill came "right out of the Andrew Mellon primer of special privilege," asserted one southern Democrat. When the Senate received the bill, it scaled down somewhat the cuts for the high income brackets, but the President vetoed the measure nonetheless, branding it as "the wrong kind of tax reduction, at the wrong time." In view of the inflationary pressures in the economy, he contended, the surplus should be used to pay off the debt rather than to cut taxes. Moreover, he pointed out, by offering a flat percentage cut for all income brackets, the bill was offering more relief to high-income recipients than to low. Truman's veto was only the second veto of a tax reduction bill in the nation's history. (Roosevelt's in 1944 was the first.) It was sustained in the House by two votes.

The Republicans continued to push for a tax cut. In July Truman vetoed a measure almost identical with the first one, but a third such bill, passed in December 1947, became law over his third veto. By that time the President was supporting a tax cut plan of his own because of the substantial surplus for the fiscal year 1947–1948, and his opposition seemed less disinterested and convincing than earlier. The Revenue Act of 1948, when it became law that April, cut rates on all personal income taxes to the extent of some $6.5 billion. No changes were made in income tax rates for corporations.

The National Security Act. In domestic affairs the one other notable achievement of the Eightieth Congress was the attempt to unify the national defense establishment. For some time the executive had been trying to move in the direction of putting the Navy, Army, and Air Force under a single head. In February 1947 the administration sent a bill to Congress providing for the creation of a single Department of Defense. Immediately the three services began to object to various features of this measure that seemed to place them at a disadvantage. As a result of their resistance, the act, as passed on July 25, provided for less centralized control than Truman's original bill, but it did set up a Department of Defense, composed of the three services under a single civilian head. A Joint Chiefs of Staff, composed of representatives from each of the services, was also created. Most important, the act placed procurement, research, and intelligence in the three services under central boards or agencies in an effort to eliminate duplication of effort. A National Security Council, including the Vice-President, the Director of Defense Mobilization, the Secretaries of State and of Defense, and the President, was created to coordinate foreign and defense policies. The first Secretary of Defense, James F. Forrestal, Roosevelt's and Truman's diligent and earnest Secretary of the Navy, was appointed on September 17, 1947.

The Democrats Stay In

If Harry Truman thought himself unworthy of and unprepared for the presidency when he took office, by 1948 he was eager to show the country that he had learned much in the interim. Many of his party, though, especially the liberal

New Deal wing, were not so pleased with him, and some even sought unsuccessfully to interest General Dwight D. Eisenhower, whose political affiliations were then unknown, in the Democratic nomination. Many other Democrats opposed Truman's nomination simply because they thought he could not win. In April 1948, only 38 per cent of the voters said they approved of his performance as President. But the President had the votes at the convention and was nominated on the first ballot, with Senator Alben W. Barkley of Kentucky as his running mate. In his acceptance speech to the convention Truman showed his mettle as a politician, announcing that he would call a special session of Congress that summer to challenge the Republican leadership to pass his program. When the Congress met and, as might have been anticipated, refused to do as Truman directed, the President was provided with a convenient whipping boy for the duration of the campaign.

Despite this advantage, Truman ran under severe handicaps. At the Democratic convention the party had been split by the insistence of northern urban liberals that a strong plank on behalf of civil rights for blacks be put into the platform in accordance with the President's own strong message on the subject earlier in the year. Two days after the Democratic convention a convention of States' Rights Democrats, meeting in Birmingham, Alabama, nominated Strom Thurmond of South Carolina as its candidate. With strong support in Alabama, Mississippi, South Carolina, and Louisiana, the "Dixiecrats," as they were soon named, threatened to take away from Truman many traditionally Democratic votes in the South. Extreme left-wing liberals, Communists, and others who thought the Truman foreign policy toward the Soviet Union was too intransigent found an advocate in Henry A. Wallace, Truman's former Secretary of Commerce, who now became the presidential candidate of the newly organized Progressive party. Wallace campaigned on a platform of social reform and a conciliatory policy toward the Soviet Union, generally opposing all measures the United States had taken in foreign affairs since 1945.

Despite, or perhaps because of, the Dixiecrat defection from the party, Truman acted after the convention in July to put into effect his promises to blacks. In two executive orders with long-range consequences, he called for an end to racial discrimination in jobs in the federal government and for the beginning of the end to segregation in the armed services. Although the desegregation of the armed services was resisted by the Pentagon, and the process took several years to accomplish, it was a major breakthrough on behalf of equality for all Americans. It was also a good example of how political self-interest can be the handmaiden of reform, since Truman's new interest in civil rights was undoubtedly spurred by his need for northern Negro votes. Even so, it was a calculated risk that at the time required courage.

The Great Surprise. After the resurgence of Republican strength in 1946 the return of the Republicans to the White House seemed assured, and Truman's personal and political liabilities only reinforced that assurance. Following an ineffectual attempt to nominate General Eisenhower, the Republicans turned again to Thomas E. Dewey, governor of New York, and the candidate of the party in 1944. Earl Warren, the popular governor of California, was named as the vice-presidential candidate. Sure of his victory, desirous of arousing hostility from no one, and contemptuous of the man in the White House, Dewey spoke mainly of the need for national unity and attacked none of the reforms of the Democratic New Deal, though they were essentially Truman's platform. If intellectuals and radio and television commentators sometimes criticized Dewey's platitudinous and fireless campaign, they nevertheless conceded, along with the public opinion pollsters, that his election was certain.

Only Harry Truman, it seemed, was not convinced. Taking a cue from the enthusiastic response to a speech he delivered extemporaneously in April, the President embarked upon a highly informal speaking tour across the country, stopping his campaign train any place a crowd could be gathered. At each stop he would launch into a freewheeling, impromptu attack on the Republicans, disdaining the aloof, statesmanlike delivery of Dewey. Again and again he castigated "that no-good" Eightieth Congress, blaming the legislation it enacted, such as the Taft-Hartley Act, or its failure to pass his own program for the ills of the nation. The enthusiastic response of the crowds he entertained in this lively fashion spurred him on to further extravagant denunciations of Republicans at the next stop. "Those fellows," he shouted, referring to the Republicans, "are just a bunch of old mossbacks . . . gluttons of privilege . . . all set to do a hatchet job on the New Deal." Often he used the timeworn rhetoric of class prejudice. "I warn you," he told one crowd, "if you let the Republicans get control of the government, you will be making America an economic colony of Wall Street." Even foreign policy was discussed in homely fashion. In Oregon he told his audience, "I like old Uncle Joe Stalin. Joe is a decent fellow but he is the prisoner of the Politburo. The people who run the government won't let him be as decent as he would like to be." By the close of the campaign, a good part of the country had been given a one-man personal appearance show by the President of the United States. By his own count, Truman traveled some 32,000 miles and delivered 356 speeches, or about ten a day, far exceeding the effort of his confident and younger opponent.

Election night in 1948 was at first mystifying and then electrifying. It was not completely unexpected that Truman should lead in the early returns, since his strength lay in the cities, which reported first. But as the night wore on, his initial lead was never lost, and sometimes it even grew. By the next morning the final vote was not yet in, but it was evident that Harry Truman would still be President. Great newspapers like the *Chicago Tribune* and respected commentators like H. V. Kaltenborn were hard to convince, but just before noon of the next day Dewey conceded that what Truman had said all along was going to happen had in fact happened. Even for those who had not voted for Truman, it was exhilarating and refreshing to have the voters turn the tables on the experts; Harry Truman never let the polltakers forget their embarrassment that night.

If on election day Truman's victory seemed a political miracle, a closer look brought forth some more plausible explanations. For one thing, the election was really very close: out of a popular vote of 50 million, Truman led Dewey by only 2 million. For another, Americans had not forgotten the Depression or the New Deal. It was evident that by associating himself with the social legislation of the New Deal, Truman drew the votes of those who had supported Roosevelt. In some respects he did better. By harping on the fall in farm prices and promising farmers the continuation of price supports, Truman recaptured the farm vote which Roosevelt had been unable to hold in 1940 and 1944. By taking the farm

A jubilant Harry Truman, a decided underdog in the presidential election of 1948, enjoys the last laugh the day after the election. *Photo: UPI*

states of Iowa, Wisconsin, Ohio, Wyoming, and Colorado, all of which had been lost by F.D.R. in the two previous elections, Truman snatched victory from seemingly sure defeat. And with the war over, the midwestern German vote, which had been drifting away from Roosevelt ever since 1940, returned to the Democrats. Finally, although the defection of the Dixiecrats cost Truman thirty-nine electoral votes and four states in the Deep South, it simultaneously guaranteed him the urban black vote in the crucial industrial states of the North. That a Democrat should win the presidency even when the South was split was new evidence of the substantial gains the Democratic party had made in the nation since 1932; it had clearly replaced the Republicans as the dominant party in the country. Wallace's appeal, once thought to be fatal to Truman's chances for retaining the liberal vote, turned out to be slight and unimportant, though it may have helped give New York to Dewey.

The Fair Deal. In his inaugural address Truman spoke of his program as the Fair Deal, defining it as an extension and codification, as it were, of the more famous New Deal. His program called for civil rights legislation, particularly a fair employment practices act to prohibit racial discrimination in jobs and an antilynching bill. He also urged upon Congress a national health program, aid for public education, and support for the construction of low-income housing. True to his pledge in the campaign, he advocated the repeal of the Taft-Hartley Act, but without success. His Secretary of Agriculture, Charles Brannan, a dynamic Coloradan who had been one of the few Cabinet officers to support

Truman's candidacy actively in 1948, advanced a radical solution to the problem of farm surpluses, also without success. The Brannan plan would have subsidized farmers while permitting farm prices to fall to natural, unsupported levels in order to allow food costs to urban consumers to drop. (Over twenty-five years later, in the Nixon administration, the plan became law, though in 1948 Congressman Nixon had been one of its opponents.)

Although Truman returned to the White House with a Democratic Congress, his program was only partly enacted. There were always enough conservative Democrats, usually from the South, to join with the Republicans to beat down his bills. The conservatives of both parties were sufficiently strong to prevent, for example, the passage of any civil rights measures during the whole four years. It would require the Negro revolution of the 1950s to bring home to both the Democratic party and the nation how overdue such legislation was.

And even when Truman did not rely upon Congress he found that his efforts on behalf of his supporters were frustrated. In order to avert a national strike of steelworkers over wages in the spring in 1952, Truman, by executive order, took over the operation of some ninety-two steel companies in the name of the government. He clearly sided with the workers in their demand for increased wages, but his primary concern was to keep production going. The steel companies, however, quickly carried the issue through the courts to the Supreme Court, which almost immediately ordered Truman to return the mills to private management. In retrospect it seems that Truman's high-handedness was the result of poor advice and planning, but the ill-conceived step caused him to leave office under a cloud. Moreover, a strike was not averted since the steelworkers left their jobs shortly after the Supreme Court found the President in the wrong.

Truman did, however, succeed in obtaining a housing act in 1949, thanks to the collaboration of Senator Robert Taft, the Republican leader; moreover, the minimum wage was raised to seventy-five cents an hour to compensate for continuing inflation. In 1950 the coverage of the Social Security Act was significantly broadened for the first time since enactment of the law fifteen years earlier. Some 10 million additional persons, largely self-employed people hitherto not covered by the act, were now included in its provisions. (Farmers, agricultural workers, and domestic servants still remained outside the social security system or any other pension scheme.) Some reorganization of the executive branch was also

THE ELECTION OF 1948

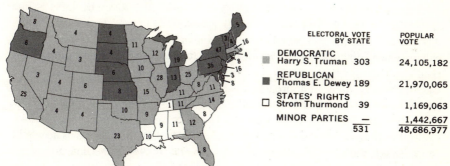

	ELECTORAL VOTE BY STATE	POPULAR VOTE
DEMOCRATIC Harry S. Truman	303	24,105,182
REPUBLICAN Thomas E. Dewey	189	21,970,065
STATES' RIGHTS Strom Thurmond	39	1,169,063
MINOR PARTIES	—	1,442,667
	531	48,686,977

undertaken after Herbert Hoover, upon the request of the President, submitted a report suggesting ways to increase the efficiency of the government. Most of the changes Truman recommended, pursuant to the Hoover Report, were accepted by Congress.

During 1949, for the first time since the 1930s, the economy slid into a slump, with some 4 million unemployed by early summer. The recession was of short duration, for by the fall an upturn was already in sight; the massive unemployment, so feared after the experience of the 1930s, never materialized. Despite the recession, however, prices continued to rise.

Mink Coats and Deep Freezers. After 1949 Truman was increasingly plagued by revelations of corruption in his administration. The Republicans endeavored to inflate some of the accounts that were coming out of congressional investigations in 1949 and 1950 into Democratic Teapot Dome scandals, but the examples of corruption were more often petty, isolated acts than indications of widespread, if hidden, malfeasance. More than petty or isolated, however, were the forced resignations of four collectors and thirty-one other officials in the Bureau of Internal Revenue because of irregularities in the conduct of their offices. Occasionally the scent of corruption came close to home, as when Colonel Harry Vaughn, the President's friend and personal aide, was shown to have accepted a deep freezer from a man having business with the government. In 1951 the Democratic National Chairman himself resigned after being charged by a congressional inquiry with "selling" influence. Although no serious scandals were ever found, the sporadic acts of corruption gave some substance to Republican charges that the Democrats were becoming careless as a result of being too long in control of the executive branch of the government.

Fair Deal and New Deal. As Harry Truman himself acknowledged, the Fair Deal was an attempt to extend the principles of Franklin Roosevelt's New Deal into a new era. It appealed to the same social groups—industrial workers, ethnic minorities, and farmers—who had been the mainstay of the early Roosevelt coalition. Moreover, like the New Deal it relied upon the federal government for the achievement of its ends, thus continuing the trend toward centralization begun at the opening of the century with Theodore Roosevelt. On the other hand, in some respects it went beyond the New Deal, as in the field of civil rights, where Truman assumed a more courageous and forthright position than Roosevelt ever had. It might also be said that Truman's vigorous support of organized labor was equally in marked contrast to Roosevelt's more cautious, even at times patronizing, approach.

The men around Truman, though, were several cuts below those who, like Harold Ickes, Harry Hopkins, Rexford Tugwell, Tom Corcoran, and Thurmond Arnold, helped make the New Deal one of the most intellectually exciting political movements in all American history. (Only the Kennedy administration would rival it.) The only member of Truman's immediate political family (below the Cabinet level) who even approached the caliber of the New Dealers was Clark Clifford, one of Truman's White House aides. Clifford was a young, personable, and talented lawyer from St. Louis who masterminded the campaign of 1948. Clifford went back to private practice in January 1950. In the mid-1960s he would reappear as an adviser to Lyndon B. Johnson, and in 1968 he became Johnson's Secretary of Defense.

The Revolution in Foreign Policy, 1947–1948

At the same time that the Truman administration was wrestling with the complicated problems of a domestic adjustment to peacetime, it was called upon to confront a dangerously deteriorating situation in Europe and in the world balance of power. The administration's response constituted nothing less than a revolution in American foreign policy. Although the roots of that revolution ran back to 1945 and 1946 when difficulties with the Russians had first become apparent, it was brought to public attention by events during the early months of 1947.

The European Economic Crisis of 1947. While the United States fruitlessly sought to settle the political state of Europe through peace treaties and conferences, the economy of western Europe labored to recover from the war. Production limped and restoration lagged. Even loans from America did not seem to help: the $3.75 billion loan made to Britain in 1946 and intended to last the British for four years would be exhausted in a year and a half. Of all the countries of western Europe aside from Germany, Britain was probably the worst off because it was so heavily dependent upon imports. Some 42 per cent of British food and raw materials came from dollar-area countries, yet only 14 per cent of British exports went to those same areas. As a consequence, Britain was running a constant deficit in dollars as it endeavored to keep its people alive. This dollar gap existed to some degree in all the countries of western Europe, for all of them depended upon American imports for a significant portion of their food and equipment.

The struggle of the British people to survive attracted world attention in January 1947, when the worst blizzard since 1894 swept down upon the island, adding new misery to old. Hundreds of villages and towns were completely isolated as telephone and telegraph lines broke and roads were made impassable by snow and ice. The digging of coal was halted because either the miners could not get to the mines or trucks and trains could not move to haul away what coal was brought up. Without fuel, railroads and factories gradually came to a standstill. The production of electricity fell off, and for a number of weeks the British government reimposed the wartime blackout in an effort to conserve fuel and power. It took four months for production to regain the level of December 1946.

That savage winter hurt all the countries of western Europe. Starvation stalked the streets in dozens of villages and cities. In France the winter destroyed 3.5 million acres of winter wheat—a blow that came on top of the shortages caused by the drought during the previous summer. The winter by itself, of course, did not cause the economic plight of Europe; the economic sickness was deeper than that. But the devastating effects of the weather brought the economic malaise of Europe to the attention of the dullest observer.

The Truman Doctrine. The most immediate result of the economic crisis was the decision by the British government to abandon its efforts to support the government of Greece in its war against Communist-supported guerrillas. Toward the end of February 1947, the British government quietly informed the United States that, as of April 1 of that year, the traditional British political and military role in Greece and Turkey would have to be abandoned in the face of diminishing dollar reserves.

Almost immediately President Truman and Secretary of State George C. Marshall, who had succeeded James F. Byrnes in January 1947, called congressional leaders to a secret meeting in the White House to discuss the British action. Marshall and Undersecretary of State Dean Acheson briefed the leaders on the gravity of the situation in the Middle East should British power be withdrawn. Even the best informed congressmen had had no inkling of how close the British government was to abandoning its traditional role as a stabilizing influence in the eastern Mediterranean. After Truman told the meeting that he thought the United States should take up the British position in the strategic area by offering aid to Greece and Turkey, Republican Senator Arthur H. Vandenberg, chairman of the important Foreign Relations Committee, remarked, "Mr. President, if that's what you want, there's only one way to get it. That is to make a personal appearance before Congress and scare hell out of the country."

On March 12 Truman did as Vandenberg advised. He appeared before a joint session of Congress to ask for $400 million in immediate economic and military aid for Greece and Turkey. "We shall not realize our objectives" of peace and order in the world, he told Congress and the American people, "unless we are willing to help free institutions and their national integrity against aggressive movements that seek to impose upon them totalitarian regimes. This is no more than a frank recognition that totalitarian regimes imposed on free peoples, by direct or indirect aggression, undermine the foundations of international peace and hence the security of the United States." The speech, received with great solemnity by Congress, aroused much discussion throughout the country. Vociferous and often strident opposition came from conservatives and left-wing liberals in unusual and uneasy agreement. Everybody recognized that the policy meant a sharp departure from the whole history of American foreign relations. The United States, for the first time in peace, was being asked to commit its military (though that was deliberately underplayed in the President's message) and economic strength to the defense of countries outside the Western Hemisphere. Moreover, the imprecise language used seemed to commit the United States to being concerned with the *internal* affairs of all the nations of the world. Although that interpretation seems to be a misreading of the intention, especially in the light of the subsequent Marshall Plan, some revisionist historians have interpreted the Truman Doctrine as the beginning of the global struggle against Communism. Actually the line of development is much less direct and consistent, but that fact in no way detracts from the novelty of Truman's call to the country. Congress placed its sanction upon this historic turn in policy when the Senate in April, and then the House in May, voted the emergency funds asked for by the President.

In his eagerness to win congressional and popular approval for the new policy President Truman virtually ignored the United Nations, mainly on the grounds that the U.N. was in no position to offer aid and, perhaps more important, because the Soviet veto might well have prevented any action at all. But public opinion polls reported that a majority of the American people were displeased with this approach, and the administration rectified what Vandenberg referred to as its "colossal blunder" by accepting the senator's amendment to the aid bill. Vandenberg's amendment provided that American aid to Greece and Turkey would be terminated if and when the U.N.—freed by prior agreement from the threat of an American veto—should vote that it deemed such aid unnecessary or undesirable.

The Crisis Deepens. Even as Congress debated the emergency aid to Greece and Turkey, it was clear to informed people that the plight of Europe was so serious that the less than half a billion dollars the President asked for on behalf of Greece and Turkey was no more than a palliative. Walter Lippmann, the noted newspaper commentator, warned that only billions of dollars of aid, along the lines of the old lend-lease arrangements, could stem the ominous decline of the European economy. When Secretary Marshall returned from an exhausting and fruitless foreign ministers' conference in Moscow in late April, he told the country: "The recovery of Europe has been far slower than had been expected. Disintegrating forces are becoming evident. The patient is sinking while the doctors deliberate." The very next day he asked George F. Kennan, an expert on Russia and the head of the Policy Planning Section of the State Department, to draw up recommendations for preventing the economic collapse of Europe.* In May, as disturbing reports of actual starvation came from Europe, the United States rushed grain to Germany, where individual rations had sunk as low as 800 calories per day.

While Kennan and his staff worked behind the walls of the State Department on a plan for European aid, Marshall prepared to broach his revolutionary idea to the people of the United States and to the world. He presented his plan, which ever after has been called by his name, in a short commencement address at Harvard University on June 5, 1947. Abandoning the strong ideological tone of anti-Communism that suffused the Truman Doctrine, Marshall based his offer on considerations of human need. "Our policy," he said, "is not directed against any country or doctrine, but against hunger, poverty, desperation and chaos." But whatever assistance is given, he emphasized, must "not be on a piecemeal basis as various crises develop. Any assistance that this Government may render in the future should provide a cure rather than a mere palliative." He also made it clear that he was not excluding the Soviet Union and the states of eastern Europe from the offer, though none of the policymakers thought Russia would accept.

Within hours after Marshall had finished speaking, Foreign Minister Ernest Bevin of Great Britain was already reading the address, a copy of which had been sent directly to him. Bevin, as he remarked later, "seized the offer with both hands." Within twenty-two days after Marshall concluded his address, the representatives of most of the countries of western and central Europe were assembling in Paris to discuss the carrying out of his idea.

The Marshall Plan. As worked out by the administration, the offer that Marshall extended to Europe in June turned out to be a bold experiment in reviving the European economy and in containing Communism by eliminating the poverty and misery on which it fed. The heart of the experiment was an

---

* Kennan had been thinking about the problem of Russian expansionism for some time. His conclusions became the primary justification for what was later called the policy of containment. Kennan argued that if Russian expansionist tendencies were firmly resisted, developments inside the Soviet Union would in time reduce the pressure for expansion, thus rendering the Communists more cooperative in international affairs. His first public statement on containment—earlier ones circulated privately in the government—appeared anonymously in the magazine *Foreign Affairs* in July 1947. Later the same statement appeared in his book *American Diplomacy, 1900–1950* (Chicago, 1951).

American grant of $17 billion to European countries, spread over a period of four years, with $6.8 billion of that figure to be expended in the fifteen months following April 1, 1948. The figures had been arrived at by the administration as a result of discussions with, and studies of, the sixteen participating nations, all of which were located west of the iron curtain. (The U.S.S.R., after some hesitation, had finally refused to have anything to do with the offer and required its satellites and its neighbors like Czechoslovakia, which was interested, to stay away from the discussions.)

The very boldness of the administration's bill, not to mention its expense, made it suspect among many people in the United States. Senator Vandenberg, who became an ardent champion of the plan in the Republican-controlled Senate, had to fight hard to overcome the suspicion in Congress. In presenting the bill to the Senate in December 1947, he called it "a calculated risk" to "help stop World War III before it starts." Within the purview of this plan, he told his colleagues, "are 270,000,000 people of the stock which has largely made America. . . . This vast friendly segment of the earth must not collapse. The iron curtain must not come to the rims [*sic*] of the Atlantic either by aggression or by default." Tirelessly he defended the plan against the charge, usually from his conservative, economy-minded Republican colleagues, that it was a gigantic "international WPA," "a bold Socialist blueprint," or a plain waste of American money.

While Congress was holding hearings on the European aid bill that fall, Europe was sinking deeper into the economic abyss. The British, in a desperate effort to reduce imports, cut each person's meat ration to twenty cents worth *per week*. In September President Truman urged Americans not to waste any food, for Europe needed all that could be spared. A few days later he asked Congress to consider immediate stop-gap aid of $580 million to prevent starvation in Europe in the coming winter. In October he called upon Americans to observe meatless Tuesdays and eggless Thursdays in an effort to conserve grain for Europe. (Cattle and poultry are heavy consumers of grain.) At his request liquor distillers agreed to a sixty-day shutdown in a further effort to save grain.

The Consummation of the Revolution. If the effects of the winter of 1946–1947 left some Americans still unconvinced of the need to help Europe, certain actions of the Russians and European Communists provided additional arguments. And the administration, desirous of getting its program for Europe approved, did not hesitate to stress the menace of Communism and Soviet military power along with its strategic and economic concerns for Europe's revival. In February 1948 Communist workers' groups suddenly took over the government of Czechoslovakia. Thus the country in central Europe whose government most Americans considered closest to their own form of democracy slipped behind the iron curtain. Nor was it any comfort to know that the largest political parties in France and Italy were Communist, that these parties slavishly supported the foreign policy of the Soviet Union, and that they were influential in the important labor unions. Soon after the Czech coup the administration received word from the usually calm American commander in Berlin that he had reason to believe a Russian attack upon western Europe was imminent. On March 17 President Truman, in an address before Congress that was carried over radio to the country, emphasized the alleged Soviet threat by pointedly identifying the U.S.S.R. as the "one nation" obstructing peace and threatening the non-Communist world. Linking the European Recovery Bill and the fear of Soviet power, he urged Congress not to put off enacting the aid bill along with universal military training and a temporary reinstatement of the draft. On March 21 and again on April 1, the Soviets obligingly provided further evidence of their truculence by placing restrictions on troops and supplies going across their zone of Germany to Allied stations in Berlin. The Berlin blockade did not start in earnest for another two months, but these moves, in retrospect, seem to have been the first intimations. On April 2 Congress passed the European Recovery Bill, granting the President about 90 per cent of the funds he had asked for the first year, but cautiously refusing to commit itself for any longer period.

The Significance of the European Recovery Program. In speaking about the Marshall Plan in later years, some American statesmen portrayed it as a remarkably unselfish act, welling up from the deep generosity of the American people. And even in the 1970s there are knowing Europeans who lived through those years who continue to speak of it in just those terms. But such descriptions are excessively generous, as revisionist American historians have recently emphasized. Americans conceived and carried out the ERP primarily because it promised to meet certain American, as well as European, needs. It aimed to revive the west European economy not only because Europe was the major trading area of the United States, but also because western Europe's revived strength was deemed essential to the security of the United States. Moreover, many Americans were literally as well as figuratively children of Europe and therefore felt a deep concern for the fate of the Old World. And finally, the ERP was a way of preventing the spread of Communism. In retrospect it seems that this last purpose received more public emphasis than it warranted, usually because the administration thought that the ingrained hostility of Americans to Communism would put the program across when other arguments would not. The emphasis was unfortunate, not only because it encouraged an unreasoning anti-Communism, but also because the European Recovery Program was much more than simply a means of containing Russian power or Communism. It was an adventurous act on the part of the American people, acting through their leaders, to deal vigorously, at a substantial cost to themselves, with a major problem. The $12.5 billion given to the sixteen participating countries between April 1948 and June 1951 was more than a means of putting the western European economy on its feet; it was part of a deliberate design to bring the economy of western Europe up to date and to encourage the introduction of new machines, new methods, and new approaches to production. Only through such a fundamental overhauling, it was correctly decided, could production reach a level adequate to maintain the inhabitants of western Europe at a decent standard of living.

Probably at no other time, except during the war years, has American influence been so directly and deeply felt in Europe as it was in the years of the ERP. American experts and advisers swarmed across sixteen countries, advising here, helping with new techniques there, cajoling reluctant European businessmen and labor leaders in still a third place, always in pursuit of that elusive productivity which for Europe meant the difference between a low subsistence economy and one that could provide a healthy and satisfying life for all classes of society. Gradually the effect became apparent. By 1951 production had increased in all the countries, with the average growth amounting to some 37 per cent in three years. Eventually, though such a goal was not included in the original plan, the ERP propelled western Europe in the direction of economic integration and unification and away from tariff walls, blocked currencies, and nationalistic self-sufficiency. Americans, always convinced of the value of their tariff-free states as a gigantic national market, could not help but think that a similar political and economic framework would work the same wonders in Europe. By the time the original Marshall Plan was coming to an end, the European Steel and Coal Community and the Common Market, both destined to come into being in the late 1950s, were already foreshadowed by the habits and practices of economic cooperation fostered among the sixteen nations by the ERP.

After the invasion of South Korea by Communist North Korean troops in June 1950, the ERP rather suddenly shifted from a strictly economic recovery program, in which no funds were to be used for military expenditures, to an adjunct of the military defense of the West. Thereafter projects were undertaken with military objectives uppermost, and the revolutionary scheme to rehabilitate and renovate the economy of Europe was abandoned only half-finished. But before it was dropped, the example of a great nation's undertaking to lend its treasure and its brains to assist the ancient continent from which it had been born had been displayed for all the world to see. Regardless of the undoubted benefit the United States reaped from the Marshall Plan, the program still stands as one of the world's most remarkable examples of an enlightened foreign policy in action. Upon the rehabilitation of Europe, after all, rested the success of the foreign policy of the United States for the next decade, from the North Atlantic Treaty Organization to the successful defense of the Republic of Korea.

Point Four. In his inaugural address in January 1949, President Truman added another dimension to the American commitment to work for the improvement of the world's economy. As the fourth point in his address, he announced that the United States would undertake "a bold new program for making the benefits of our scientific and industrial progress available for the improvement and growth of underdeveloped areas." In subsequent years American technicians spread around the globe, assisting primitive farmers to become less so, introducing better means of disease prevention and cure, and generally helping to bring the labor-saving and life-saving technology of the West to the unproductive economies of Asia, Africa, and South America.

An Unprecedented Commitment. The capstone to the arch of Truman's policy of containment of Russian Communism was the North Atlantic Treaty Organization. Early in 1948, after the Czech coup and as the Soviets were tightening controls over Berlin, Great Britain, France, Belgium, Luxembourg, and the Netherlands joined together in a mutual defense pact. Later in the year, when these Brussels Pact countries, as they were called, asked the United States to associate itself with them, the Truman administration suggested that the number participating be increased. In the final agreement twelve countries on both sides of the north Atlantic joined the alliance; the number was increased to fourteen in 1952, when Turkey and Greece became members. In article five of the treaty all the signatories agreed that "an armed attack against one or more of them in Europe or North America shall be considered an attack against them all." But the kind of assistance expected of any signatory was only that which could be constitutionally provided—a clause demanded by the American constitutional requirement that only Congress can declare war.

The signing of the treaty at Washington on April 4, 1949, was an historic moment in the diplomatic history of the United States. For the first time during peace, the United States had obligated itself to come to the assistance of nations in Europe. This obligation was the strongest yet in the course of the diplomatic revolution that had begun only four years earlier with the ratification of the United Nations Charter. American attitudes had indeed come a long way since World War II when President Roosevelt had informed Stalin and Churchill that, after the war was over, the American people would not permit United States forces to be stationed in Europe for more than two years at the most. The North Atlantic Treaty encountered little opposition in the Senate, passing, with the vigorous help of Senator Vandenberg, by a vote of eighty-two to thirteen on July 21, 1949. In early 1951 General Eisenhower was brought back from his retirement post as president of Columbia University to serve as Supreme Commander of the new twelve-nation force. By 1953 NATO counted sixty ground divisions and 5000 planes at its disposal, as compared with the sixteen divisions that could have been mustered in 1950 against an estimated 125 Russian divisions. There was still no equality of force between NATO and the Russians and there never would be. But the Russian striking force now necessary for an attack would be so large that it could not be organized without detection far in advance of the assault. There would thus be time for further defensive actions to be taken. Perhaps even more important, the participation of the United States in these forces insured an American response to any attack from the East and thus made such an attack less likely.

The Berlin Blockade. One of the reasons the United States and western Europe established NATO was the Russian threat to Berlin. Indeed, soon after the European Recovery Program went into effect the simmering conflict between the United States and the Soviet Union over Germany boiled up to a new level of danger. In early 1948 the United States reformed the currency in the western zone of Germany to help rehabilitate that devastated country. The Soviets, still fearful of and hence opposed to a united Germany that would be friendly to the West, saw in the American move a threat to the economy of its zone in eastern Germany, since the new and sounder currency would also circulate in West Berlin, which was well inside the Russian zone.

The Russian response to the currency reform was the closing of all rail, auto, and barge routes to West Berlin. The United States, Great Britain, and France were faced with the choice of going to war over the question of access to Berlin or of abandoning the change in the currency. Then another possibility was suggested: to supply Berlin by air, since the Western powers had their own airfields in Berlin. Thus began the gigantic airlift of more than 3000 tons of food, fuel, and raw materials each day, which the 2.5 million people living in the western zone of the city needed. To carry out the job, an almost uninterrupted line of planes flew across the Soviet zone of Germany every day and night for over ten months. This prodigious feat of organization, courage, and stamina captured the imagination of the West, restored the sagging morale of the West Berliners, and saved the city. The Russians, perhaps recognizing that they were already pressing hard against the limits of Allied tolerance, did not use their military aircraft to disrupt the airlift. Not until May 1949, however, were the ground transportation facilities again open to the West. By then the airlift had clearly demonstrated the ability of the Allies to supply Berlin through the winter, when fuel for heating needed to be brought in, as well as in the summer.

The establishment of NATO and the successful reopening of access to Berlin marked the end of the great effort to prevent a threatened domination of Europe by Russia and Communism. In retrospect the likelihood of a Russian invasion of western Europe seems much less than at the time. Indeed, revisionist historians have argued that the revolution in American foreign policy was really a thrust for American economic and political domination of Europe under the guise of resisting Russian threats. This view, however, seriously underplays western Europe's own quite independent perception and fear of Russian pressure. It also lacks any substantial evidence of such intention from American sources, though American officials certainly hoped to keep open trade with as much of Europe as possible. Moreover, the revisionist view ignores the fact that Russian actions at the time did not always appear as restrained or limited as they seem to have been in retrospect. The Western leaders of the 1940s had just finished a war against another dictator who had in fact dominated Europe. It seemed natural, if careless in retrospect, to apply the lessons learned then to resist another dictator who seemed bent on the same course.

The revisionist argument has not gone unnoticed by those once at the center of policymaking. Dean Acheson, one of the architects of American policy during these years, defended American actions while admitting that some of the charges of the revisionists might have some merit. Two decades after the revolution in foreign policy, Acheson wrote in his memoirs that "a school of academic criticism has concluded that we overreacted to Stalin, which, in turn, caused him to overreact to the policies of the United States. This may be true. Fortunately,

EUROPEAN DEFENSE ALLIANCES

- NATO members in Europe, 1949 (or by date of admission)
- Warsaw Pact members, 1955

Figures indicate millions of dollars of Marshall Plan aid.

perhaps, these authors were not called upon to analyze a situation in which the United States had not taken the action it did take." Furthermore, without access to Russian government documents it is difficult to know what Russian intentions were in western Europe, especially if Russia had faced no opposing military force of consequence. And finally, as R. L. Richardson has pointed out, "it is obvious, as the revisionists insist, that war-weary Russia was unwilling to provoke a war with the United States, but it is equally obvious that without the American presence, Russia would have dominated war-weary Europe."

The successful containment of Russian and Communist influence and power in Europe did not end the pressure upon the Western nations. As will be seen in the next chapter, just as new bulwarks were being thrown up in Europe, unexpected challenges were emerging in Asia. But even before the Communist threat was felt in Korea, the fear of Communism in the United States gave birth to a domestic witch-hunt that surpassed even the excesses of the Red Scare at the end of the First World War.

The Great Fear, 1949–1954

In 1789, early in the French Revolution, a nameless fear seized the peasants of France. For months, afraid yet without knowing the source of that fear, they went on a rampage against the Old Regime, burning, looting, and killing those they suspected of opposing the revolution. Historians have called this emotional outbreak *La Grande Peur*. A similar, though less violent, outburst of irrational fear seemed to grip the American people during the five years between 1949 and 1954. Like the French peasants who feared that the landlords were launching counterrevolution, the American people in those years feared that international Communism was so powerful and so pervasive that its agents might strike anywhere, from within the country as well as from without. As long as the Great Fear persisted, suspicion corroded hitherto healthy and trustful relations among Americans. Friends became circumspect with one another; people feared to exercise their fundamental right to sign petitions to their government; teachers were compelled to swear that they were not Communists; United States senators trembled before one of their number who had appointed himself the grand inquisitor of Communists; the State Department and other government agencies summarily fired all employees who had ever been even remotely connected with leftish causes; and the overseas information service of the United States was subjected to a humiliating investigation by two young men whose antics made their country the laughingstock of Europe.

The roots of the Great Fear were to be found in the deteriorating international situation in Europe during 1946 and 1947. The uncovering in February 1946 of a Soviet spy ring in Canada, in which several Canadian Communists were involved, dramatized the fact that domestic Communists were likely recruits for espionage on behalf of the Soviet Union. In the context of the developing contest between the Western nations and the Soviet Union, the loyalty of Communists and Communist sympathizers in government became a subject of intense popular and political concern and inquiry, abroad as well as in the United States. The British government, for example, removed a number of Communist governmental employees from sensitive positions because their loyalty was questionable. The very existence of the Soviet Union gave the Great Fear a more objective justification than the Red Scare of 1919, when Bolshevik strength in international affairs was a figment of the imagination. In March 1947 President Truman, responding in part to Republican assertions of Communists in government as well as the general fear of disloyalty in government, ordered a check of all federal employees to find out if any should be dismissed for Communist party affiliation or sympathy. Later that same year a permanent board was set up to evaluate charges of disloyalty brought against government employees.

The federal loyalty program quickly became a target of many liberals because the loyalty of employees was ascertained by examinations of their past acts and affiliations—a procedure that might or might not be an accurate measure of present loyalty. Moreover, it was also evident that merely unconventional or radical ideas unrelated to any Communist or disloyal affiliation were often taken by the authorities as evidence of disloyalty. Although all persons concerned admitted that no one possessed a constitutional right to be employed by the government, the practice of dismissing people from jobs they had competently filled for many years simply on the basis of dubious charges against their loyalty endangered the liberties of American citizens.

On the question of Communists in government the Truman administration found itself in a dilemma. The President and most of his administration, as subsequent actions like the veto of a Communist control bill would show, did not believe at any time that Communist subversion was a serious domestic threat. Indeed, the Truman administration did much to resist the mindless anti-Communism of McCarthyism. Yet the administration could not ignore the Communist issue domestically because it had played up the Communist threat internationally when seeking to win popular and Republican support for its foreign policy. The failure to make a clear and consistent distinction between Communism as a political doctrine and as Soviet expansion had come home to roost. Part of the reason that the distinction was not made more sharply was that in the minds of American policymakers it was not always clear; they easily slid from opposing Russian power to opposing Communist ideas. That lack of clear distinction would plague American policymakers in subsequent administrations as well.

The Uncovering of Communist Spying. If the establishment of a loyalty program and the administration's emphasis upon the Communist threat abroad alerted the public to the dangers of Communist espionage, the revelations before congressional committees and in open court of actual spying for the Soviet Union justified the loyalty program to a large number of Americans. In 1948, the same year that the government of Czechoslovakia was taken over by a minority of well-organized Communists, a witness told a congressional committee that she had received classified information from government employees for transmission to the Soviet Union when she was a Russian agent before the war. Another former Communist and Russian agent, Whittaker Chambers, by then a respected senior editor of *Time* magazine, told the same committee that he too had received secret information from Communists employed in the State Department in the late 1930s.

In 1949, as the threat of Russian Communism abroad continued to grow, the search for Communist plots within America reached a new high. That was the year in which the Communists gained complete control of China and the Soviet

Union successfully exploded its first nuclear device, thus breaking the American monopoly. That was also the year of the trial of eleven leaders of the Communist party of the United States, charged by the government under the Smith Act of 1940 with conspiracy to advocate the overthrow of the government by force and violence. The trial lasted over ten months, filled with bitter exchanges between the defense attorneys and the judge, and ended in the conviction of the accused. While the trial was going on, more revelations of Communist espionage continued to reach the front pages of the nation's newspapers.

By this time fear of Communists and their sympathizers was spreading beyond government. In June 1948 the University of California required all of its 4000 faculty members on pain of dismissal to swear that they were not Communists. (A year later 157 faculty members were fired for refusing to take the oath.) The National Education Association, the leading organization of teachers in the country, voted in July that Communist teachers should be barred from all schools. In September at Peekskill, New York, a pleasant country town just north of New York City, a bloody, hate-filled, anti-Communist riot broke out. Thousands of angry, fearful men and women stoned and manhandled a group of admirers of the black singer Paul Robeson because of his known sympathy with the Soviet Union. Some 145 people were hurt in the resulting melee.

The Hiss Case. Although Alger Hiss was not technically charged with spying or with being a former Communist, his trial for perjury in 1949 was certainly the most sensational of the several public examinations of Communists in government. It was also the most divisive. Part of the testimony of Whittaker Chambers when he appeared before the House Committee on Un-American Activities in 1948 concerned Hiss, who had been a State Department employee in the late 1930s and early 1940s, but who by 1948 was president of the highly respected Carnegie Endowment for International Peace. Chambers testified that he had received from Hiss secret State Department documents for transmission to the Soviet Union. Hiss at first denied ever knowing Chambers, but later conceded that he knew Chambers slightly under another name. Under oath Hiss categorically denied ever passing secret documents to Chambers or anyone else. Although the formal charge brought against him was no more than perjury—the statute of limitations precluded any more serious charge—to most Americans the trial of Alger Hiss, which began in May 1949, was a trial for espionage, if not for treason. (After Hiss' conviction, former President Herbert Hoover wrote Congressman Richard Nixon, who had been a defender of Chambers, "At last the stream of treason that has existed in our government has been exposed in a fashion all may believe.")

The emotions stirred by Hiss' two trials—the jury could not agree in the first one—ran deep. Hiss, carefully groomed, well-educated, highly respected, and strongly supported in his first trial by eminent figures in public life, stood in sharp contrast to the unkempt Chambers, who, though by then prosperous, testified candidly, almost embarrassingly, to his early dissolute, irresponsible life as a writer, Communist agent, and professional liar. To those people who had always suspected that the New Deal was soft on Communism, Alger Hiss—who had been a minor figure in the Roosevelt administration—seemed living proof that they had been right all along. Liberals who distrusted renegade Communists and disliked anyone who reported the activities and ideas of former friends to vindictive congressional investigating committees refused to believe that Hiss could be guilty, even when he was convicted and sentenced to five years in prison. Max Lerner, a liberal commentator, wrote after the trial, "There is a difference between the legal verdict of a jury and the moral verdict each of us must render to himself." Hiss' innocence, despite the verdict of the jury, remained an article of faith among many liberals, even though during the trial Hiss was unable to counter some very damaging evidence brought against him. Efforts toward obtaining a new trial, though strenuously pushed, were fruitless.

Spies and the Bomb. Until 1950 most of the allegations and evidence of Communist infiltration of the government pertained to the years before the war. In 1950, however, the double-headed fear of domestic Communists and Russian military power came together in a new and frightening combination: the public learned that American Communists had helped steal the secrets of the nuclear bomb for the Soviet Union. The first report of such activities came from abroad in February 1950, when the British government announced the arrest of Klaus Fuchs, a German-born physicist who was then employed at the British government's nuclear energy establishment at Harwell and who during the war had worked at Los Alamos, New Mexico, on the development of the first nuclear bomb. Fuchs soon confessed to giving scientific information on the nuclear bomb to the Soviets. In May the Federal Bureau of Investigation, which had been responsible for alerting the British to Fuch's treachery, arrested an American, Harry Gold, as an accomplice of Fuchs. During the summer months other Americans, including Julius and Ethel Rosenberg, were arrested for having taken part in a conspiracy to obtain and pass secret information on the nuclear bomb to the Soviet Union. When brought to trial, all of them were found guilty; the Rosenbergs were executed in 1953 for their part in the conspiracy while the others received long prison terms.

To these sensational revelations the Congress responded with the Internal Security Act of 1950, passing it over a veto in which Truman denounced the measure as "the greatest danger to freedom of speech, press, and assembly, since the Alien and Sedition Laws of 1798." Among other restrictions, the act required Communist and Communist-front organizations to register with the government and to identify as Communist all their official mail and literature. The most severe of all the provisions of the act, and one that measured the extremity of congressional concern, was the clause that authorized the government to place all Communists, citizens and aliens alike, in concentration camps whenever a national emergency should occur. (That provision was repealed in 1970.)

The Rise and Fall of McCarthy. The arrests and trials of Communists, along with the revelations of Communist espionage, continued during 1951 and 1952, but the most significant element furthering the Great Fear in these years and after was the rise to prominence of Senator Joseph R. McCarthy. Like Alger Hiss, the Republican junior senator from Wisconsin seemed to trigger tremendous emotion in the American people. To many Americans he appeared to be the most forthright and effective opponent of Communists in the nation. To those who suspected his motives and doubted his allegations of Communist infiltration of government he seemed to be the greatest menace to democratic government in our history. From hindsight it appears that he was not quite either. McCarthy's anti-Communism was shallow—largely a handy vehicle for achieving personal glory and

For a brief time Joseph McCarthy and his young aides wielded immense power as they investigated the loyalty of government officials. *Photo: Eve Arnold—Magnum*

reelection. His following, which at times was huge, posed no serious political threat, for it received no program from its leader—apparently McCarthy had none. He was a product and a perpetuator of the Great Fear, but he could not survive it.

McCarthy gained prominence as an anti-Communist in 1950, when he announced in a speech at Wheeling, West Virginia, that at least fifty-seven Communists were working in the State Department. The Senate later cleared the department of the charge of harboring Communists, but McCarthy's allegations of Communists in government, though never any more soundly based than the first one, continued. In the atmosphere of the Great Fear his power to intimidate government officials and private citizens grew alarmingly, aided by extreme anti-Communist Democrats as well as Republicans. When, as a result of the Republican victory in 1952, McCarthy became chairman of the Senate Committee on Government Operations, he gained a new and effective platform for his attacks. He and his committee proceeded to investigate the State Department, the overseas information service, and any other aspect of government that interested them. He did not hesitate to encourage employees of the executive branch to reveal to him confidential information from their departments. Whole sections were turned inside out as the State Department tried vainly to satisfy McCarthy's standards of purity in matters of Communist infiltration. Inasmuch as McCarthy was the self-appointed authority on the subject, no organization could ever be clear of the charge if he did not consent to the clearance.

As the foregoing suggests, McCarthy was not partisan in his allegations; he attacked the administration of the Republican Eisenhower as vigorously as he had that of the Democratic Truman. Indeed, so powerful was he felt to be that during the 1952 campaign Eisenhower agreed to speak from the same platform with him and to delete from his speech passages praising General George Marshall, even though Eisenhower deeply resented the attacks McCarthy had made earlier in the Senate upon the general.

Imprisoned in the grip of the Great Fear, many Americans supported the senator despite his failure to uncover any Communists in government or to strengthen the security of the United States. As late as January 1954 a Gallup poll reported that 50 per cent of the American people viewed McCarthy and his activities with favor. Few of his wild allegations seemed excessive in the anxious atmosphere of the Great Fear. When the senator sent two young, untrained assistants to survey the United States information centers in the capitals of Europe, people on two continents gasped to think that such irresponsibility could be countenanced in a great democracy. Yet so substantial was the fear of McCarthy that responsible officials whom his investigators suspected of disloyalty were obligingly fired.

McCarthy's power to frighten, however, came to a surprisingly abrupt end. The turnabout began in 1954 with a thirty-five-day Senate investigation of the senator's alleged attempts to interfere in the operation of the Army. During those hearings millions of Americans saw for themselves on their television screens the famous Communist hunter's unprincipled, crude, and bullying tactics, which he now directed against the representatives of the United States Army. Many now began to have second thoughts about McCarthy's integrity and intentions as a fighter against Communism. Even before the Army hearings were concluded, McCarthy became the subject of a hearing himself before a select committee of the Senate inquiring into his conduct as a senator. For years he had insulted and impugned the motives of his fellow senators. Now, at the conclusion of the inquiry, the Senate condemned his conduct; sixty-seven of his colleagues voted against him, though a mere twelve months before only Senator William Fulbright of Arkansas had been willing to stand out against an appropriation for McCarthy's committee. Though he suffered no actual loss of senatorial privileges, McCarthy's influence and power did not survive his condemnation. He soon went into a physical decline, dying in 1957. The effects of his activities were not so quickly removed. As President Eisenhower wrote a decade later, "McCarthyism took its toll on many individuals and on the nation. No one was safe from charges recklessly made from inside the walls of congressional immunity. . . . Innocent people accused of Communist associations or party membership have not to this day been able to clear their names fully." And twenty years later his name is still used in Europe as well as in America to describe unfair and untrue allegations in the name of anti-Communism.

In 1954 the perceived Russian threat to the balance of world power and therefore to the security of the United States and Europe was as great as when the Great Fear first enveloped Americans, but by that date, as the end of McCarthyism showed, they no longer thought that the internal enemy was as dangerous as the foreign. As a consequence, they could turn their attention from a tortured, unending search for traitors in their midst to the maintenance of vigilance abroad.

SUGGESTED READING

There are several single-volume books that cover the years between the end of World War II and the sixties, but none does the job with a livelier style or greater anecdotal richness than Eric Goldman, *Crucial Decade—and After* * (1960). John Brooks, *The Great Leap: The Past Twenty-five Years in America* * (1966) emphasizes social and intellectual changes.

The question of the origins of the Cold War has spawned a literature of considerable size and contentiousness. Basic to the revisionist position is a general study on American foreign policy, William Appleman Williams, *The Tragedy of American Diplomacy* * (rev. ed., 1962). Not all revisionists are of Williams' philosophical outlook, but all emphasize the responsibility of the U.S. more than that of the U.S.S.R. for the beginning of the Cold War. Two revisionist studies of the Cold War period in general are Stephen Ambrose, *The Rise to Globalism: American Foreign Policy Since 1938* * (1971) and Walter LaFeber, *America, Russia, and the Cold War, 1945–1971* * (1972). More detailed revisionist studies are Lloyd C. Gardner, *Architect of Illusion: Men and Ideas in American Foreign Policy* (1970) and Joyce and Gabriel Kolko, *The Limits of Power: The World and United States Foreign Policy, 1945–1954* (1972). The Kolkos' interpretations need to be approached more critically than most. Specific criticisms of the revisionist outlook, particularly as it stems from a New Left perspective, have begun to appear. Least satisfactory because it limits itself to textual criticism is Robert James Maddox, *The New Left and the Origins of the Cold War* (1973). Robert W. Tucker, *The Radical Left and American Foreign Policy* * (1971) is still the best full-length critique. The most profound criticism is to be found in J. A. Thompson, "William Appleman Williams and the 'American Empire,'" *Journal of American Studies,* 7 (1973). J. L. Richardson, "Cold War Revisionist: A Critique," *World Politics,* July 1972, is also very good. Several essays, both for and against revisionism, provide argument and enlightenment in Richard S. Kirkendall, *The Truman Period as a Research Field: A Reappraisal, 1972* (1974).

Much of the literature on the Cold War has not been involved in the revisionist argument, though virtually all has been affected by it. The fullest, and rather official, view of the diplomacy of 1945–1946 is the authoritative Herbert Feis, *Between War and Peace: The Potsdam Conference* * (1960); see also his *From Trust to Terror: The Onset of the Cold War, 1945–1950* (1970), a survey of broader scope. Adam Ulam, *The Rivals: America and Russia Since World War II* * (1971) makes almost no concessions to the revisionists. The best general discussion of the origins is John Lewis Gaddis, *The United States and the Origins of the Cold War, 1941–1947* * (1972), though Gaddis fails to discuss the revisionists directly.

A number of printed sources for the period are already available. Harry S. Truman's *Memoirs,* 2 vols. (1955, 1956), is indispensable, if dull reading. Secretary of State James F. Byrnes has written of his activities during these crucial years in *Speaking Frankly* (1947), and Dean Acheson has given his view in *Present at the Creation: My Years in the*

* Available in a paperback edition.

State Department* (1969). Walter Millis and E. S. Duffield, eds., *The Forrestal Diaries* (1951) provides important information on attitudes within the Truman administration. *The Private Papers of Senator Vandenberg,* edited by A. H. Vandenberg, Jr. (1952), offers insight into the private thoughts of a leading Republican senator of the time. Another view from inside the State Department is provided by Charles E. Bohlen, *Witness to History: 1929–1969,* the memoirs of a leading Russian expert and U.S. foreign service officer.

There is not yet a scholarly biography of Truman, but Richard Kirkendall is writing one. A sketchy but useful volume on Truman before he became President is Frank McNaughton, *This Man Truman* (1945). Jonathan Daniels, *The Man of Independence* (1950) and Cabell Phillips, *The Truman Presidency* (1966) are by journalists favorably disposed toward their subject. Probably the closest thing to a scholarly survey of the Truman years is Richard S. Kirkendall, ed., *The Truman Period as a Research Field* (1967) in conjunction with the revised volume of 1974 already referred to. The excellent compilation B. J. Bernstein and A. J. Matusow, eds., *The Truman Administration: A Documentary History* (1966) can be profitably supplemented by the essays from a radical point of view in B. J. Bernstein, ed., *Politics and Policies of the Truman Administration** (1970). For a judicious discussion of early atomic energy policy see B. J. Bernstein, "The Quest for Security: American Foreign Policy and International Control of Atomic Energy, 1942–1946," *Journal of American History,* 60 (1974).

There are now a number of monographic studies on particular aspects of the Truman years. Susan M. Hartmann, *Truman and the 80th Congress* (1971) critically analyzes Truman's use of the Republicans. Truman's movement into civil rights is discussed favorably and in great detail in Donald R. Coy and Richard T. Ruetten, *Quest and Response: Minority Rights and the Truman Administration* (1973). H. A. Mills and Emily C. Brown, *From the Wagner Act to Taft-Hartley* (1950) puts the principal labor legislation of the Truman administration into historical perspective. Arthur F. McClure, *The Truman Administration and the Problems of Post-War Labor, 1945–48* (1969), carries the story beyond Taft-Hartley. Generally favorable, but also balanced and full, is Alonzo L. Hamby, *Beyond the New Deal: Harry S. Truman and American Liberalism* (1973). On politics in general during Truman's administration, one of the most valuable and interesting is Samuel Lubell, *The Future of American Politics** (1952). For the election of 1948, as well as other elections, consult Volume 4 of the valuable cooperative work, A. M. Schlesinger, Jr., and F. L. Israel, *History of American Presidential Elections, 1789–1968* (1971).

An engrossing book on the innovations in the Truman foreign policies, written by a participant, is Joseph M. Jones, *The Fifteen Weeks** (1955). George F. Kennan, *Memoirs, 1925–1950* (1967) contains elegantly written recollections of the containment policy as seen by the author from inside the State Department. Kennan is usually critical of how the administration conducted foreign policy. Much more critical, and from a radical point of view, is Joyce and Gabriel Kolko, *The Limits of Power,* already referred to.

One of the major controversies of the period is treated with understanding in Alistair Cooke, *A Generation on Trial: U.S.A. v. Alger Hiss* (1950). Hostile to Hiss, but important for understanding the temper of the times, is the memoir of Hiss' accuser, Whittaker Chambers, *Witness* (1952). Probably the best study so far of McCarthy and the anti-Communist crusade is Richard H. Rovere, *Senator Joe McCarthy** (1959); Earl Lathan, *The Communist Controversy in Washington* (1966) is a scholarly study, emphasizing hatred for the New Deal, rather than fear of the Soviet Union, in explaining anti-Communism. Richard M. Freeland, *The Truman Doctrine and the Origins of McCarthyism* (1972) unsuccessfully seeks to place primary blame for McCarthyism on Truman's foreign policy.

The loyalty program is straightforwardly analyzed, along with a discussion of the British government's "purge" of Communists, in Eleanor Bontecou, *The Federal Loyalty-Security Program* (1953). The argument that McCarthyism arose from an earlier Populism is refuted in Michael Paul Rogin, *The Intellectuals and McCarthy: The Radical Specter* (1967). Alan Barth, *The Loyalty of Free Men* * (1951) is a journalist's contemporary indictment of enforced conformity, loyalty oaths, and McCarthyism. Edward A. Shils, *The Torment of Secrecy* (1956) is good on putting the American fears and excesses of those years in historical and sociological perspective. Owen Lattimore, *Ordeal by Slander* (1950) reveals, from the author's personal experience, how McCarthy destroyed one expert on Asia. A vigorous defense of McCarthy is William F. Buckley, Jr., and L. Brent Bozell, *McCarthy and His Enemies* * (1954).

CHAPTER TWO

A FOREIGN POLICY FOR THE COLD WAR

WARS HAVE A WAY of getting out of hand, of releasing forces and evoking reactions that surprise the participants. The Second World War was no exception. Americans suddenly discovered in 1948–1949 that as a result of the war against Hitler, Russian armies were now in the center of Europe. Americans had exchanged the threat of German for Russian power. To thinking men and women, this new development did not negate the once imperative reasons for the war against Germany, but it did show that even for a victor war could have unexpected and undesirable consequences.

The Three-pronged Revolution in Asia

The Collapse of Colonialism. If the results of the war in Europe dropped new problems into the laps of Americans, in western Asia the results were bewildering. One of the ironies of the war was that the victors lost as much territory as defeated Japan and considerably more than Germany. The great colonial powers of Europe—Great Britain, France, and the Netherlands—which had ruled far-flung empires in Asia for as long as three centuries, found that the conclusion of hostilities in Europe also ended their authority in Asia.

The local movements against the colonial powers had begun before the war, but the intrusion of the Japanese into southeast Asia gave a new impetus to the independence movements. As Asians the Japanese did their best to cultivate nationalist sentiment against the Western powers in the countries they overran, especially when it became evident in 1944 that the Allied powers would soon reoccupy their colonies. The world had long known of the Indian movement for independence, but suddenly in 1944 and 1945 it learned of similar movements in French Indochina, Malaya, Burma, Ceylon, and the Dutch East Indies. Thus when the western European powers returned to their former colonies, they found widespread popular unrest, loud demands for independence or autonomy, and sometimes, as in Indochina and the Dutch East Indies, armed rebellion against their colonial authority.

One by one the European powers made the only possible response: they got out of Asia, some more gracefully than others. The United States, having promised the Filipinos their independence before the war, was ready first. Final independence was granted to the islands on July 4, 1946. The British, hard pressed by the losses of the war and now ruled by a Labour party government opposed to colonialism, recognized the direction in which the tides of change were running in Asia more quickly than did the Dutch and French. In February 1947 the British government announced its intention of granting independence by the following year to its valuable if unruly colony of India. Bloody riots between Muslims and Hindus split the Indian subcontinent into India and the newly created Muslim country of Pakistan. On August 15, 1947, both India and Pakistan became independent within the framework of the British Commonwealth of Nations. Less than six months later two other important British colonies, Ceylon and Burma, gained their independence. In 1948 also, in western Asia, the British relinquished their authority in Jordan and Palestine, where they had been the dominant power since the First World War. The preparation of the Malay states for independence took somewhat longer, partly because the country was so disunited and partly because a fierce guerrilla war first had to be fought against

Communist rebels. Nevertheless, in August 1957 Malaya became an independent state. Although Singapore, the once great bastion of British power in Asia, still flew the Union Jack, it gained its independence in 1963. Thus, of the many areas once under British control in Asia, only the pinpoint of Hong Kong remained. All over Asia the sun was indeed setting on the British Empire.

Not all the European powers in Asia recognized the shape of the future. The Dutch, though faced with a colonial rebellion when they returned to the East Indies, were not willing to grant it independence. For several years they fought strenuously against the nationalist forces, even though most of the world considered their cause lost and their ambition outmoded. In late 1949 they were compelled to agree to the complete transfer of power to the new nationalist government of the United States of Indonesia. Although in western Asia the French relinquished their control over Lebanon and Syria in 1946, in eastern Asia they resembled the Dutch, unable to accept the reality of the nationalist movements for independence. For almost a decade after 1945, the French struggled to suppress a continuous, large-scale military rebellion in Indochina. The most persistent of the nationalist elements was the Communist-led Vietminh, which had assumed authority from the Japanese in 1945. The climax of the long fight against the Vietminh came in 1954, when French resistance to this manifestation of the new Asian nationalism drew the United States into novel commitments in southeast Asia. These commitments and their consequences are more properly discussed later; here it is sufficient to note that in 1954 the French finally abandoned their eighty-year-old sovereignty over Indochina. In 1974 the colonial era could be said to have come to an end, for in that year Portugal, which had founded the first overseas empire during its naval explorations in the sixteenth century, announced the abandonment of its empire in Africa.

The Nature of Anticolonialism. Historically nationalism is a European phenomenon, originating and reaching its earliest flowering on that continent. But in expanding their power and their culture around the globe during the heyday of imperialism in the nineteenth century, the great colonial nations of Europe introduced nationalism to an Asia that barely knew either the word or the idea. Thus the whirlwind of nationalism that the colonial powers reaped in 1945 and after had actually been sown by the colonial powers themselves.

But if in that sense Asian nationalism was a product of the West, in a more fundamental sense it was anti-Western—a revolt against Europe. The greatest fact in the minds of these former colonial peoples was their hatred of Western colonialism. For them there was nothing abstract about the term; its definition was drawn from decades and sometimes centuries of their own history. The countries they associated with that hated experience were the principal allies of the United States in Europe: Great Britain, France, Belgium, and the Netherlands. Efforts by the United States to counter this liability by portraying the Soviet Union as an imperialistic and colonial-minded power came to nought for a very good reason. While American assertions about the imperialistic nature of Soviet policy may have been true in the abstract, to the new nations of Asia the Soviet Union simply was not a colonial power in their sense of the word; the Communists had no colonies in Asia and Africa. Since the Soviet Union and other Communist states were free of the taint of that colonialism, the emerging nations could—and did—deal with them as potential friends. Actually, however, most of the new nations, fearing to jeopardize their independence by close association with either camp in the Cold War, preferred to be neutral in their international posture. But even that neutralist position caused difficulties. During the Eisenhower administrations, for example, Secretary of State John Foster Dulles severely criticized the policy of neutralism among the emerging nations. At one point he announced that neutralism, except under very special circumstances, was "an immoral and shortsighted conception." At other times he seemed to think of it as a way station on the road to Communist despotism.

In the 1950s the nationalist revolution in Asia, which was the great new fact of international relations on that continent, spread to Africa as well. By that time, too, it was evident that to the urge for national independence had been added the drive for economic growth and an improved standard of living. But national independence, the history of the postwar years makes clear, is much easier to achieve than economic advancement. Virtually all the new countries were at best peasant countries, devoid of capital, modern agricultural techniques, or an industrial base. Furthermore, in their desire to improve their economic status as rapidly as possible they looked to the wealthy countries of western Europe, to the United States, and to the Soviet Union for help. In this way the rise of the independent countries of Asia and Africa has had ramifications beyond the decline in the power of the former colonial powers, important as that has been. It has also meant that Asia, Africa, and to a certain extent Latin America became areas in which the Western nations competed against the Soviet Union and Communist China. In short, a whole new realm of Cold War competition opened up as a result of the Asian revolution and its spread to Africa.

Winning the support of these new countries was not easy for the United States. As a leader of the West and a power with economic and financial connections throughout the world, the United States wanted a stable community of nations. But in the underdeveloped parts of the globe, disorder and instability were the conditions of existence. During the 1950s and the early 1960s the Russians, less dependent on and less involved in world trade and finance, thought they could only gain from change and upheaval. They welcomed economic breakdown and political instability in a way the United States could not. Americans may have approved emotionally of the nationalist ambitions of the emerging peoples and of their hope for economic betterment, but American economic and strategic interests were more likely to be hurt by upheaval and change than were the Communists'. The contrast in outlook was most evident in the Congo crisis of 1961. The United Nations hurriedly sent in troops and supplies to restore order after the breakdown of government there soon after the Belgians left, while the Communist states looked with favor and anticipation upon the upheaval. Since 1965, as will be seen in Chapter Four, the Russians have assumed a more traditionally big power attitude toward such examples of political instability, as their mediation in the Indian-Pakistan border war, the Vietnam settlement, and the Middle East war of 1973 make quite clear. For a while in the 1960s Communist China took the place of Russia as the primary outsider in the world and as the nation that felt it had more to gain than to lose from political disorganization in the world. But since 1971, as the visit of President Nixon to China signaled, China too has apparently abandoned its outsider's role. This means that the newly independent states of Asia and Africa will have less freedom of action in the future for they cannot count on playing off one big power against another. Nor can they expect much financial aid from the United States. Foreign aid appropriations fell steadily as the sixties came to an end and ceased almost entirely in the 1970s. As one rather cynical Englishman wrote in 1973, "In most developed countries, aid now has only two not very powerful lobbies behind it, the churches and the young."

Effects of Anticolonialism in the U.N. One immediate consequence of the nationalist movements in Asia and Africa has been the alteration in the alignment of forces in the United Nations. As a result of the Cold War, and especially since the United States, during the Korean War, succeeded in having the General Assembly assume the power to make recommendations to member states when a threat to the peace arose, the General Assembly has superseded the Security Council as the most important body of the United Nations. But if the General Assembly avoids the paralysis the veto causes in the Security Council, it suffers instead from equality of voting: a vote by a small state like Costa Rica is equal to that of the Soviet Union or the United States. Such a procedure puts a premium upon numbers while ignoring the reality of power—always a dangerous practice in government. Between 1945 and 1965, when U.N. membership was 116, fifty-five new countries from Asia and Africa gained admission. These nations, held together by their newness and their anticolonial origins, constituted a formidable voting bloc. For most of them American resistance to Communist power in Asia and Europe was at best a secondary concern, as their voting, year after year, for the admission of Communist China against American desires quite clearly showed. At the same time, the U.N. itself has suffered in authority as its actions have been controlled by many weak states, and consequently the two superpowers have sought increasingly to settle world problems between themselves, as in the Middle East wars of 1967 and 1973.

The Transformation of Japan. The second prong of the revolution in Asia was the impact of the American occupation of Japan. Although ostensibly the representative of all the Allied powers that helped defeat Japan, the American commander in Japan, General Douglas MacArthur, was in fact the sole authority during the occupation. Under his command the United States not only stripped Japan of all its colonies, including Formosa and Korea, but deliberately undertook to destroy the old Japan. A thoroughgoing and successful agrarian reform program redistributed the land to the peasantry, and a new constitution brought back parliamentary institutions. The constitution also reduced the emperor from a god to a mere symbol of national unity and removed the army from politics and government. Women were enfranchised for the first time and granted increased freedom in society. As Edwin C. Reischauer, an authority on Japanese history and ambassador to Japan under President Kennedy, wrote, "During the early postwar years in Japan, MacArthur played the role not only of the most radical American revolutionary of modern times but also one of the most successful." In accepting the revolution, the Japanese went so far in their new constitution as to repudiate, with the support of MacArthur, the waging of war or the maintenance of armed forces. Japan seemed on the way to complete abandonment of its militaristic tradition and its imperialistic ambitions in Asia.

When the Korean War broke out in 1950, however, the United States and its non-Communist allies of World War II hastened to conclude peace with Japan, despite the objections of the Soviet Union. The treaty of peace was signed in September 1951, and in a separate agreement the United States was permitted to retain military bases in Japan. The United States also encouraged the Japanese to rebuild some of their dismantled military machine as a defense against the rise of Communism in China. In the 1960s Japanese economic strength and prosperity made evident that it could not remain for long as a nonmilitary power. It was the wealthiest and economically strongest nation in Asia. By the early 1970s Japan was the third greatest industrial power in the world. That fact alone, regardless of the wish to keep its military power at a minimum, made Japan a world power.

The Rise of Chinese Communism. The third element in the Asian revolution was the conquest of China by the Communists. When the war ended in 1945, China was accorded the status of a great power by the United States and Great Britain. It received, for example, a seat as a permanent member of the Security Council of the United Nations. Most people assumed that Generalissimo Chiang Kai-shek would now establish himself as the head of the legitimate government of all China. Even Josef Stalin at the close of the war made a treaty recognizing the generalissimo's government rather than that of the Communist leader Mao Tse-tung. But the Chinese Communists with a sizeable army were stronger than most observers thought, partly because the Russians turned over to them the Japanese equipment in Manchuria.

The United States, anxious to work out a peaceful settlement between Chiang and Mao, struggled through 1946 and 1947 to establish some basis for agreement. At the suggestion of President Truman, General George C. Marshall traveled to China in 1946 in an effort to compose the differences between the two forces, but to no avail. Chiang, long an opponent of Communism, would not have Communists in his government, and the Communists, scenting success in the wind, would not disband their army. By the end of 1947 the two forces were engaged in open civil war, during which it became increasingly evident that Chiang did not enjoy the support of the masses of Chinese. His government, always dictatorial, was also blatantly corrupt and inefficient.

The Fall of Chiang Kai-shek. The progress of the Communists, whose forces were concentrated in the north, was at first slow and uneven, then swift and complete. By the end of 1948 they had captured all of Manchuria and were ready to challenge Chiang in China proper. Early in 1949 north China was in Communist hands, and the generalissimo nominally resigned his offices in an effort to hold off further Communist penetration, but without effect. In September Mao Tse-tung announced the formation of the People's Republic of China, with its capital at ancient Peiping (now Peking) in the north. By the end of that year the principal cities of south China were in Mao's hands, while Chiang Kai-shek and the remnant of his army fled to the island of Formosa some hundred miles off the southeast coast. The Soviet Union extended diplomatic recognition to the new regime in October, and in February 1950 a mutual assistance agreement and pact of alliance was signed in Moscow by the Soviet Union and the new Chinese People's Republic. With ratification of the pact in April, Communist power in Asia was consolidated and the stage was set for its expansion.

The triumph of Communism in China came at precisely the time when the end of the Berlin blockade and the creation of NATO marked the diminution of the Russian Communist threat in western Europe. Now a whole new area seemed open to Communist expansion. In making the decision to render assistance to western Europe in 1947–1948, the United States had in effect elected to abide by whatever results Chiang, without massive aid from the United States, could achieve in Asia. In 1947–1949, as in the Second World War, Europe, with its highly skilled population and technically advanced society, came first on the American scale of priorities. The dependence upon Chiang, however, proved to be misplaced, for he could not stop the advance of the Chinese Communists. It was not accidental, therefore, that the next test of American foreign policy should come in Asia; there American power was weakest and its allies almost impotent. When the American representative, John Foster Dulles, came back from the foreign ministers' meeting in Paris in June 1949, he told Senator Vandenberg, "The Politburo knows that it has lost the Cold War in western Europe; . . . it's nervous about holding its European satellites; . . . it's preparing to concentrate largely on Asia." Read today, his remark reveals one of the major flaws in the American outlook toward Communist states in the 1950s. For Dulles was assuming a unity among the various Communist states around the globe that was not necessarily there. Only in the 1960s would it become clear to American leaders that Communist countries were not a monolith, to which the American response must always be of the same intensity or degree of concern. But at the time, and especially in the light of Communist military aggression soon after Dulles made his observation, a belief in a worldwide, closely coordinated Communist effort at expansion seemed quite plausible.

The Korean War

The Fateful Decision. On Saturday night, June 24, 1950, President Truman was sitting in the library of his home in Independence, Missouri, when the telephone rang. It was the Secretary of State, Dean Acheson. "Mr. President," he said, "I have very serious news. The North Koreans have invaded South Korea." Truman, deeply shocked, replied that he would fly to Washington immediately, but Acheson, desirous of not alarming the country, asked him to stay in Independence until the nature and extent of the invasion had been definitely ascertained. Meanwhile Acheson secured the President's permission to call the Security Council of the United Nations into immediate session. The next day brought the news that the invasion was in deadly earnest; the President hastily left Independence for Washington to confer with his military and diplomatic advisers. On the way to Washington, as he told the story later, he ran over in his mind the possible actions which the United States, already heavily committed in Europe, should take if the North Koreans refused to heed a cease-fire order from the Security Council. To Truman the invasion was a rerun of the old movie of Hitler's aggressions in the 1930s. "If this was allowed to go unchallenged," he wrote later, "it would mean a third world war, just as similar incidents had brought on the second world war." The President's advisers agreed that assistance must be given, and airdrops of supplies for the South Korean army were authorized that same Sunday. At the same time the President ordered the American Seventh Fleet in the western Pacific to take a position in the strait between the mainland and the island of Formosa in order to forestall a possible Chinese

Communist invasion of Chiang Kai-shek's last stronghold. (This last decision, understandable in the context and excitement of the surprise attack by the Korean Communists, marked a sharp change in policy which had far-ranging consequences. Up until then the United States had stayed out of military involvement in the Chinese civil war; thereafter it was a defender of Chiang's repudiated regime on Formosa and by the same token an avowed enemy of the Chinese Communists. The American action probably also influenced the Chinese Communists in their decision to enter the Korean War later in the year.)

Limited aid to the South Koreans soon proved inadequate. On Monday Syngman Rhee, the president of South Korea, appealed directly for United States intervention, as the surprisingly powerful North Korean army, sweeping everything before it, compelled Rhee's government to flee from its capital at Seoul. Truman, moving cautiously but resolutely, now ordered American air and naval forces to support the South Korean forces, but not to attack targets north of the thirty-eighth parallel, the border between the two Koreas. The following day, June 27, the United Nations Security Council branded the North Koreans aggressors because they had refused to heed an earlier call for a cease-fire. It also called upon all the member states to aid the South Korean government. The administration, which had worked hard to secure the backing of the United Nations, immediately declared that the American forces were acting on behalf of the world organization, but added that the interposition of the Seventh Fleet was an action of the United States and not of the United Nations.

On July 7 the Security Council recognized the United States as the leader of the U.N. forces, and President Truman named General Douglas MacArthur, already the commander of American forces, the chief of the U.N. army. By this time the United States had found it necessary to commit ground troops to Korea, for it was evident that unless substantial ground support was forthcoming, the Communists would conquer the whole peninsula in a matter of days. President Truman authorized the first troops, at MacArthur's request, on June 30. At that time the United States counted not more than ten and a half infantry divisions and one armored division in its entire army.

The Background. From the beginning the Korean War was a strange business, certainly the least clearly defined war Americans had yet fought. The very border over which the aggression occurred was artificial, being but the arbitrary line at which Russian and American occupation troops agreed to meet in 1945. For years the line was the scene of numerous border clashes provoked by both sides, neither of which recognized the other as a legitimate government. Syngman Rhee, the head of the South Korean government, a Princeton graduate and a long-time Korean nationalist, was bent upon unifying his country, by force if necessary. So seriously did the American authorities view Rhee's intentions that they refused to supply his army with aggressive weapons like tanks and heavy artillery. The Russians took no such precautions, permitting the North Koreans to build up the well-trained, well-equipped force that made possible their spectacular early successes.

There is some reason for believing that the Russians and North Koreans did not expect the United States to intervene in the defense of Korea. In early 1949, at about the time the United States and Soviet occupation forces withdrew from both parts of Korea, General MacArthur, publicly describing the Pacific Ocean

THE KOREAN WAR,
JUNE 25–NOV. 24, 1950

→ U.N. offensive of
Sept. 15–Nov. 24

as "an Anglo-Saxon lake" and defining the American defense perimeter in the western Pacific, omitted Korea. Less than a year later Secretary of State Dean Acheson, addressing the National Press Club, again left Korea outside the United States defense line in the western Pacific. Almost pointedly he said that those countries outside the perimeter should, if they were attacked, look for aid from the United Nations. Did these statements encourage the North Korean attack? Many Republicans later said they did; no one yet knows. In his memoirs, the Russian leader Nikita Khruschev later said that the impetus for the attack came from the North Koreans and that Stalin and Mao Tse-tung approved.

The Russian boycott of the U.N. going on at that time as a protest against the denial of a seat to Communist China supported the argument that the Soviet leaders were surprised by American intervention. Thus when the resolution for United Nations intervention came before the Security Council, the Soviet delegate, Jacob Malik, was absent and could not veto it. Even though Trygve Lie, the Secretary-General, urged Malik to attend the meeting that was to vote on military intervention in Korea, Malik, much to the relief of the United States, refused to break his boycott. He did later, but by then his power to hamstring the U.N. operations in Korea was gone. The question remains: why did the Russians permit the U.N. to act in Korea?

The Entrance of the Chinese. To the Communists, to most Americans, and to the world, the month of August 1950 demonstrated how low American nonnuclear military power had sunk since 1945. The North Koreans pushed the South Koreans and the whole American Eighth Army down the peninsula to its tip around the port city of Pusan. Evacuation seemed imminent. Actually the situation was not as bad as it appeared. As early as July 7 MacArthur had told the administration of his plan to recoup the situation as soon as United States forces in Korea had been built up. On September 15 his forces carried out a highly

CHINA

NORTH KOREA

River

Yalu

Chongchon R.

SEA OF JAPAN

Pyongyang

Armistice line, July 1953

38° — 38°

CHINA

Seoul

Inchon

Han R. retreat

Line of U.N.
Jan. 24, 1951

YELLOW SEA

Kum R.

THE KOREAN WAR,
NOV. 25, 1950–JULY 27, 1953

SOUTH KOREA

•Taegu

☐→ Communist offensive
of Nov. 29, 1950–Jan. 24, 1951

☐→ U.N. counteroffensive
of Jan. 25–Nov. 27, 1951

Pusan

successful surprise landing at Inchon, the port of Seoul, far behind the North Korean lines, while at Pusan the American and South Korean armies attacked in great force. Large segments of the North Korean army were thus trapped in a gigantic pincer, while the rest of the army was forced to retreat rapidly, suffering enormous losses. On September 28 Seoul was liberated, and the following day Syngman Rhee reestablished his government there. Three days later MacArthur ordered his troops to move north of the thirty-eighth parallel, calling on the North Koreans "forthwith to lay down your arms and cease hostilities under such military supervision as I may direct."

On October 15, 1950, the President flew out to the American base at Wake Island in the Pacific to meet with MacArthur. There the supremely confident general told the President that the war would be won and the conquest of all Korea completed by Thanksgiving. The Chinese Communists, he assured the President, despite some buildup of their troops in Manchuria and their protests over the crossing of the thirty-eighth parallel, would not intervene in the war. The next day, unknown to the U.N. command at the time, the first military units of Chinese "volunteers" crossed into Korea. Meanwhile the U.N. forces pushed north. On October 26 the first U.N. troops, a contingent of Koreans, reached the Yalu River, the border between Korea and China. Through the darkness they peered across the river into Communist China. The main U.N. force was still some twenty to thirty miles south. Soon after their arrival at the Yalu the advance group of Koreans was ambushed and driven back with heavy losses by units of the Chinese army denominated volunteers to preserve the fiction that China was not entering the war. The following night several full divisions of Republic of Korea (R.O.K.) troops were attacked and forced back; when United States Eighth Army troops went to the aid of the R.O.K., they too were assaulted and forced south. When all U.N. troops had to be pulled back some fifty miles from the Yalu, it became evident that the Chinese Communists had entered the war in force. In retrospect it is clear that the decision on the part of the United States and the U.N. to advance north of the thirty-eighth parallel was a mistake. Nothing in the end was gained by it, and in view of the Chinese warnings it is highly probable that the Chinese would not have entered the war if the North had not been invaded.

Both as a military operation and as a symbol of united action against aggression, the war was completely changed by the Chinese intervention. The triumph of U.N. persistence, power, and audacious strategy at Inchon was suddenly followed by a series of costly and humiliating defeats as the U.N. forces were driven back down the peninsula and forced once again to evacuate Seoul. It was clear that unless the Chinese could be halted, hope of completely clearing Korea of Communists would have to be abandoned.

Aware of this fact, MacArthur increasingly importuned Washington for permission to attack the Chinese across the Yalu, in what he referred to as their "sanctuary." But Truman and Acheson, acutely aware of the obligations of the U.S.S.R. to China under the mutual security pact of February 1950, believed that any such action would expand the war into a global conflict. Though it went unnoticed at the time, neither the Chinese nor the Russians attacked the American sanctuary in Japan, a vital staging area for the successful prosecution of the war in Korea. The Russians refrained probably for the same reason that the Americans respected the Manchurian sanctuary: to keep the war from becoming a nuclear exchange between the great powers.

But if the United States was spared a nuclear war, a limited war in a place far from American shores imposed frustrations and tensions upon a people accustomed to an all-out drive for victory culminating in the enemy's unconditional surrender. In December 1950 a draft board in Montana refused to call up another man until General MacArthur was authorized to use the atom bomb as he saw fit in China. Truman's popularity as measured by public opinion polls rose and fell during his first five years in office, but after January 1951 a majority of the people consistently opposed him. After the Chinese invasion "Truman's War," as the conflict in Korea was dubbed, became increasingly unpopular. Not even during the War of 1812 had Americans been called upon to accept such indefinite and limited goals in their warmaking. Never before had the limits of American power been so frustratingly evident. They would be again, however, in Vietnam.

The Dismissal of MacArthur. One measure of the discontent stemming from the war was the furor stirred up by Truman's removal of General MacArthur from his command in Korea in April 1951. For several months the general had been privately and publicly proclaiming his irritation at having to refrain from striking at the Chinese at their staging areas in Manchuria. Although such statements by the United Nations commander evoked alarm among the other powers supporting the U.N. effort in Korea, Truman hesitated to take any strong action against the popular MacArthur other than to warn him against making such remarks in the future. For three weeks before the Chinese struck in force across the Yalu, Acheson reports in his memoirs, both military and civilian officials in Washington hesitated to warn MacArthur that his troops were in danger of a major attack, so fearful were they of the general's wrath and popularity. But when a letter from the general criticizing administration policy

Generals Douglas MacArthur and Matthew Ridgway (with live grenades on chest) touring the front lines in Korea. After his dismissal by Truman, MacArthur was succeeded by Ridgway. *Photo: UPI*

was read from the floor of the House of Representatives, the President could no longer ignore his insubordination. MacArthur's removal from command was swift and public.

The domestic reaction was equally quick and revealing. Within twelve days after the announcement over 27,000 letters and telegrams had been received at the White House, as compared with fewer than 2,000 after the announcement of Roosevelt's court-packing plan in 1937. Congressmen received telegrams instructing them to "Impeach the little ward politician stupidity from Kansas City"; "Run the United Nations back to Switzerland"; "Impeach the imbecile."

In San Gabriel, California, a crowd hanged the President in effigy; in Los Angeles the city council adjourned "in sorrowful contemplation of the political assassination of General MacArthur." In Ohio and Massachusetts flags were lowered to half-staff. Upon his return to the United States the general received a stupendous welcome in New York and throughout the country; the two houses of Congress respectfully invited him to address them. The Armed Services and Foreign Relations Committees of the Senate scheduled elaborate hearings to inquire into his removal.

In the course of the hearings from May 3 to June 25, some 2 million words of testimony from the principal military and diplomatic figures in the country were entered in the record. The public press and air waves were filled with criticisms of limited war in Korea and with revelations of American strategic plans and capabilities. Yet when the record was complete, it was evident that MacArthur's recommendations amounted to carrying the war into China in order to oust the Communists from all of Korea. As General Omar Bradley said, speaking as chairman of the Joint Chiefs of Staff, to have extended the fighting to the mainland of Asia would "involve us in the wrong war, at the wrong place, at the wrong time, and with the wrong enemy." Later Truman put it this way: "I knew that in our age, Europe, with its millions of skilled workmen, with its factories and transportation networks, is still the key to world peace." After all, the recovery of Europe under the Marshall Plan had only begun and the threat of Russia there had not yet completely receded. To become involved in a war with China might expose Europe to attack.

The Effect and Significance of the Korean War. Before the armistice was negotiated in mid-1953, American deaths reached over 37,000; the wounded and missing reached levels several times that figure. To many Americans the war remained a bewildering and frustrating experience. It was sneeringly called "Truman's War," or "that police action," in derogation of the evasion the President used to answer the charge that he had committed the country to war without congressional authority. In fact Senator Robert A. Taft, the leading Republican in the Senate, publicly accused the President of usurping authority in sending troops to the Korean War. The limited character of the war and the resulting frustration were also used by Communist hunters like Senator Joseph McCarthy to lend credence to their charges that the administration was not wholeheartedly fighting Communism at home or abroad.

Charles Bohlen, the long-time Russian expert and diplomat, saw the war as a turning point in United States relations with the Soviet Union and the world. Acheson and others, Bohlen wrote, incorrectly interpreted the war as a sure sign that Stalin's Russia sought to dominate the world, especially since in 1949 Russia had exploded its first nuclear weapon. The one clear military advantage that the United States had was now gone. The result in the United States was a drive to expand American military power. In 1950, Bohlen pointed out, the United States had only the North Atlantic alliance bases and a handful of others in Asia. But by 1955 the United States had "about 450 bases in thirty-six countries and we were linked by political and military pacts with some twenty countries outside of Latin America. It was the Korean War and not World War II," Bohlen quite accurately concluded, "that made us a world military-political power."

Yet more positive gains had been made, too. This had been the first war ever fought by an international organization dedicated to preserving peace with an international army. By the end of 1950 some twenty nations had sent units or help of some kind to Korea; by the time the fighting ended, forty-two nations had offered assistance to the defense of South Korea. Moreover, the war demonstrated that collective security backed by American power and commitment would work, for the North Korean invasion had been halted and turned back. (When the American ambassador told French foreign minister Robert Schuman of Truman's decision to intervene in Korea, Schuman's eyes filled with tears. "Thank God this will not be a repetition of the past," he said.)

Domestically the war forced the administration into adopting economic controls once again. Both income and excise taxes were raised in 1950, and in January 1951 the President signed into law a new excess profits tax. In early 1951 the government was compelled to restrict civilian use of steel, rubber, and aluminum to keep war production going. Wage increases were also discouraged in an effort to prevent price rises. But the rigid price controls and rationing procedures that had been used during the Second World War were not necessary in this much smaller struggle. Indeed, by the end of 1952, though the fighting continued in Korea, the military production buildup had reached its peak and economic controls were gradually eliminated. In fact, many Americans who had no relatives in the armed forces in Korea hardly knew there was a war at all—a fact that made the war even more frustrating and unpopular among those whose sons or husbands were fighting in Asia.

The End of the Korean Fighting. Once the intervention of the Chinese made evident that a conquest of the whole peninsula by the U.N. forces was out of the question, the administration tried its best to break the virtual stalemate as speedily as possible. The Communists, however, were not so eager; they were willing to talk about an armistice, but they were not willing to agree to it without argument and bargaining. As a result the war, now virtually a military stalemate on a line just north of Seoul, dragged on into the new administration of Dwight D. Eisenhower. In the middle of 1953, despite a last-minute maneuver by Syngman Rhee, who opposed some of the armistice terms, the fighting halted along a line that gave the South Koreans slightly more territory than they had possessed before the attack three years earlier. The new President, personally very popular and unassociated with the frustrating war in the first place, was able to win acceptance for a good deal less than full victory. Truman probably could not have won popular support for such a conclusion to a war.

The armistice of July 1953 terminated the fighting, but it did not end the split in Korea; that, like the division of Germany, could not be healed until the deeper and more significant antagonism between Communist and capitalist regimes which the superpowers had encouraged was ended.

The "New Look" in Foreign Policy

A Republican Version of Foreign Policy. Although in many respects the new Eisenhower administration continued to pursue the foreign policy goals established under Truman, it sought to introduce new means of achieving them. As representatives of the party that had long criticized containment as too passive,

Eisenhower and his Secretary of State, John Foster Dulles, wanted to try more active means to defeat the Russians. In theory the party was interested in doing more than simply countering Communist advances, but in practice it was not united on how a new approach to foreign policy should be carried out. As will be shown in the next chapter, the Republican party in 1953 and after was deeply split between the internationalists, represented by Eisenhower and Dulles, and the neo-isolationists, or continentalists, of whom Senator Taft (and later that year, Senator William R. Knowland of California) was the spokesman and Senator McCarthy was a vociferous extremist. This latter group in the party—and sometimes it virtually dominated in foreign affairs—generally resisted foreign aid and doubted the value of NATO and other commitments in Europe. Hence it was usually unprepared to support more vigorous action in foreign affairs, despite its emotional hostility to the allegedly passive policy of containment. Furthermore, the party's traditional economic and political conservatism made it reluctant to spend larger sums of money or to break new paths.

Convinced that the Democrats under Truman had been spendthrifts, the new administration wanted to balance the budget by reducing expenditures in general, and in foreign affairs and defense in particular. Since the Defense Department was the most costly agency in the government, it received the first attention of the economizers, despite warnings that cuts in military expenditures might endanger national security. This urge to economy throughout the Republican party put a restraint upon the administration's ability to break out of the policy of containment.

The "new look" in foreign policy, as it came to be called by the press, was a deliberate attempt to reduce defense expenditures at the same time that new approaches to foreign policy were introduced. Behind the new look lay the assumption that by a careful and deliberate use of the new technology of war— that is, rockets, nuclear weapons, jet aircraft, and carriers—security could be purchased at a lower financial cost than under the Democrats. An irreverent reporter summarized it as "a bigger bang for a buck." The administration, especially Secretary of the Treasury George Humphrey, was convinced that unless the international commitments of the United States were brought into line with its economic capabilities, the well-being of the nation would suffer. Eisenhower later wrote in his memoirs that maintaining economic strength, of which a balanced budget was an important element, was part of national defense. The United States, said Secretary Humphrey, had "no business getting into little wars. If a situation comes up where our interests justify intervention, let's intervene decisively with all we have got or stay out."

Early in 1953 the administration tried to break out of the containment policy of Truman by announcing that the Seventh Fleet, patrolling the waters of the Formosa straits, would no longer inhibit an attack by Chiang Kai-shek's troops upon the Communist Chinese mainland. Although this action, known as "unleashing" Chiang, had long been demanded by the extremists in the party, it did not galvanize the Nationalist government on Formosa; two years later the administration felt it necessary to put Chiang "back on the leash." In April 1953 Secretary of State Dulles told the world that the United States did not consider the "captive peoples" of eastern Europe "a permanent fact of history." The implication was that the United States would not accept forever a policy of merely containing Russian power; it looked to a time when that power would be rolled back.

Furthermore, although Eisenhower and Dulles represented the internationalist wing of the Republican party, they thought that the Democrats had been too eager to have the United States assume the heaviest burden of European defense. Actually, in the last years of the Truman administration the Democrats, under the prodding of Secretary of State Dean Acheson, had also been moving to build up Europe's self-defense. Acheson, for example, had urged German participation in NATO in order to counter Russian superiority in ground forces. That course, however, had not been acceptable to the western European nations. Instead those nations suggested a new European Defense Community in which the armies of all the participants, including Germany, would be pooled. In this way fears of a revived, independent German military power would be assuaged. In 1953 the plan was being debated, but French fears of any form of German rearmament raised serious doubts that it would be accepted. Piqued by what he considered French irresponsibility in the face of a common menace, and mindful of the administration's desire to cut United States military expenses, Secretary of State Dulles in December 1953 publicly threatened an "agonizing reappraisal" of American policy toward Europe unless France accepted the European Defense Community. The French parliament, nevertheless, in August 1954 voted down EDC. The military cooperation of the nations of western Europe was salvaged only by a compromise plan offered by Anthony Eden, Prime Minister of Great Britain. Eden suggested a looser "Western European Union" and, in a notable departure from British tradition, committed four British divisions to permanent station on the continent. German rearmament, also provided for in Eden's proposal, began at the end of 1954.

The Policy of Massive Retaliation. Perhaps the most notable expression of the new look in America's military policy was Secretary Dulles' threat of retaliation against the Soviet Union or Communist China directly, regardless of where an attack began. Dulles set forth his position in a public address on January 12, 1954, before the Council on Foreign Relations. "The basic decision," he said, "was [*sic*] to depend primarily upon a great capacity to retaliate, instantly, by means and at places of our own choosing." With such a policy, he explained, the Department of Defense could shape military policy to fit American needs. "That permits a selection of military means instead of a multiplication of means. As a result, it is now possible to get, and share, more basic security at less cost."

The new policy had the wholehearted concurrence of the civilian head of the Defense Department, Charles E. Wilson. One general has written that he heard Wilson say, "We can't affort to fight limited wars. We can only affort to fight a big war, and if there is one that is the kind it will be." The administration's new look placed heavy emphasis upon air power—a shift that was quickly reflected in the distribution of expenditures among the three services. Between 1953 and 1955 the size of the ground forces was cut one third and the Navy 13 per cent, while the Air Force was enlarged. The budget for 1955 showed a decrease of over $4 billion for the Army, a $1.5 billion cut for the Navy, but an increase of $1.2 billion for the Air Force.

The crisis in the Middle East, which will be discussed later in this chapter, required the Eisenhower administration to halt temporarily the reduction in the number of ground troops, but the policy of depending mainly upon the Air Force and nuclear retaliation prevailed throughout both Eisenhower administrations. This narrowing of options available for the defense of the country and for the conduct of foreign policy was strenuously opposed by three of the chairmen of the Joint Chiefs of Staff. All of them—Generals Matthew Ridgway, James Gavin, and Maxwell Taylor—wrote books criticizing the policy after their retirement from the service. Later Maxwell Taylor became an adviser to President Kennedy when that President reversed the new look approach to defense. During 1957 Secretary Wilson announced two 100,000-men cuts in the armed services, and after the Middle East crisis of 1958 the Department of Defense informed the nation that the growing perfection of long-range missiles (intercontinental ballistic missiles) had allowed the department to put into effect "a new concept" of United States global military strategy. This new plan placed greater emphasis upon the I.C.B.M. as compared with the intermediate-range vehicles. A week later the Secretary of Defense recommended reductions of 71,000 men for the coming year. In subsequent years Sherman Adams, Eisenhower's principal presidential assistant, pointed out that the President believed that nuclear weapons would be used in any large war of the future and that to keep a large standing army was wasteful. In Eisenhower's mind expenditures for such an army jeopardized the government economy that he wanted to characterize his administrations.

The Middle East crisis, however, did compel the administration to recognize that "little," or limited, wars might require some adjustment in defense plans. As a result a new Strategic Army Corps was established in 1958, composed of 150,000 paratroopers and infantrymen who were maintained within the continental United States for instant air transportation to trouble spots anywhere in the world. But it was not until the Kennedy years and the Berlin crisis of 1961 that the new look, with its dependence upon air power and nuclear weapons, was definitely abandoned in favor of a broader range of military responses to threats to American interests.

A New Era in International Affairs

The Death of Stalin. On March 5, 1953—the same year that the Eisenhower administration took office in Washington—Josef Stalin died. Several months of confusion ensued before it became clear who would be Stalin's successor. At first it seemed to be Georgi Malenkov, the new premier and a slavish follower of Stalin. Also prominent from the first was Nikita Khrushchev, the short, stocky, uneducated son of an impoverished miner. Reacting strongly against the terroristic iron rule of Stalin which had engulfed even the immediate subordinates of the old dictator, the new leaders played down any particular one of their group. Instead they talked about "collective leadership." As was learned later, however, a struggle for dominance by one man was going on behind the scenes. Early in July 1957 it was announced that Malenkov, Molotov, and one other old supporter of Stalin, all of whom had been prominent in the new collective leadership, had been dismissed from their posts in the government and in the party. Malenkov, in a decided improvement over the usual Stalinist practices, was not killed but was instead appointed director of a remote hydroelectric station, while Molotov, reputed by Secretary Dulles to be one of the world's great diplomats, was sent as Soviet ambassador to Outer Mongolia. Now that his possible rivals for power had been removed, Khrushchev emerged in March 1958 as the successor to Stalin's one-man rule. He became premier as well as first secretary of the party.

In addition to sparing the lives of his rivals, Khrushchev showed in other ways that he was quite a different kind of leader from Stalin. Ebullient where Stalin was taciturn, outgoing and talkative where Stalin was suspicious and secretive, the new leader proved to be Communism's and Russia's most persistent and tireless world salesman. He traveled to as many non-Communist countries as would have him, including the United States, where in 1959 he talked with everybody, parrying criticisms with humor or heavy sarcasm. Everywhere he predicted the triumph of Communism and praised his country's achievements. With the rise to power of Khrushchev Soviet policy, if it did not change in fundamentals, altered greatly in style. It became flexible, energetic, quick to take advantage of changes in the world scene, cleverly attuned to propaganda advantages, and especially resourceful in appealing to the interests and fears of the emerging anticolonial nations of Asia and Africa.

The advent of Khrushchev marked more than a change in personality; it also announced a new Soviet view of international relations. At the Twentieth Congress of the Communist party of the Soviet Union (1956), at which he denounced Stalin and his use of terror, Khrushchev also announced that the old Marxist-Leninist dictum that war between socialism and capitalism was inevitable no longer held. "At the present," he told the Congress, "the situation has changed radically," by which he meant the new power of the Soviet Union in the world.

On his tour of the United States in 1959, Nikita Khrushchev took many Americans by surprise with his apparent openness and good humor. *Photo: Elliott Erwitt—Magnum*

Capitalist states, he admitted, would still act in a belligerent manner, "but war is not a fatalistic inevitability." This shift in the old line was pregnant for the future, since it indicated for the first time publicly that the Russian leaders recognized that no one could win a nuclear war. That change in Russian outlook was to be not only the basis for the ideological split between the Soviet Union and Communist China, which first became noticeable in 1959–1960, but also the foundation for a new relationship between the United States and the Soviet Union.

Thus in both Washington and Moscow the year 1953 marked a dividing line between two eras. By then the world had moved from the atmosphere of the immediate postwar years, in which the issues left over from the war were paramount, into an era in which new forces were at work. Perhaps the most striking alteration was that Europe by now had definitely ceased to be under serious threat from the Soviet Union—and everyone knew it. The European Recovery Plan, NATO, and a new, expanding prosperity had done their work. At last people of all classes were enjoying the fruits of the industrial might of Europe. Automobiles, refrigerators, washing machines, television sets, and a thousand and one products of a consumers' society were now coming into the homes of the European working class for the first time. With a booming economy and a prosperous people, western Europe had regained its confidence; the fear of a Russian thrust to the rim of the Atlantic had virtually disappeared. In fact, the nature of the Communist threat was now quite altered. The danger of military aggression was being replaced by threats of internal subversion and exploitation of unrest in the new nations emerging in Asia and Africa.

Testing the New Look. As we have seen, dependence upon air and naval power and the massive destructive power of nuclear weapons constituted the heart of the Eisenhower-Dulles alternative to containment. That policy was dictated in large part by a concern for financial economy and a desire to use the new technology of war to maximum advantage. The flaw in attempting to employ the threat of nuclear war in dealing with any act of aggression, regardless of its size or place, was that the American monopoly of nuclear and hydrogen weapons no longer existed. By 1953 the Soviet Union had exploded both fission (nuclear) and fusion (hydrogen) devices and was presumably in a position to inflict upon the United States as much damage—if not more, considering the concentration of the American population and industry—as American forces could upon Russia. The "balance of terror" which thus ensued undermined the ability of any policy of "massive retaliation" to meet local and limited acts of aggression, Russian inspired or not.

The hard truth of the dilemma, even without nuclear weapons being involved, was evident in March and April of 1954 in the crisis in French Indochina. The French forces there, having fought the Communist-led Vietminh ever since 1945, found themselves about to suffer a decisive defeat at Dienbienphu. In response to French appeals for air assistance from the United States, several military and civilian figures in the administration, including Vice-President Nixon, counseled support, though not with nuclear weapons. Public opinion, however, when informed of the matter, was violently opposed to American involvement. President Eisenhower took the same view and no American air support was sent. Without American military assistance the French forces capitulated. During the summer at a conference in Geneva the French agreed to a cease-fire, which ended French power in Indochina.

Alarmed by the loss of French Indochina, Secretary Dulles sought to bolster resistance to Communist penetration in the rest of southeast Asia by a new multinational defense treaty, creating the Southeast Asia Treaty Organization, the signatories of which were Thailand, Australia, New Zealand, the Philippines, Pakistan, and the United States. Concluded in September 1954 and modeled after the NATO agreement, SEATO expanded American military commitments tremendously but did little to increase the available power for meeting those obligations. Conspicuous by their absence from the new organization were other important states of southeast Asia: Indonesia, India, Ceylon, and Burma, all of which preferred to stay out of such an agreement in the interest of retaining their neutralist foreign policies.

The Geneva Conference, 1955. One sign that a new stage had been reached in the Cold War was the interest among the Western nations in holding a meeting of the heads of government of the Big Four powers, especially the United States and the Soviet Union. A meeting at the summit, as Winston Churchill called it, might help bring some relaxation of tensions and some progress in the long, fruitless search for a disarmament formula. By the summer of 1955 the administration was prepared to consider a meeting at Geneva with the Russians, the French, and the British. Eisenhower by this time was hopeful that some step might be taken which would reduce the suspicion between the West and the East and put a halt to the arms race, especially in nuclear weapons. The meeting took place in July 1955 with Khrushchev and Nikolai Bulganin, at that time the Soviet premier, representing the Soviet Union.

Although the public statements that issued from the conference were optimistic and the pictures of the four heads of state always showed them smiling, it was evident by the third day that the differences between the West and East were not being appreciably reduced by the discussions. The Russians, though, were apparently impressed by the earnestness of Eisenhower and perhaps for the first time began to question their unceasing public assertions that the West wanted war.

On the fourth day Eisenhower made a dramatic effort to move the conference off dead center. After reading some remarks about American disarmament policy he laid down his papers, took off his glasses, and, looking directly at the Russian delegation, offered a new proposal for disarmament. Obviously deeply sincere and almost beseeching in his effort to reach the Russians, Eisenhower suggested that both nations "give to each other a complete blueprint of our military establishments from beginning to end, from one end of our countries to the other; lay out the establishments and provide blueprints to each other. Next, to provide within our countries facilities for aerial photography to the other country . . . where you can take all the pictures you choose and take them to your own country to study. . . ." The suggestion was intended to be only the beginning of a broader plan to relieve both sides of the oppressive fear of another and more devastating Pearl Harbor. Since both superpowers were developing missiles capable of delivering nuclear and hydrogen bombs within a matter of minutes, the fear was realistic. But despite Eisenhower's high hopes, the proposal aroused only suspicion in the Russians. Six years later Khrushchev told President Kennedy that he thought the plan was no more than a way to carry on espionage in the Soviet Union. The Americans were so fearful of another Pearl Harbor that within a year after the Russian rejection of the "open skies" idea, Eisenhower authorized secret reconnaissance flights across Soviet territory. In 1960 these flights would turn out to be more than simply a means of getting intelligence.

Although the open skies idea involved practical difficulties and reflected Eisenhower's naiveté in international relations, it certainly demonstrated the willingness of the United States to think anew about disarmament, and it convinced millions of people of the President's genuine desire to dissipate the dark and sluggish cloud of war that hung over the world. The open skies proposal, like the conference itself, also offered evidence that the administration was adjusting its policy in the face of the new posture of Soviet leaders since 1953.

The Suez and Hungarian Crises. Two tests of American policy took place almost simultaneously in November 1956. The more important occurred in Egypt. Ever since 1952 Egypt had been going through a revolution from above, led by young, nationalistic army officers. The revolutionary leaders wanted to rid their country of its historic dependence upon Great Britain and to efface the humiliating defeat at the hands of the Israelis in the Palestinian War of 1948. Politically the revolution reached a climax with the deposing of the corrupt King Farouk in 1953 and the proclamation of a republic. The new republic, bent upon ridding Egypt of all vestiges of British power, pushed for the withdrawal of British troops from the Suez Canal, a goal that was reached in July 1954, when the British promised to bring home within two years all their troops in the canal region. That same year a young, ardently nationalist colonel, Gamal Abdel Nasser, became head of the revolution and the government. Ambitious and bold on behalf of his country's nationalist goals, Nasser appealed to both the Western powers and the Soviet Union for military and economic aid. And at the same time that he was negotiating with the United States for financial assistance to construct a giant dam on the upper Nile at Aswan, his government recognized the Communist government of China. Irritated by this playing of both sides, Secretary Dulles cancelled the negotiations for American aid in the building of the Aswan dam. One week later, in July 1956, and two months after the departure of the British troops, Nasser moved to take over the Suez Canal. Contrary to its treaty obligations, Egypt nationalized the canal, which was owned largely by French and British stockholders. The European powers, heavily dependent upon the Middle Eastern oil that passed through the canal, protested vehemently. Then on October 25 Israel, provoked by repeated minor acts of aggression by Egyptian forces on their common border and encouraged secretly by England and France, crossed the Egyptian frontier in force. Ten days later, as planned, British and French paratroopers dropped on Egyptian soil in an effort to recapture control of the canal and hopefully to oust Nasser.

At almost the same time that British and French troops were invading Egypt, Russian tanks were entering Budapest in Hungary to put down a revolt of the Hungarian people against the Communist regime there. Relentlessly and ruthlessly the Russian army crushed the inadequately armed Hungarian rebels, while Khrushchev threatened Britain and France with nuclear bombing by long-range missile if they did not withdraw their forces from Egypt.

Both the Suez and Hungarian incidents took the United States government by surprise. The French and British, unsure of the American attitude toward their intentions in the canal area, had failed to inform Washington of their plans. Angry that allies of the United States should ignore his views and deeply concerned over the possible Russian response to the armed attack on Egypt, Eisenhower threw the influence of the United States government at home and at the U.N. against the French and British. With both American and Russian as well as world opinion aroused against them, the British and French governments agreed to a cease-fire and the withdrawal of their troops. Israel also withdrew its troops in response to a resolution of the U.N. General Assembly. A United Nations force was hastily created to patrol the border between Israel and Egypt— the first such force in history. Nasser's army, much less prepared than he had led the world and his own people to believe, was thereby saved from certain defeat.

Preoccupied with the Egyptian situation, the United States and the other Western powers were unwilling to take any action about Hungary other than to publicize the plight of the Hungarian people in the United Nations. Indeed, the circumstances and the location of Hungary in the center of Europe, far from any Allied territory, precluded any action short of direct war with the Soviet Union. Later Eisenhower wrote that he had feared that Russian insecurity about Poland and Hungary, both of which were resisting Communist rule, might be triggered into a world war if the United States made any threatening move. To assuage Russian apprehensions, the United States reaffirmed its earlier promise not to ally itself with either Hungary or Poland against the Soviet Union.

The Eisenhower Doctrine. The attack upon Egypt by Britain, France, and Israel threw Nasser and those countries that supported him, like Syria, into closer association with the Soviet Union, which was credited with stopping the invasion by its missile rattling. Rumors of Soviet infiltration of the Middle East through friendship with Nasser circulated in late 1956 and 1957. Washington became increasingly worried about the possibility of Russian influence becoming permanent and extensive in that unstable and turbulent region. As a result in March 1957, in response to an appeal from President Eisenhower, Congress passed a resolution affirming American intentions to aid any country in the Middle East that seemed threatened by Communist penetration.

The test of the Eisenhower Doctrine, as it was soon called, came in the spring of 1958. During May, in the former French colony of Lebanon on the shores of the eastern Mediterranean, the pro-Western government came under increasing threats from its few local Communists and Arab nationalists and from the pro-Nasser government of neighboring Syria. Fearful that it could not survive, the Lebanese government appealed to the United Nations for support. Before any action was taken at the U.N. the pro-Western monarchy of Iraq was overthrown by a friend of Nasser. To Eisenhower and his advisers this latest eruption in the Middle East seemed a prelude to a Nasser-Russian attack on Lebanon. As a result, the United States on July 15, under the authority of the congressional resolution of the preceding year, rushed 3500 troops to Lebanon. The same day the British flew 2000 men into Jordan to bolster its pro-Western regime against possible attack. No attacks occurred and by August the crisis was over, with the pro-Western governments in the two countries secure. American and British troops were entirely withdrawn in October.

By 1957, then, the administration had come full circle in its attitude toward Russian expansion. Once extremely dubious, if not contemptuous, of the validity of containment, it was now prepared to do its best to carry out that doctrine since it had found the policy of massive retaliation too cumbersome a tool for dealing with the kind of local crises that seemed to characterize the Communist threat after the Korean War. One other lesson had been learned. After the Middle Eastern crises of 1956 and 1958 it was evident that Moscow was not the only source of instability in the world. Rising nationalism in western as well as eastern Asia, not to mention Africa, was injecting a new and disruptive element into world politics.

The President as Missionary. One sign of the influence of the new nations was the strenuous efforts of the two superpowers to win their support. In the late 1950s Khrushchev made several tours of Europe and Asia, especially to professedly neutral countries like India, to "sell" the Russian position on war and peace. Whether influenced by Khrushchev's example or by his own concern over the accelerating arms race, Eisenhower, despite two heart attacks and a serious abdominal operation in the preceding four years, undertook three extended foreign tours within six months in 1959–1960.

These attempts to win the approval of world opinion for American policy were related to Dulles' resignation in April 1959 because of ill health. Dulles had always been the most adamant member of the administration in dealings with the Russians. He had opposed, for example, the meeting of heads of government at Geneva in 1955. With Dulles gone, a more personal and relaxed approach to foreign policy came to the fore. Even before Eisenhower embarked upon his trips,

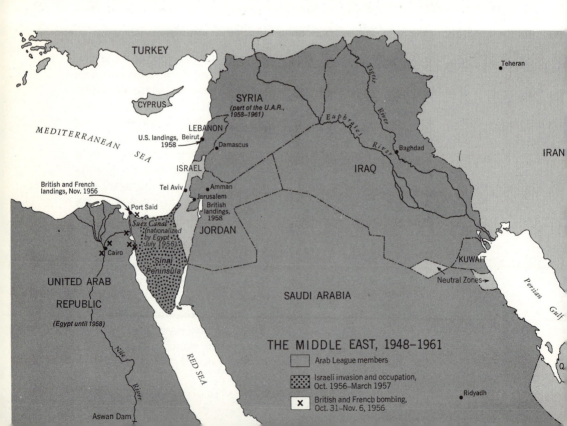

THE MIDDLE EAST, 1948–1961

☐ Arab League members

▨ Israeli invasion and occupation, Oct. 1956–March 1957

☒ British and French bombing, Oct. 31–Nov. 6, 1956

and within three months of Dulles' resignation, Vice-President Nixon made a trip to Moscow where he presented the American view of world affairs to the Russian people at the opening of the United States exposition at a trade fair and engaged in a famous "debate" with Khrushchev.

The President was acutely conscious that his years in the White House were fast drawing to a close. Though he never reveled in the job, he nevertheless saw it as an opportunity; personal visits might further his great ambition to secure a lasting peace. He told the American people just before he left on the first trip in December 1959, "During this mission of peace and goodwill, I hope to promote a better understanding of America and to learn more of our friends abroad."

The first trip, which was to India, the Middle East, and southern Europe, was the longest: nineteen days to stop in eleven countries on three continents, for a total of 22,000 miles. Eisenhower's welcome in India was perhaps the most overwhelming in a career studded with mass greetings: an estimated one million people turned out to hear and see him in New Delhi. Crowds almost as large met him in Karachi, Pakistan, and Teheran, Iran. In late February 1960 he embarked upon a two-week tour of Latin America, where he was well received, though only a year before Vice-President Nixon had been stoned and spat upon in Peru and Venezuela. The President's third foreign tour, in June 1960, however, was quite different from the previous two.

For some months anti-American sentiment in Japan had been growing among students and left-wing organizations. It came to a climax on June 11 when James Haggerty, the President's press secretary, arrived in Tokyo to make preparations for the President's arrival some days later. Haggerty's car was surrounded by a yelling, prancing, stone-throwing mob at the airport, necessitating the rescue of the American officials from their besieged automobile by a U.S. Marine helicopter. Later demonstrations against the United States reached such proportions that the Japanese government requested the President to cancel his scheduled visit. As a consequence the President visited only Taiwan, the Philippines, and Korea.

The U-2 Incident. The Japanese riots against the United States that summer were undoubtedly encouraged by a spectacular failure of American foreign policy earlier in the spring. On May 5, less than two weeks before the heads of the three Western powers were scheduled to meet with the Russians at another summit meeting in Paris, the Soviet government announced that its armed forces had shot down an American espionage plane deep within Soviet territory. The United States at first denied the allegation, saying that the unarmed U-2—a high-altitude reconnaissance plane—had been on nothing more than a routine weather mission along the borders of the Soviet Union. This answer to the Soviet charge proved to be highly embarrassing to the United States. The next day, May 7, Premier Khrushchev triumphantly and indignantly informed the Soviet parliament that the pilot of the American plane, now in the hands of the Soviet authorities, had confessed that his mission had been to fly across the Soviet Union from Pakistan to Norway, photographing military installations. The plane had been brought down at Sverlovsk, 1200 miles inside the Soviet border.

Confronted with the evidence, the United States admitted the truth of the Soviet charges but defended them—in Eisenhower's phrase—as "a distasteful but vital necessity" to protect the world against another Pearl Harbor. The flights had actually been going on since 1956, but heretofore apparently no Soviet rocket had been able to reach the high-flying U-2. The administration's aberrant interpretation of international law evoked much opposition inside and outside the United States—De Gaulle called it "this . . . absurdly ill-timed violation of Soviet air space"—and was in effect abandoned when Eisenhower announced on the eve of the Paris summit meeting that the flights were being halted. (President Kennedy later refused to renew the flights on the grounds that the risks involved were not worth the information gained.)

The whole U-2 affair dealt American prestige a heavy blow, since it caught American authorities in a deliberate, official falsehood. Moreover, considering the closeness in time of the flight to the convening of the Paris meeting, it suggested a recklessness in American activities that most people in the United States and the West in general did not associate with the hitherto cautious Eisenhower. But some of the opprobrium piled upon the United States government both at home and abroad dissipated on May 16, when Khrushchev broke up the conference before it began by demanding that Eisenhower apologize for the flights. Two days later, when it was apparent that the President was not going to apologize, Khrushchev held a two-and-a-half-hour press conference during which he furiously castigated the United States and Eisenhower for permitting the flights. Back in Moscow in June, Khrushchev insulted the President personally during a press conference and brought Soviet-American relations to a new impasse. A majority of the Senate Foreign Relations Committee, after holding hearings on the U-2 incident, concluded that the administration had mishandled the matter and that without the incident the Paris conference would probably have been held as scheduled. Eisenhower's cherished hope of a new relationship with the Soviet Union went aglimmering.

Troubles Nearer Home. Also during 1960 American relations with a new regime in Cuba deteriorated ominously. Ever since 1956 a young revolutionary, Fidel Castro, had been fighting a guerrilla war in the Sierra Maestra mountains against the regime of General Fulgencio Batista, the dictator of Cuba. Castro's forces grew in strength as more and more people recognized the corrupt and tyrannical character of Batista's regime. On January 1, 1959, the rebels moved out of the hills and mountains; Batista, seeing the handwriting on the wall, fled the country. The following day Castro's bearded revolutionaries entered Havana to proclaim a new order in Cuba. The United States, hopeful that Cuba was now on the way to a more honest and democratic government, recognized the new regime in a matter of days. Castro, a striking giant of a man with a full beard, made an unofficial goodwill tour of the United States during which he received an enthusiastic welcome, both publicly and privately, visiting with Vice-President Nixon and other dignitaries of the government.

Events back in Cuba, however, aroused American misgivings about the new regime. Arbitrary military trials that ended in the execution of hundreds of so-called war criminals and widespread confiscations of property were especially disturbing. That summer the United States officially expressed its concern to Castro over a new agrarian reform law which the United States asserted was taking American property without adequate compensation.

The American protests did not stop the Cuban confiscations. Indeed, during 1959 and early 1960 the Cuban government assumed an increasingly anti-American attitude in both word and deed. Over a billion dollars worth of American business assets in Cuba were confiscated without compensation. That the Cuban government harbored Marxists and was very friendly toward the Soviet Union and Communist China did not diminish American anxieties. (Later, in his memoirs, Eisenhower said that he had refused to see Castro during his visit in 1959 because he believed the Cuban to be a Communist sympathizer.) A visit to Cuba by a high Soviet official in February 1960 resulted in the extension of $100 million in credits and an agreement by the Soviets to purchase 5 million tons of Cuban sugar over the next five years. Fearful that these and other trade arrangements with the Soviet bloc were precursors of Soviet economic and political domination, the United States took strong measures to express its disapproval. In late May the United States ended all economic aid to Cuba, and in July, at the recommendation of Congress, the President cut the imports of Cuban sugar by 95 per cent. Sugar was not only Cuba's main export, but the United States was the island's biggest customer. The immediate Cuban reaction was more name calling and public displays of anti-Americanism in the plazas of Havana. By the close of 1960 Cuban-American relations were a source of widespread public and congressional concern, irritation, and frustration.

Deeply disturbed by the increasingly anti-American and pro-Soviet character of the Castro regime, the administration quietly undertook countermeasures. In March 1960, two months before the public announcement of the cut in the sugar quota, it approved a plan for the secret military training of anti-Castro Cuban refugees for an invasion of the island. The training took place in remote sections of Guatemala, under the direction of the U.S. Central Intelligence Agency. The actual invasion was postponed because of the American presidential elections, but both the military leaders in the government and the CIA pressed the new President, John F. Kennedy, for an invasion early in 1961. The aim was to mount the invasion before the arrival in Cuba of new Soviet-built jet airplanes which would threaten its chances of success.

Kennedy found himself in a quandary about the invasion; he had not been privy to its organization, yet he was now expected to countenance it. New in the job and desirous of not appearing weak in the face of military insistence upon going through with the plan, he agreed to it. His one requirement was that United States forces not be involved in the actual invasion, though he permitted them to assist in bringing the refugee-soldiers from Guatemala to Cuba. The invasion was badly planned and even more ineptly executed. For one thing, the newspapers in the United States learned of the secret training camps and so eliminated the element of surprise. For another, the size of the force was wholly inadequate and American intelligence as to Castro's strength and popular support was wide of the mark. The 1500 Cubans who landed at the Bay of Pigs in April 1961 were easily crushed in a matter of hours by Castro's superior air and ground forces. The invaders neither got to the hills to carry on guerrilla warfare, nor did their attack trigger the popular uprising they had expected. Castro was simply stronger militarily and politically than the Cuban refugees and American intelligence had believed.

The Bay of Pigs was a fiasco from any point of view. As a power play it was inexcusable, since no real power had been committed by the United States; thus the scheme was bound to fail. As a violation of international law and the inter-American agreements it put the United States in the position of supporting the kind of subversive activity it condemned when perpetrated by Communist states. Kennedy was shaken by his first venture into foreign policy. Manfully he accepted full responsibility for the humiliating experience, but he recognized that he had accepted advice he should have questioned closely. Two days after the fiasco he asked Theodore Sorenson, his close assistant, "How could I have been so far off base? . . . All my life I've known better than to depend on the experts. How could I have been so stupid, to let them go ahead?" But because he had let them go ahead, he felt a responsibility for the invaders who languished in Castro's prisons. Later he managed to arrange for their return to the United States.

The Bay of Pigs incident had an enormous impact on Europe. American prestige, already shaken by the U-2 incident, plunged to a new low. As in the U-2 incident, the United States was caught in an official lie which called into question the government's future credibility. At the United Nations Adlai Stevenson, the American representative, had categorically denied that his country was involved in the attack when the charge was made by the Cuban delegate. (Stevenson had not been told of U.S. complicity.) In Latin America the Cuban fiasco undercut the strenuous efforts of the United States to overcome Latin American hostility, which American intervention and Dollar Diplomacy had aroused in the early years of the century. Now, after thirty years of practicing the Good Neighbor policy, the United States had given new grounds for cries of "Yankee Imperialism" which went up from Mexico City to Buenos Aires.

The Bay of Pigs did more than lower American prestige in Europe and Latin America; it prepared the way for a more dangerous confrontation in the Western Hemisphere with the Soviet Union itself.

SUGGESTED READING

The complexities and myriad details of the international politics of the 1950s are clearly discussed from somewhat different points of view in Jules Davids, *America and the World of Our Time* (rev. ed., 1962) and John Spanier, *American Foreign Policy Since World War II** (2nd rev. ed., 1965), the latter taking a "hard-nosed" *Realpolitik* approach. Less interpretative but more complete is Wilfrid F. Knapp, *A History of War and Peace, 1939–1965* (1967), the work of an English scholar. Louis J. Halle, *The Cold War as History* (1967) surveys the postwar international situation with detachment and insight, arguing for an abandonment of the fears and anxieties that have caused the United States to overextend itself around the world. Hugh Seton-Watson, *Neither War Nor Peace** (1960) is a comprehensive and informed survey of the international situation during the 1950s. One of the few general defenses of American policy in these years to also confront the revisionist argument is Raymond Aron, *The Imperial Republic* (1974). A. Doak Barnett, *Communist China and Asia: A Challenge to American Policy* * (1960), Edwin O. Reischauer, *The United States and Japan* (3rd ed., 1965), and Cecil V. Crabb, Jr., *The Elephants and the Grass: A Study of Nonalignment** (1965) are good introductions to particular areas of American concern as the Cold War spread beyond Europe.

The literature on the Korean War is a fast growing one, and only a few items can be mentioned here. The best general account of the war is by a Briton, David Rees, *Korea:*

* Available in a paperback edition.

The Limited War (1964). T. R. Fehrenbach, *This Kind of War* * (1963) is a detailed military history, drawing the moral that the United States must never let down its guard. Glenn D. Paige, *The Korean Decision* (1968) is a detailed analysis of the decision to intervene. Ronald J. Caridi, *The Korean War and American Politics* (1968) is useful but not definitive. Douglas MacArthur, *Reminiscences* * (1964) and Matthew Ridgway, *The Korean War* (1967) are the recollections of the two U.S. commanders in Korea, each of whom saw the war in quite a different light. John W. Spanier, *The Truman-MacArthur Controversy and the Korean War* * (1959) is the best study of perhaps the most critical episode in the history of civilian-military relationships in the United States. The best work on the Chinese intervention is Allen S. Whiting, *China Crosses the Yalu* (1960), which shows that the Chinese gave ample warning of their intention to counter the move north of the thirty-eighth parallel. Allen Guttmann, ed., *Korea and the Theory of Limited War* * (1967) is a good introduction to the crucial place of that war in strategic military thought. The traditional interpretation of the war has been criticized in I. F. Stone, *The Hidden History of the Korean War* (1952), which is by a liberal journalist, and in Joyce and Gabriel Kolko, *The Limits of Power* (1973), by two radical historians. The Kolkos have been well taken to task in William Stueck, "An Exchange of Opinion: Cold War Revisionism and the Origins of the Korean Conflict: The Kolko Thesis," *Pacific Historical Review*, 42 (1973), 537–575, which includes two responses by the Kolkos.

Eisenhower's foreign policy is hostilely analyzed in Norman A. Graebner, *The New Isolationism: A Study in Politics and Foreign Policy Since 1950* (1956). Paul Peeters, *Massive Retaliation: The Policy and Its Critics* (1958) is a defense of the administration's foreign policy under Dulles. Very critical of Dulles is Herman Finer, *Dulles Over Suez* (1964), which deals with the Middle East crisis of 1956. An excellent, if critical, analysis of Dulles the man as well as the Secretary of State is Townsend Hoopes, *The Devil and John Foster Dulles* (1973). James M. Gavin, *War and Peace in the Space Age* (1958) and Maxwell D. Taylor, *Uncertain Trumpet* (1960) are books by high Army officers who objected to the Eisenhower administration's policy of "more bang for a buck." David Wise and Thomas B. Ross, *The U-2 Affair* (1962) is an exciting play-by-play journalistic account of that regrettable incident. Richard M. Nixon, *Six Crises* (1962) discusses in a sympathetic manner some foreign policy decisions within the administration. Dwight D. Eisenhower, *Waging Peace* (1965), the second volume of his memoirs, is indispensable for the administration's point of view on foreign policy. See also other studies of the Eisenhower administration discussed in the Suggested Reading for Chapter Three.

FROM COMPLACENCY TO ACTIVISM

*I*N 1948 GENERAL EISENHOWER could have had either the Democratic or the Republican nomination for the presidency, but he respectfully and steadfastly refused both. At one point he painstakingly set forth reasons why a military man like himself, who had spent his whole life outside of civilian pursuits, would not be the proper man for the office. Cogent as his arguments may have been, they could not erase the fact of his immense popularity and the respect in which he was held. As the journalist Marquis Childs pointed out, the American adoration of Eisenhower in the postwar years was comparable only to the English idolization of the Duke of Wellington after his defeat of Napoleon. Nor was it forgotten that the Iron Duke became England's postwar prime minister.

The Election of 1952

After 1948 the Democrats were no longer interested in Eisenhower, for in public statements as president of Columbia University the general had made clear that his political views were Republican. He deprecated, for example, the Democrats' concern with social security and health insurance by saying that those who wanted security could find it in prison. Thus, in trying to convince him that it was his duty to run for President in 1952, the Republicans had a clear field. Even Eisenhower's appointment as Supreme Commander of the North Atlantic Treaty Organization forces in December 1950 did not seriously interfere with the mounting Republican effort to nominate him. Especially interested in his candidacy were leading members of the eastern, internationalist wing of the party, which had supported Thomas Dewey in two previous campaigns. In fact, it was Dewey in 1950–1951 who did most to talk up Eisenhower's candidacy, despite the general's refusal to commit himself.

The Eisenhower Story. Born in 1890 in Denison, Texas, Dwight David Eisenhower was raised in Abilene, Kansas, one of five brothers in a family of decidedly modest income. It was the mother who held the family together and who left the enduring impression on the five sons. Never a studious boy but much interested in sports and physical activity, Dwight went to work after high school. Then, at the age of twenty and largely by chance, he was successful in his try for an appointment to the United States Military Academy. At West Point he broke rules, though never to the extent of being dismissed, and was no more than a fair student. In sports Eisenhower excelled and, but for an injury, might have become one of Army's star football players. After West Point his life followed the pattern for officers in the peacetime Army: frequent changes from one dull post to an even duller one, with promotions slow in coming and pay barely adequate. For a while in the thirties he served in Paris and in Manila under General Douglas MacArthur.

After twenty years of active duty Eisenhower had reached only the rank of major. Then came the Second World War, bringing new activities, rapid promotion, and a new sense of purpose. As a kind of protegé of General George C. Marshall, the chief of staff, Eisenhower now moved up quickly in rank; within two years he went from colonel to full general and to the command of the mightiest army ever assembled. With victory in Europe his name became known to every American and most Europeans; his popularity may well have exceeded that of any other public figure in the twentieth century. Eisenhower's radiant

Dwight Eisenhower shortly after winning the Republican nomination. *Photo: UPI* smile, warm manner, and genuine interest in and respect for people made him a natural political candidate. Moreover, his meteoric rise from truly humble origins fitted in well with the American tradition of presidential nominees.

The Republican Convention. During the spring of 1952, despite the general's refusal to say whether he was a candidate or not, those who wanted him continued to act as if he were. And sure enough, just before the Republican nominating convention opened on July 11, Eisenhower resigned his military commands and announced his willingness to try for the nomination. His most formidable opponent was Senator Robert A. Taft, the acknowledged leader of the midwestern, isolationist wing of the party, which dominated the grass-roots organizations. But as had been true for the preceding two conventions, the eastern, internationalist faction of the party controlled a majority of the delegates. In the very first days of the preliminary meetings the Taft supporters were beaten on a procedural matter; it was thus made clear which way the balloting would go. Despite valiant efforts to prevent it, and amid many public, as well as private, expressions of bitterness by the Taft forces, Eisenhower was nominated on the first ballot. His partner in the race was Richard M. Nixon, senator from California, who a few years before had made a name for himself as the member of the House Committee on Un-American Activities who had unmasked Alger Hiss.

The Democrats' Problem. Remembering Franklin Roosevelt's four terms, the Republican Congress in 1947 succeeded in adding the Twenty-Second Amendment to the Constitution. Although the incumbent, Harry Truman, did not come under its limit of two terms for the presidency, in March 1952 he announced that he was not a candidate. Truman's first choice for his successor was his friend Chief Justice Fred M. Vinson, but Vinson would not leave the Court. Early in 1952 Truman began to talk of the possible candidacy of the first-term governor of Illinois, Adlai Stevenson. Stevenson was not widely known outside of his state and Washington, D.C., where he had worked during the war. Moreover, he was genuinely interested in completing his record as governor. Repeatedly Stevenson told the press and the politicians who were interested in his candidacy that he was not available. But for lack of a more popular candidate and because Stevenson was an accomplished speaker, an exceptionally literate writer, and a good campaigner, the pressure upon him continued. Not quite prepared to remove himself irrevocably from the race, Stevenson found himself drafted for the nomination after a three-ballot fight with Estes Kefauver of Tennessee. Stevenson's was probably the first true draft since Garfield's in 1880. In an effort to heal the wounds of the 1948 campaign over civil rights, the convention named a moderate Southerner, Senator John J. Sparkman of Alabama, as Stevenson's vice-presidential candidate.

A Popular Campaign. During the conventions and campaign in 1952, more people than ever before watched at first hand the process of choosing a President. The extensive television coverage of the two conventions, which cost $11 million, enabled viewers to have better seats at the mammoth gatherings than most of the participants. The most spectacular use of television during the campaign was Senator Nixon's defense of his probity. Early in the campaign a newspaper revealed that a group of wealthy California businessmen had been contributing to a special fund for Nixon while he was a senator. Inasmuch as Eisenhower was making much of the lax financial standards of the Truman administration, the revelation about Nixon could not be passed over. Eisenhower, obviously taken aback by the incident, waited several days before deciding whether Nixon had become a political liability. Meanwhile Nixon appeared on a nationwide telecast in which he missed no opportunity to present himself as a wronged person who had never accepted a dishonest dollar in his life. Nor did he overlook a chance to cast innuendoes at the Democrats, as when he referred to his wife's "respectable Republican cloth coat"—a sly reference to the mink coat scandals of the Truman administration. So overwhelmingly favorable was the response to Nixon's fight for his political life that Eisenhower quickly decided he was a definite asset in the campaign.

The Republicans attacked the Democrats from a number of angles. Since this was still the era of the Great Fear, charges of corruption and Communist infiltration of government were heard widely. But unquestionably the most telling issue was the unpopular Korean War. "We are suffering from a new kind of K.K.K.," said Stevenson's manager late in the campaign, "Korea, Communism, and corruption." Since the Republicans had not had a President since Hoover, the Democrats hammered home the poor record of the Republican party in the Great Depression. Recognizing the powerful appeal of this argument, Eisenhower acted to counter it. Again and again during the campaign he promised to mobilize the resources of government to combat a depression if one should occur while he were

Governor Adlai Stevenson addressing a crowd in Paterson, N.J., during the 1952 presidential campaign. Many who first heard Stevenson in 1952 became his unswerving supporters through two more presidential campaigns. *Photo: UPI*

President. His promise signaled his public acceptance of the New Deal revolution.

Almost from the outset Stevenson was running behind the general. Yet his serious attention to what he considered the issues of maintaining domestic prosperity and securing a permanent peace abroad, and his literate, often witty speeches captured the imagination of millions of people who had never heard of him before. Not since the days of Woodrow Wilson had the voters been treated to the urbanity and precision of language which characterized almost every one of Stevenson's carefully prepared and lucid speeches.

Recognizing that Korea was the key to the election, Eisenhower in late October announced that, if elected, he would immediately "forego the diversion of politics . . . to concentrate on the job of ending the Korean War. . . . That job," he pointed out, "requires a personal trip to Korea. I shall make that trip. . . . I shall go to Korea."

Pre-election polls and post-election analyses amply demonstrated that the war was actively disliked by most Americans, not so much because it was a war, but because it was being fought under circumstances Americans found hard to accept. In October 52 per cent of those polled voluntarily listed Korea as the main issue in the election. Moreover, as the MacArthur hearings had made clear, most Americans did not like the limited aims and therefore the self-imposed restrictions under which the administration chose to carry on the war. With no victory in the usual sense possible, the war had a hopeless air, which the Republicans did not hesitate to emphasize. As one Truman supporter told a reporter in 1952, "I'm against this idea that we can go on trading hills in Korea indefinitely." One southern Democrat put it more directly: "If the war is settled by November, I'll be for Stevenson. If not, it's Ike. If we can't get a truce I figure we'll need a military man around to clean things up." The polls showed that 75 per cent of those concerned about the war thought Eisenhower would end it sooner than Stevenson. Even prosperity, which ordinarily works to the advantage of the party in power, was turned against the Democrats that year. Many voters felt that the good times at home were being purchased at the cost of American blood in Korea. In short, the charges of corruption and Communist infiltration of government were only secondary. But in conjunction with the war, they added up to an insuperable handicap for Stevenson, especially when placed beside the fame and prestige of Eisenhower.

The Measure of Eisenhower's Victory. The popular vote for Eisenhower was overwhelming: 33.9 million to Stevenson's 27.3 million: this disparity was exceeded by that in the electoral college: 442 to 89. Eisenhower's vote-getting power was attested by his running 15 per cent ahead of his party's vote for Congress and by his decisively breaking into the solid South for the first time since 1928. Border states like Missouri, Kentucky, and Maryland, middle southern states like Tennessee and Virginia, and deep southern states like Texas and Florida all trooped into Eisenhower's column. Despite his internationalist position, he captured the isolationist belt of the Middle West. Of the 57 counties in the nation which had consistently deserted the Republicans ever since 1928, Eisenhower gained back 31; he carried counties in both the North and the South that had never voted for a Republican President. Eisenhower was the first Republican since 1928 to attract substantial support from all classes as well as from all sections of the country.

THE ELECTION OF 1952

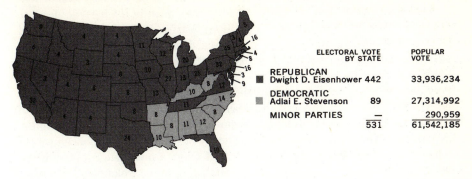

	ELECTORAL VOTE BY STATE	POPULAR VOTE
REPUBLICAN Dwight D. Eisenhower	442	33,936,234
DEMOCRATIC Adlai E. Stevenson	89	27,314,992
MINOR PARTIES	—	290,959
	531	61,542,185

In voting for a general, the country was giving voice to its weariness with partisan politics, for in America, unlike continental Europe, Army officers were almost ostentatiously detached from politics. Many U.S. Army officers, like General George Marshall and Eisenhower himself before 1948, refrained from voting in order to symbolize their lack of political partisanship.

Eisenhower's break into the South was still another measure of the increasing role of urban voters in elections. Studies have shown that 85 per cent of white-collar voters in southern cities voted for Eisenhower—an echo of early twentieth-century political history, when northern cities had been a stronghold of Republican voters. Moreover, in 1952 urban, middle-income voters in the South, long strongly Democratic, swung to Eisenhower; and the lack of unions in the South meant that the urban working class there, traditionally conservative anyway, would not follow the pattern of northern urban workers, whose unions closely tied them to the Democratic party.

Across the nation Eisenhower sliced into the old Roosevelt-Truman coalition by capturing substantial Irish and German (both Catholic and Protestant) votes and making inroads in the traditional Democratic allegiance of Poles. Women of all classes and backgrounds seemed to favor Eisenhower over Stevenson, who was divorced. In November women voted heavily for Eisenhower, and their ballots made up a larger proportion of the electorate than men's.

As befitted a victory of such proportions, Eisenhower entered the White House with Republican majorities in both houses, but because he was unable to carry congressional candidates to victory with him in his personally successful invasion of Dixie, these majorities were rather slim. On the other hand, many of the Southerners, though Democrats in name, were more sympathetic to the Republican program than to some of the liberal aims of their own party. With these men Eisenhower could work.

Building a New Republican Party

The Republican Problem. Ever since the Depression and the advent of the Second World War there have been two Republican parties. The division between them has been evident in both foreign and domestic policies. Although by the 1940s the majority of Americans accepted most of the New Deal measures as permanent features of American life, conservative Republicans continued to reject them. Nevertheless, by 1948 a significant segment of the party leadership, headed by Thomas Dewey of New York, Earl Warren of California, and Harold Stassen of Minnesota, was quite prepared to accept the New Deal revolution as a fact of political and social life. Moreover, after 1941 this same wing of the party, best represented by Senator Arthur Vandenberg, espoused an internationalist position in foriegn policy, supporting the United Nations, the Marshall Plan, and NATO. Yet although this eastern, liberal, internationalist wing managed to control the presidential conventions beginning in 1940, it did not constitute a majority of Republicans. Indeed, the tendency of the typical Republican was to follow the lead of figures like Senator Taft of Ohio, a moderate conservative in domestic politics (see p. 15) and a continentalist, if not an isolationist, in foreign policy. At one time Taft denounced NATO as "so dangerous as to commit the United States to a cause beyond its capacity," while he denounced the U.N. as "an utter failure as a means of preventing aggression." His book *A Foreign Policy for Americans,* published in 1951, set forth his deeply felt conviction that American commitments in Europe should be severely curtailed, if not abandoned completely. After 1950 when Senator Vandenberg, the Republican architect of bipartisanship in foreign policy, withdrew from the Senate because of a fatal illness, Taft's views dominated Republican councils in Congress. After Taft's death in 1953 his views were perpetuated by William F. Knowland of California, whose literal-minded singleness of purpose equalled Taft's, but who fell far short of the Ohioan in sharpness of mind and intellectual discipline. Taft and Knowland enjoyed the enthusiastic support of extreme anti-Communists and supernationalists from the Midwest like Senators Joseph McCarthy of Wisconsin, John Bricker of Ohio, and William Jenner of Indiana.

One of the potent arguments advanced to persuade Eisenhower to run in 1952 was that he alone would be able to tame the party's lingering isolationism and remake the Republicans into a party ready to meet contemporary issues with modern principles. Unless that could be done, advocates of his nomination pointed out, their party would never be anything more than a minority in the politics of the nation. The challenge appealed to Eisenhower, and for the first years of his administration he tried, with some success, to remake the Republican party. But in all his actions as President the division within the party complicated his mission and limited his success.

Eisenhower the President. One of the persistent themes of the Democrats during the campaign had been that a military man like Eisenhower would be sure to assume a dangerously aggressive tone in dealing with Congress, the nation, and the world. Experience revealed, however, that nothing was less to be feared. From the beginning of his tenure until the end of his second term, Eisenhower in the White House was the opposite of the stereotype of a general. Indeed, he refused to lead Congress; it is difficult to talk about an Eisenhower program since most of the legislation of the Eisenhower years originated not in the White House, but in Congress. Newspaper reporters, used to the vigorous leadership of Harry Truman and Franklin Roosevelt, were astonished when Eisenhower refused to comment upon pending legislation on the grounds that to do so would be to interfere with the legislative branch during its deliberations. The President consciously subordinated his own ego, usually giving credit for ideas and plans to the Cabinet or the administration rather than to himself. He not only seemed to think of himself as an equal member of a team; he even went so far as to remove himself from active involvement in the functions of government. His second-in-command, Sherman Adams, kept problems away from the President as much as possible, bringing only the truly unresolvable to the chief executive for decision. A hundred years after the demise of the Whig party, politically sophisticated observers were surprised to find a Whig in the White House again.

Actually a large part of the explanation for Eisenhower's limited conception of his office stemmed from his military experience. People forgot that his military experience had never included the field command of men in battle, but at its culmination had involved the coordinating of huge, disparate armies and the reconciling of differences among allied nations joined in a common military enterprise. His great service as Supreme Commander of NATO forces, as during the war, had been his unsurpassed ability to reconcile diverse interests and secure cooperation between conflicting personalities. As a general he had acted as a mediator and a compromiser of differences, and under the circumstances probably nothing else would have worked. As President he operated in a similar fashion.

Leaders Under Eisenhower. At a press conference in January 1954 the President set forth in general terms, in the involved syntax for which he became famous, the philosophy of his administration. "When it comes down to dealing with the human in this country and his government, the people in this administration believe in being what I think we would normally call liberal, and when we deal with the economic affairs of this country, we believe in being conservative." In practice the administration showed itself to be more liberal than many Democrats had expected. But it was also true that Eisenhower was deeply concerned with avoiding the unbalanced budgets of Truman, for balancing the budget was what the general meant by being conservative in economic affairs.

In keeping with his economic principles and the character of the Republican party, Eisenhower chose a preponderance of businessmen for his Cabinet officers. One of the quips of the day was that it was a Cabinet of eight millionaires and a plumber, the last being a reference to Martin Durkin, Secretary of Labor. Durkin, whose appointment was described by the forthright Taft as "incredible," was a union leader and a Democrat. Eisenhower appointed him as a gesture of national unity in case of labor strife. Durkin resigned after eight months because of differences over the Taft-Hartley Act; he was replaced by a businessman. Despite the influence of Taft in the party, in the Cabinet his only ally was Ezra Taft Benson of Utah, the Secretary of Agriculture. Benson was an ardent advocate of free enterprise in agriculture as in business, and during his tenure he undertook a campaign to have farm price supports steadily reduced in the interest of reducing the mounting farm surpluses. In this endeavor, however, he was opposed consistently, and usually successfully, by the farm interests in both parties in Congress.

The two most influential members of the administration were Secretary of State John Foster Dulles and George Humphrey, the Secretary of the Treasury. Dulles, who had long experience in diplomatic affairs under several administrations, virtually controlled American foreign policy during his years with Eisenhower. Again and again Eisenhower told the press that Dulles, in his estimation, knew more about foreign policy than any other man in the nation. Before 1941 Dulles had been an outspoken isolationist, but as Secretary of State he extended the military and moral commitments of the U.S. farther than any of his predecessors.

George Humphrey dominated domestic policies as Dulles did foreign. A self-made millionaire from Ohio, Humphrey, like the President himself, was raised in a small town, but in an upper-middle-class family. As a businessman Humphrey was firmly committed to the removal of government interference from business enterprise. A balanced federal budget was as much his goal as it was Senator Taft's. From the beginning Humphrey conceived of himself as the watchdog of the Treasury. At the time of his appointment, he is supposed to have made one request of the President. "I want you," he told Eisenhower, "if anyone asks you about money, to tell them to go to see George."

Immediately below Humphrey in influence within the administration was Charles E. Wilson, the Secretary of Defense. As president of General Motors Wilson had made a good record as an executive willing to work fairly and responsibly with labor unions. Like Humphrey, he conceived of his job as the head of the national defense establishment as largely that of financial watchdog. Wilson was in complete agreement with the policy of depending upon a few advances in military technology, which would allow defense expenditures to be reduced. Many generals in the Pentagon thought him rigid in his conception of the proper defense for the nation. One embittered chief of staff later said of him, "He was the most uninformed man, and the most determined to remain so, that has ever been Secretary."

Removing Government from the Economy. The first Eisenhower administration intended to be a businessman's government in the best sense of that phrase. It was not intended that government should be subservient to business interests, as was often the case in the 1920s, but rather that the interests of business would be recognized and the interference of government in business minimized. Thus as early as February 6, 1953, the administration abandoned all economic controls left over from the early days of the Korean War. The administration also curtailed or abandoned government manufacturing enterprises which competed with private business, preferring instead to have government buy its supplies and services whenever possible fron private enterprise. At one time the President even entertained a hope of selling the Tennessee Valley Authority. In March 1953, for example, he told the Cabinet, "By God, if ever we could do it, before we leave here, I'd like to see us *sell* the whole thing, but I suppose we can't go that far."

Paramount among the new administration's policies was the drive for a balanced budget. At the time, and later when he came to write his memoirs, Eisenhower saw a balanced budget as the principal achievement of his administration and the essential difference between the administrations of his Democratic predecessors and his own. To achieve a balanced budget, however, something more than minor economies was necessary if taxes were not to be raised. Almost as soon as he took office Eisenhower cut back the amounts allocated in the Truman budget for foreign aid and military equipment—the amount provided for foreign aid alone was reduced by over a billion dollars. But despite his concern for economy the new President would not cut spending deeply enough to balance the budget immediately, because to do so would endanger national security. As will be seen a little later, this compromise quickly got him into trouble with his party, which wanted a balanced budget the very first year.

Other policies and acts of the administration strengthen this picture of a government trying to minimize governmental interference in and restrictions on business. In agriculture, for example, Congress was asked to enact flexible price supports so the President could lower farm prices to reduce the surplus that had been piling up for years as a result of price supports. Over the long run, the administration hoped to bring agricultural prices under the control of the market, something that had not been true since 1933. With the so-called Dixon-Yates contract, the administration also sought an alternative to the expansion of public power facilities. It refused to approve a new steam plant for the Tennessee Valley Authority in 1953 when it became evident that more power was needed in the Memphis area. Instead the government made a contract with a private power syndicate (Dixon and Yates) to supply the electricity. In time the Democrats in Congress succeeded in invalidating the contract, which they viewed as an attack on public power in general and the TVA in particular. They had not forgotten that Eisenhower had once described the TVA as an example of "creeping socialism." In the field of nuclear energy the administration also favored private over public enterprise. In 1956 the Atomic Energy Commission authorized the development of electric power from atomic energy by private industry. By the end of the year seventeen plants were planned or under construction by private firms.

Similarly, on the matter of offshore oil rights the administration supported the position of oil companies and businessmen in general. The Truman administration had convinced the United States Supreme Court that the oil-rich submerged lands off the Gulf Coast belonged to the federal government and not to the states. Conservationists and liberals believed that federal administration of this natural resource would be less liable to private pressure and abuse than control by the states. Hence they supported the Truman policy; the states, of course, and the oil companies opposed it. The Eisenhower administration, acting on the principle that the states should be given as much jurisdiction and authority as was consistent with the national interest, supported legislation that overturned the Supreme Court decision and awarded control over the disposition of offshore oil to the states, notably Texas and Louisiana.

In domestic policy, in short, Eisenhower was clearly a conservative. In some respects he was even more conservative than Senator Taft. For example, in 1960 the President admitted to his chief assistant, Sherman Adams, that he could not have gone along with Taft in such matters as federal aid to education and support of public housing, both of which Taft strongly supported. In Sherman Adams' words, Eisenhower saw his administrations as "the first great break with the political philosophy of the decades beginning in 1933."

In at least two respects, however, Eisenhower and his supporters accepted New Deal-Fair Deal policies without question. One was the willingness to take governmental measures to avoid a depression. When in 1954 the economic indices showed a decline in the economy, Eisenhower urged his advisers and subordinates to prepare plans for the necessary antidepression measures. When in March the number of jobless reached 3.7 million, or 5.8 per cent of the labor force, the President in the privacy of the Cabinet meetings expressed grave concern, indicating that Republicans as well as Democrats by now agreed that halting a depression was a prime responsibility of government (even though then, and later in another recession, the administration took only minimal antidepression actions). The President and the Republican Congress also supported an expansion of the social security system in the very first year of the new administration.

The President and Congress. For most of his eight years in the White House Eisenhower did not enjoy a Congress composed of a majority of his own party. Yet in some respects his two years with a Republican Congress caused him more pain and difficulty than his six with a Democratic one. Certainly it is true that the Democrats, somewhat awed by his enormous popularity, and themselves generally dominated by moderates and conservatives, did not find working with Eisenhower difficult. This was not true of the conservative members of his own party who ran Congress in the years 1953–1954. Senator Taft, until he relinquished his Senate leadership in 1953 because of failing health, was the acknowledged head of the conservatives in the party and in the Senate. The President, determined to work closely with the party in an effort to heal its deep split, encouraged Taft to see him as often as he wished and without appointment. But the President's cultivation of Taft and his supporters could not eliminate all the conflicts between the executive and the legislature or between the two wings of the party. Even more than the administration, for example, Taft wanted a balanced budget. That first year Eisenhower, despite many cuts in expenditures, could not achieve a balance between income and outgo. When informed of this at a meeting with the President, Taft exploded, banging the table and shouting, "Now you're taking us right down the same road Truman traveled. It's a repudiation of everything we promised in the campaign." Inwardly incensed by the outburst, the President outwardly controlled himself. Patiently he tried to explain that any further cuts would endanger the national defense. Taft was not convinced, but he did not denounce the administration's policy in public.

The other Republicans in Congress took much the same attitude as Taft. Although the President voluntarily cut more than a billion dollars from the mutual security budget inherited from the Truman administration, the Republicans in Congress were still not satisfied. Even after the President went before Congress to plead for his bill without any cuts, the fiscal conservatives joined with the extreme nationalists to slash still another billion from the foreign aid budget. The President's recommendation for a three-year extension of the reciprocal trade agreements was cut by the Republican Congress to one year. His request for new housing was also sharply cut by Congress. *The Congressional Quarterly Almanac* for 1953, taking note of how often the President was opposed by his own party in Congress, calculated that the Democrats saved the President's measures fifty-eight times in that one year. So uncooperative were the Republicans that in the middle of 1953 Eisenhower was talking privately about the desirability of forming a new party which would more accurately reflect his views.

The most striking and dangerous example of the conflict within the Republican party and between Congress and the President was the controversy over the Bricker amendment. In 1953 Republican Senator John Bricker of Ohio offered a constitutional amendment that would have seriously reduced the treaty-making power of the President. In the case of *Missouri* v. *Holland* (1920) the Supreme Court had held that through treaties the power of the federal government could be enlarged beyond the limits otherwise set by the Constitution. The Court based its judgment on the constitutional provision that treaties were "the supreme law of the land." In fact, however, treaties had never been used to enlarge federal powers in any important field. And there were few instances even in minor fields where federal power had been expanded through treaties. Nevertheless, Senator Bricker and his supporters feared that radical social and economic changes would be introduced through the "backdoor" of the treaty-making power. The Bricker amendment would have postponed the effective date of all treaties until Congress or the states passed supporting legislation that would be valid without a treaty.

President Eisenhower and Secretary of State Dulles strongly opposed the amendment on the grounds that it would greatly hamper the conduct of foreign policy. But in the era of the Great Fear a majority of congressmen agreed with Bricker. In 1953 the administration was able to force a postponement of a vote on the issue, but early in 1954 the proposal for an amendment came up again, this time with widespread support from members of Congress and from patriotic organizations throughout the country. Although a majority of senators voted for it, their numbers were insufficient to make up the necessary two thirds. A modified but still objectionable form of the amendment was offered by a conservative southern Democrat a little later. It was defeated by only a single vote in the Senate: thirty-one to sixty. Of the supporting votes, Republicans cast more than half.

The President and His Party. Conflicts between the President and his party in Congress like that over the Bricker amendment were actually skirmishes in the long war waged by the President to refashion the Republicans into an internationalist party. One way the President sought to influence the party was by campaigning for its candidates. In the congressional elections of 1954 he took the unprecedented action of touring the country in vigorous support of Republican congressmen. Over and over again he called the voters' attention to the disadvantages, not to mention dangers, inherent in a government divided between two parties, and hence the desirability of his having a Republican Congress with which to work. (In point of fact, the Democratic congressmen supported him more consistently on foreign policy than the Republicans.) But despite Eisenhower's campaigning the congressional elections of 1954 ran true to form in that the opposition party made gains. The Democratic majorities that were achieved in both houses and the seven new Democratic governors boded ill for the success of the President's "modern Republicanism."

The Election of 1956. By 1955 the great majority of Republican leaders, regardless of their attitudes toward Eisenhower's political philosophy, knew that he was their greatest popular attraction since Warren G. Harding. And so it was foregone that he would be the Republican candidate in 1956, once he had recovered completely from a heart attack in the fall of 1955. Eisenhower himself accepted the nomination because his central goal of establishing a secure peace in the world still eluded him. The 1955 Geneva Summit Conference had given him some reason to believe that he had established a better relationship with the Russian leaders than any other high American official had been able to do since the Cold War began. He also cherished the hope of making permanent the changes he sought in his party. At the convention that summer he was renominated by a grateful party, with Richard M. Nixon once again his running mate.

Meanwhile the Democrats had chosen Adlai Stevenson again, this time on the first ballot. The fight among the Democrats occurred over the vice-presidency, with John F. Kennedy of Massachusetts and Estes Kefauver of Tennessee battling for the place. Kefauver won, but not before many southern delegates had given their support to Kennedy. That a Roman Catholic should have won southern support suggested that the South's opposition to Al Smith in 1928 on religious grounds was now more history than political warning. (The thought was not lost on Kennedy or those who hoped to make him President some day.) The Democrats sought to avoid the rupture of 1948 over civil rights by remaining silent on the controversial Supreme Court decision on the desegregation of schools. For its silence the party was to suffer among southern Negro voters.

Stevenson, eager to run this time, carried on a whirlwind campaign. His speeches were not so intellectually exciting or so witty, but he had been warned that wit in politics did not add up to victory. The Republicans depended upon having produced "Peace and Prosperity," as their slogan phrased it, but the real appeal was the President, as the great number of people, especially teen-agers, wearing "I Like Ike" buttons attested. Stevenson tried to counter the popular cult of Ike by seriously discussing the dangers of further testing of nuclear and thermonuclear bombs, but the administration officially and the Republicans unofficially squelched him by contending that a cessation of tests would endanger the national defense. The Hungarian and Suez crises, which broke into the headlines just before the voters went to the polls, did little to harm Eisenhower's high place in the public mind, despite the fact that both events constituted rather obvious failures in the conduct of American foreign policy. If the two crises had any effect, it was merely to reinforce the feeling of most Americans that at such times the general was more needed than ever.

The Strange Victory. As the public opinion polls had predicted, Eisenhower won easily; his percentage of the popular vote had been surpassed only by Roosevelt in 1936 and Harding in 1920. Stevenson's total vote of 26 million was slightly smaller than in 1952. The vote in the electoral college was 457 to 73. Once again Eisenhower broke into the now less than solid South, taking Virginia, Tennessee—though the latter was Kefauver's native state—Louisiana, Florida, and Texas, among the states of the old Confederacy. Somewhat of a surprise was the decided shift of southern blacks to Eisenhower, probably because of the Supreme Court decision on school segregation. The shift was especially evident in the cities, where Eisenhower's strength in the South was concentrated.

The real surprise was that, despite his tremendous personal victory, Eisenhower was unable to bring a Republican Congress back to Washington with him. He ran 6.5 million votes ahead of congressional Republicans. Even his former Secretary of the Interior, Douglas McKay, campaigning in Oregon for the Senate, was defeated. The Democrats retained their small but sufficient majorities in both houses. Not since 1848 had a President failed to carry at least one house in his election; for a popular President like Eisenhower to fail to do so was unprecedented. The common explanation for the paradox was that the majority of voters were still wary of the Republican party, especially on domestic issues, but that they trusted Eisenhower. In the minds of many liberal Republicans the Old Guard of the party, which had opposed welfare legislation under Roosevelt and Truman, still dominated Republican councils; such voters might not be able to support the party, but they would vote for the President. Moreover, Eisenhower

THE ELECTION OF 1956

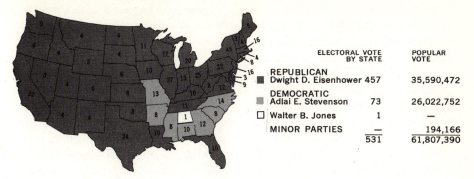

	ELECTORAL VOTE BY STATE	POPULAR VOTE
REPUBLICAN Dwight D. Eisenhower	457	35,590,472
DEMOCRATIC Adlai E. Stevenson	73	26,022,752
Walter B. Jones	1	—
MINOR PARTIES	—	194,166
	531	61,807,390

had still not altered the old image of the party in the minds of the independent voters. It was also true that Eisenhower's real appeal had always lain in his apparent lack of partisanship; probably many voters who supported him did not take him seriously when he said he needed a Republican Congress. After all, hadn't he gotten along quite well with the Democratic Congress? Actually Eisenhower's strong partisanship has often been underestimated. In his memoirs, for example, he wrote that the defeat of Richard Nixon in 1960 was "my principal political disappointment. . . . I cannot ascribe any rational cause for the outcome," since in his opinion Nixon was clearly the better man. He also made a strenuous effort, he further tells us, to prevent Douglas Dillon from serving in the Kennedy Cabinet, because Dillon was a Republican and a former member of his Cabinet. Eisenhower apparently also thought of himself as a more activist President than many historians have. Much later he talked about his foreign policies with pride: "The United States never lost a soldier or a foot of ground in my administration. We kept the peace. People asked how it happened—by God, it didn't just happen, I'll tell you that."

Eisenhower's Second Term

Divided Government. Throughout his whole second term Eisenhower had to work with a House and Senate controlled by Democrats. In the midterm elections of 1958, Democratic majorities in both houses reached proportions not seen since the middle 1930s. Leading Republican conservatives like Senators William Knowland and John Bricker lost their seats in 1958. That same year only two Republican newcomers managed to counter the nationwide Democratic tide: Nelson Rockefeller, running for governor of New York, and Barry Goldwater, contesting for a Senate seat in Arizona. As a result the President conceived his job to be the protection of the taxpayer from the potentially, if not actually, wasteful Democratic Congress. When Congress passed salary increases for government employees in 1957, the bills were all successfully vetoed by the President. Early in 1958 when a recession that had begun the previous August began to evoke congressional and public apprehension, labor and business groups alike demanded tax cuts as a means of pumping more purchasing power into the economy. The seriousness of the recession was attested by the report in April from the Federal Reserve Board that the index of industrial production had dropped 11.7 per cent since the previous August—the biggest decline since the Great Depression. Despite this fact, the President refused to endanger his first balanced budget by recommending tax cuts. Only with great reluctance did he sign a $3.375 billion federal highway bill which the Democratic Congress passed as an antirecession measure.

When in August 1958 it became clear that the recession was over, the President returned quickly to his adamant stand against spending. Characteristically he saw the issue in moral, not modern economic terms. In January 1959, for example, he told legislative leaders that Democratic spending had to be held down: "We've got to convince Americans that thrift is not a bad word." In 1959 he vetoed a public works bill which he stigmatized as a pork barrel; the House sustained his veto by a single vote. When he vetoed a second such bill it was passed over his veto—the first overridden veto in his experience as President. Right down to the end of his tenure he was resisting congressional spending. In June 1960 he vetoed a 7.5 per cent pay increase for federal employees, but the veto was overridden, largely because it was an election year, by the Democratic Congress. As we have seen earlier, a similar concern for economy was evident in administration policy on military expenditures. The administration's willingness to let the economy stagnate out of concern for inflation would be a major Democratic issue in the campaign of 1960.

The Griffin-Landrum Act. One of the three principal pieces of legislation of Eisenhower's second administration was the Labor-Management Reporting and Disclosure Act. (The other two were the Civil Rights Act of 1957 and the National Defense Education Act of 1958. See pp. 84 and 90.) The act grew out of congressional hearings on labor union corruption and racketeering. In a sense the bill was a continuation of the philosophy of the Taft-Hartley Act, since the underlying assumption in both acts was that labor unions and especially their leaders needed to be federally controlled for the protection of union members as well as the public. The act set up a bill of rights for union members to protect them against assessments and coercion by their leaders. It also required unions to make public, largely for the benefit of their members, all expenditures and all payments made to officers. Unions were also required to hold regular elections of officers. The act was one of the achievements to which Republicans pointed with pride in the campaign of 1960, though many conservative Democrats had supported the bill from the outset.

The New Movement for Negro Rights

The Supreme Court Decision of 1954. On May 17, 1954, in the hushed, ornate chamber of the Supreme Court of the United States, Chief Justice Earl Warren read a unanimous opinion. The case was *Brown, et al.* v. *Board of Education of Topeka, et al.,* in which black children contested statutes that required their segregation from white children in public schools. The heart of the question, the Chief Justice said, was, "Does segregation of children in public schools solely on the basis of race, even though the physical facilities and other 'tangible' factors may be equal, deprive the children of the minority group of equal educational opportunities?" The answer of the Court was, "We believe that it does." These historic words marked the climax of a half century of persistent effort by Negro rights organizations to reverse the Court's acceptance of racial segregation. Specifically rejecting the conclusion in the case of *Plessy* v. *Ferguson* of 1896, the Court now announced that "in the field of public education the doctrine of 'separate but equal' has no place. Separate educational facilities are inherently unequal" in 1954, whatever they may have been in an earlier period when the Fourteenth Amendment was adopted.

Although the Court's decision was momentous, it was not a complete surprise. Ever since the late 1930s the Court, under the guidance of four different chief justices, had been striking down discriminatory laws and practices. In 1938, for example, the state of Missouri was told that an out-of-state law school for black Missourians did not meet the requirement of the Fourteenth Amendment for equal treatment of all citizens. Then in 1944 in *Smith* v. *Allwright,* the Court decided that Democratic primaries in the southern states, which were the real elections because the Republican party was virtually nonexistent there, could not exclude Negro voters. Four years later the Court specifically refused to uphold real estate agreements that discriminated against buyers on grounds of race. In 1950 Texas was told that its separate law school for blacks was not equal to that open to white students and hence was unconstitutional. The culmination was the great decision of 1954 on public school segregation.

Though quite definite in its condemnation of segregation, the Court was still fully aware of the difficulties that would arise in carrying out the decision. As a result the Court postponed for a year its specific orders to the school districts for which the decision had been made. But communities in West Virginia and Delaware, and the cities of Baltimore and Washington, none of which was directly involved in the case, voluntarily began to desegregate their schools in September 1954. In its second school segregation decision, on May 31, 1955, the Court laid upon the local school boards the responsibility for drawing up plans for desegregation; they were also to bear the burden of proof for any delay in desegregating. The Court called upon the states, through their school boards, to end segregation within a "reasonable time," but it refused to set a deadline for the completion of the change. For all those who regretted this omission by the Court, there were many others who were thankful that the Court had given the South, where the changes would be most resisted, time to adjust to the alteration in well-established educational practices. One consequence, though, was that the delay permitted the formation of organizations and pressure groups determined to resist desegregation. During 1955 and 1956 white citizens' councils formed all over the South, dedicating themselves to obstructing desegregation through every legal means, and sometimes through illegal intimidation of officials and school boards as well.

Resistance to implementing the decision was strongest in the Deep South, where no effort was made to admit blacks to previously all-white schools. Even in eastern Tennessee, not usually thought of as extreme on the race question, an angry mob at the little town of Clinton forced the halting in September 1956 of the first attempts to desegregate the local high school. In February of the same year a shouting, threatening crowd of students and townspeople forced the first black student at the University of Alabama to withdraw. By the middle of the year some 350 school districts in nine states had desegregated, but none of these districts was in the Deep South; there the line was firmly held.

The Montgomery Boycott. At the very time that the Deep South was resisting the movement toward equalization of educational facilities, southern Negroes were displaying a new militancy which belied the argument of many southern whites that blacks were content with the segregated status quo. On December 5, 1955, the 50,000 black residents of Montgomery, Alabama, began a boycott of the local busses in protest against segregation and discrimination by the bus company. The boycott continued for months, with as many as 95 per cent of the black population of Montgomery participating, often at great personal sacrifice. Although ninety-two of the black leaders, of whom twenty-five were ministers, were arrested under an old law as a means of breaking the boycott, the protest continued. The principal leader of the movement was the Reverend Martin Luther King, Jr., a young minister from Atlanta who had just come to Montgomery to accept his first church. A Doctor of Philosophy from Boston University, King won national recognition and eventually the Nobel Peace Prize for his advocacy of nonviolence in the face of violence and riot. Militant in his determination to win equality for his race, he nonetheless counseled love for those who opposed him. The United States Supreme Court upheld a lower court on November 13, 1956, in striking down segregation on the busses of Montgomery.

Civil Rights Legislation, 1957 and 1960. Three years after the Brown decision, desegregation was still proceeding very slowly. Aside from a few school districts in western Texas, North Carolina, and Tennessee, virtually no states south of the border states had taken the first steps toward desegregation by the summer of 1957. Nevertheless, the pressure for further breaks in the color line continued to mount. Now the drive was for protection of black voters in the South. After long debate and delaying action by southern congressmen, Congress in August 1957 passed the first Civil Rights Act since the Reconstruction. A large part of the credit for the passage of the act was due the majority leader in the Senate, Lyndon B. Johnson, a Texan and a Democrat. Despite its novelty, the act had been so watered down in getting through Congress that it proved inadequate in protecting black voters. Consequently, three years later a second Civil Rights Act was passed to increase the powers of the Justice Department in seeking to compel local officials to register blacks.

Despite the new laws, voting by blacks in the South remained far less, proportionately, than by whites. Part of this disparity, of course, resulted from continued resistance, covert and overt, on the part of southern election officials and from intimidation by local groups of whites. A large part, however, also stemmed from the blacks' lack of interest and political inexperience. Hence Negro organizations and leaders organized campaigns to overcome the widespread political apathy, timidity, and ignorance among southern black people. Yet the resistance of southern whites to Negro voting was so obviously effective that within five years Congress and the national administration would feel it necessary to enact even stronger federal protections for black voters in the South.

The Little Rock Crisis. At a news conference on July 17, 1957, while Congress was debating a controversial provision of the Civil Rights Bill, a reporter asked President Eisenhower whether he knew that under existing statutes he possessed the power to use federal troops to enforce the desegregation of the schools in the South. The President replied that he had been so informed, but then went on to say, "I can't imagine any set of circumstances that would ever induce me to send federal troops . . . into any area to enforce the orders of a federal court, because I believe that the common sense of America will never require it." Within two months the unimaginable occurred.

Arkansas is not a deep southern state, and it had already taken some steps toward desegregation. In September 1957 five of the state's school districts, including one in the city of Little Rock, were scheduled to carry out plans for the grade by grade integration of the public schools. Five days before classes were scheduled to begin, on August 29, a state court forbade the Little Rock School Board to carry out its integration plan, on the grounds that information from Governor Orval Faubus indicated violence would ensue if the plan were put into effect. A federal court countermanded the state court's injunction, but the night before the school was to open the governor ordered contingents of the national guard to surround Central High School. When nine black students sought entrance, their way was barred by the troops. Because the federal court insisted that the school board's plan be put into effect, the situation at the high school was a direct clash between the authority of a federal court and that of the state. Minds leaped back across a century to Andrew Jackson and South Carolina's nullification.

President Eisenhower was extremely reluctant to intervene in the explosive situation—he was a Whig President, not a Jacksonian. Moreover, he was not publicly committed on the issue of desegregation. Throughout his presidency he had refused to express publicly a belief in the rightness of the Supreme Court decision of 1954, feeling that to do so was improper for the President. (Later, in his memoirs, the President said he had approved of the decision all along.) In 1957 he rejected a private request from Martin Luther King to go into the South to uphold the morality of desegregation as a means of countering the widespread white resistance. Apparently Eisenhower did not view segregation as a moral issue.

Whatever his views on desegregation, Eisenhower never harbored any doubts about the supremacy of the federal government and the necessity of upholding its courts. For all his belief in limiting federal power, the President could not ignore Faubus' defiance of the federal court. After a request from the governor for a conference, the President met with him and a temporary truce was arranged. Soon thereafter the situation at the high school eased as the soldiers were replaced by policemen. On September 23 the black children were permitted to enter, but over a thousand protesters and rowdies surrounded the school, shouting and threatening. As a result the school authorities sent the Negro children home before the end of classes. The next day, when the crowd refused to disperse upon a presidential order, Eisenhower incorporated the Arkansas National Guard into the United States Army—thus putting them under his command instead of the governor's—and dispatched a thousand troops of the 101st Airborne Division to Little Rock. Grimly the paratroopers with fixed bayonets took up their positions around the school, dispersed the mob, and for the next few weeks escorted the black students through the corridors of Central High to their classes.

The newspaper pictures of federal troops protecting nine young Negroes from an angry mob in the center of a large American city shamed most Americans and shocked the world. Little Rock became a worldwide symbol of the dangerous consequences of the unresolved conflict in the American mind between racism and equality. Not since the Civil War had public officials so openly defied the authority of the United States; not since the Civil War had the basic understanding which underlies all democratic government deteriorated to such an extent that only naked force could compel compliance with law. In order to reduce tensions in the community, the federal troops were withdrawn two months later and replaced by the federalized Arkansas guardsmen, who remained on the school grounds for the remainder of the school year.

White students look on as heavily guarded black students arrive at Little Rock Central High School. The scene would be reenacted, with variations, in other states, North and South, as the drive for integrated education continued. *Photo: UPI*

The immediate effect of the Little Rock crisis was a hardening of southern resistance to school desegregation. Arkansas and Virginia enacted "massive resistance" laws, which were intended to close the schools if integration seemed to be in the offing, and a number of cities in both states did suspend public schooling for a year or more. But the prospect of an end to public education soon produced a popular reaction against massive resistance. Conservative businessmen, ministers, mothers worried over the education and safety of their children, and friends of law and order in general began to recognize the uselessness and the danger of such resistance. Slowly, painfully, tentatively, the moderate people of the South, of whom there were many, began to organize. By 1960 massive resistance was over. In 1960–1961 integration came to the Deep South for the first time, though again not without violence and harassment of the black children and the whites who chose to accept integration. That year both Louisiana and Georgia opened at least tokenly integrated schools. The three most adamant states of the Deep South—Alabama, Mississippi, and South Carolina—did not permit any breaches in their patterns of segregation on any level until the Kennedy administration increased federal pressure. Outside of these three states, token integration at the university level had been proceeding without serious incident for several years.

The Sit-In Movement. Like the Montgomery bus boycott of 1955, the so-called sit-ins showed that the drive against segregation was more than a protest by a few northern black organizations or a handful of southern liberals. Masses of blacks in the South were joining the protest. No longer could it be argued that dissatisfaction with segregation was caused by northern agitators or was the attitude only of blacks who had left the South. In February 1960 a completely unorganized group of black college students in Greensboro, N.C., instituted a new form of protest against segregation. They contested the exclusion of Negroes from lunch counters in the local Woolworth five-and-ten by simply sitting at the forbidden lunch counter and refusing to leave when denied service. The practice, which usually resulted in the immediate shutting down of the counter, was taken up by black students in other towns and cities. Sometimes they were joined by white students. The tactic quickly became a national form of protest. Violence rarely resulted because the sitters-in steadfastly refused to respond to taunts or provocations, even when white hoodlums physically attacked them or burned them with lighted cigarettes. Around the nation local authorities arrested as many as 1500 sit-in students for trespass, but by the end of the year several national chain stores had desegregated their lunch counters in 112 southern and border state cities.

Those stoical, well-disciplined sit-in students, quietly reading their books while making their protest, suggested an even greater self-control and moral content in the Negro protest movement. Even some southern newspapers commented on the moral superiority of these black students over the rowdies and hoodlums who baited them. Very noticeable in this new means of protest was a religious undertone that echoed the important part black ministers in the South were playing in most of the demonstrations and protest activities. A deep religious commitment had long been associated with southern blacks; it was now being shaped into a peaceful but remarkably effective weapon of social change.

The National Implications of the Negro Rights Movement. Ever since the First

World War the most common form of black protest against the segregation patterns and limited job opportunities in the South was migration to the North. By the end of the 1950s black migration to the industrial cities of the North was creating problems there too. The black population of fourteen of the largest metropolitan areas in the North grew almost 80 per cent between 1950 and 1960, while the total population of these areas increased only 19 per cent. Housing, schools, and recreational facilities open to Negroes streaming into Chicago, New York, Detroit, and other large northern centers did not expand proportionally. Increasingly blacks complained of being compelled to live in ghettos in the North and of being forced to attend inadequate, overcrowded schools. Moreover, many pointed out, the housing patterns in these northern cities, by separating the races, produced separate and unequal schools which sometimes were as inadequate as those established by law in the South.

The large number of Negroes now concentrated in northern cities presented problems not only because they were confined to black ghettos, but also because they were the poorest, least educated, and least skilled portion of the population. Organizations like the black-led Urban League pointed out that most blacks were rural in background and that in the fifty years since 1910 the black population of the United States had changed from being 70 per cent rural to being 70 per cent urban. That fact in itself was a demographic change productive of much social unrest. When blacks came to the big cities they were faced not only with the pressing disabilities of racial discrimination, but also with the challenges of a new urban environment. Clashes with the police and social maladjustments may not have been inevitable, but they were to be expected.

In short, as the South wrestled with its age-old problem of how to fit Negroes into traditionally white America, northern cities were also finding out that legal segregation was not all that blacks objected to or had a right to object to. Housing and job opportunities that were truly open to all would have to prevail if black discontent and protest were not to grow and fester in the North. A measure of the need as well as the lateness of the hour was the eruption of extensive violence in the ghettos of northern cities in 1964 and after (see pp. 114–15).

Sputnikitis

Embarrassed or disquieted as many white Americans might be over the unsavory publicity segregation and incidents like Little Rock brought them, they felt secure in their pride in the scientific, technological, and industrial advances of their prosperous society. After all, the United States had been the first nation to split the atom and fuse hydrogen. Then came October 4, 1957.

The Russian Sputnik. On that day the Soviet Union announced that Russian scientists and technologists had placed a man-made satellite in orbit around the earth. Sputnik I, the Russians called it. Even before Americans could attempt to equal the Soviet achievement, Russian scientists on November 3 sent up Sputnik II, which was large enough to carry a live dog. In contrast, the first American effort, a Navy Vanguard rocket, exploded on the launching pad in early December. Not until January 31, 1958, were the anxious Americans at Cape Canaveral, Florida, able to launch the first Explorer satellite. Though it went higher than the two Sputniks, its weight was a mere 18 pounds as compared with

184 for the first Sputnik and 1160 for the second. Americans were dismayed by the demonstrated ability of the Soviet Union to surpass them technologically and shocked to reflect on what it meant militarily. Throughout the world Soviet scientists received wide public acclaim. It would take time and much humility before the Americans would catch up with the Russians.

With the scientific and, to a lesser extent, the political prestige of both countries hinging upon successfully orbiting hardware, satellites were hurled into the skies in profusion during 1958. By 1961 the advent of the first Sputnik had evoked six separate series of American space efforts, each more ambitious than the preceding.

The Military Implications of Sputnik. The feverish activity in space was provoked by something more than a desire for international prestige and scientific inquiry, though these motives were not absent. The heavy vehicles the Russians shot into space in 1957–1958 indicated that they possessed a rocket of much greater power than anything available to the armed services of the United States. Thus behind the space contest was a missile race. Before the first Sputnik was sent into orbit, President Eisenhower had depreciated a Russian announcement in August that the Soviet army possessed a missile capable of attaining a speed in excess of 13,000 miles per hour with a range of 5,000 miles. Prior to the firing of Sputnik the United States had twice failed to launch its Atlas intercontinental ballistic missile. And even when the missile was lifted off its pad it traveled no more than 500 miles before plunging into the ocean in the south Atlantic missile range.

After Sputnik public and congressional pressure grew for an acceleration of the missile program. So strong was the national concern and dismay that the President felt the necessity on November 7, soon after the second Sputnik went up, to reassure the nation. He also named James R. Killian, president of the Massachusetts Institute of Technology, to be his special adviser on science and technology. On January 7, 1958, Eisenhower asked Congress for $1.37 billion to expand and accelerate the missile program. Congress almost immediately granted him all but $100,000 of his request. The budget of $73.9 billion which the President proposed for 1958–1959 was the largest peacetime budget in American history. As a result, the United States began to develop a new array of weapons.

The rocket arsenal of the United States contained a spectrum of instruments, ranking from little bazookas, which enabled a single infantryman to stop a tank, through the short- and medium-range weapons like Nike and Thor, which could be used against planes, troop formations, and ships, to the giant intercontinental ballistic missile (I.C.B.M.), which, as its name implied, could span oceans and devastate cities with its nuclear warhead. Most spectacular of all was the 1500-mile-range Polaris, which could be fired from a submerged nuclear-powered submarine. Because the submarine would be constantly moving beneath the surface—it could remain submerged for months at a time—it would be an almost impossible target for an enemy to locate and destroy. The first in a series of such submarines, equipped with sixteen nuclear-bomb-tipped Polaris missiles, went on regular patrol in the north Atlantic on November 15, 1960. Thus, as a result of Sputnik, the two major powers began a missile race that forecast a fantastic kind of push-button war in which only minutes might elapse between the declaration of war—if there was even that—and the slaughter of millions in a thermonuclear holocaust.

The Debate over Education. One further consequence of the Sputniks was a furious national debate on the character and goals of American education. Americans had always been deeply concerned with education, valuing it highly and relishing its successes in a country composed of a great variety of nationalities and language stocks. Shocked by the recently demonstrated Russian superiority in technology and science, public figures and others proceeded to lay the blame for American inferiority in science and technology on the American educational system. Actually criticisms of public education—the heart of the American system—had been widely heard before Sputnik. Books like Professor Arthur Bestor's *Educational Wastelands* (1953), Mortimer Smith's *The Diminished Mind: A Study of Planned Mediocrity in Our Public Schools* (1954), and Rudolph Flesch's *Why Johnny Can't Read* (1955) all attested to the growing feeling in the 1950s that American education was not demanding enough of the nation's children. Principally under attack was a misunderstood version of progressive education. In the 1920s and 1930s some schools had gone to the extreme of making "adjustment to life" a central function of education and of offering courses appropriate to such an approach that were without meaningful content. As a result, all aspects of progressive education came under attack. Critics like Bestor and Smith demanded more "old-fashioned" training: memorization, more intellectual discipline through the study of traditional subjects, and more emphasis on mathematics, languages, and sciences.

Thus when the Russian Sputniks began to orbit, the ground was well prepared for a critical examination of American education. That same November in which the second Sputnik appeared in the sky, the United States government itself issued a 200-page study, *Education in the U.S.S.R.,* which focused attention on the rigorous methods of Russian education. Noticeable in the report was the large amount of time spent in the study of sciences, languages, and mathematics by the children of the nation which had produced the first man-made satellites. Less than two months later a report of the Rockefeller Brothers Fund, a highly respected research organization, recommended a complete examination of American education. The debate was on. Suddenly scientists became the darlings of press and public, and publicists vied with one another in trying to discover means by which young Americans could be encouraged to become scientists. Each year the newspapers reported with new pride the increasing percentage of graduating high-school students who elected to study science, mathematics, or foreign languages in college.

The administration and Congress responded to the national mood by enacting, on September 2, 1958, the National Defense Education Act, which suggested in its very title the new connection between national defense and the schools. The law authorized the spending of $887 million over a period of four years to encourage instruction and study in science, mathematics, and modern foreign languages. Included in that sum was $82.5 million in scholarships for graduate study in these fields and a $295-million loan fund for college students. It was the first major federal effort in support of higher education since the land-grant college act of 1862.

Although the shock of Sputnik awakened Americans at least temporarily to the desirability of study in science and languages, the promised reevaluation and restructuring of American education as a whole never came about. For a while there was a new emphasis upon "excellence," but no fundamental changes or even experimentation resulted. The well-known traditional educator Robert M. Hutchins, former president of the University of Chicago, spelled out the irony of Sputnik and education. "History will smile sardonically," he wrote in 1959, "at the spectacle of this great country's getting interested, slightly and temporarily, in education only because of the technical achievements of Russia, and then being able to act as a nation only by assimilating education to the cold war and calling an education bill a defense bill." By the Johnson years Sputniks were no longer necessary to justify federal aid, as we shall see in the next chapter. But there still would be no searching national examination of what the schools ought to do or how they should do it.

The Election of 1960

The Campaign. Because of the Twenty-Second Amendment, 1960 was the first election year in which neither party was kept on tenterhooks waiting to find out whether the incumbent would run again. As a result, even before the convention the Republicans had a good idea who their candidate was to be; Vice-President Nixon made no secret of his ambition to succeed Eisenhower. When toward the end of December 1959 Governor Nelson Rockefeller of New York, Nixon's only serious rival for the nomination, withdrew from the race, the field was clear for Nixon. His nomination was clinched when Eisenhower let reporters know definitely during the spring that Nixon was his choice. As expected, at the Republican convention in Chicago in July Nixon was nominated on the first ballot, with Henry Cabot Lodge, the United States ambassador to the United Nations, as his running mate.

The Democratic convention was much less decisive. Indeed, a number of hopeful candidates, especially Senators John F. Kennedy of Massachusetts and Hubert Humphrey of Minnesota, had been campaigning unofficially for almost a year before the convention and, in Kennedy's case, planning for it even longer. In the course of the six months before the convention met in Los Angeles, Kennedy succeeded in effectively eliminating Humphrey by winning the primaries in Wisconsin and West Virginia. Within certain segments of the party there was still sentiment for Adlai Stevenson, who had captured the imagination and allegiance of many intellectuals and idealists, though Stevenson himself was once again troubled by self-doubt and indecision. The conservatives in the party, especially those in the South, gave their support to Senator Lyndon Johnson of Texas, the amazingly successful and shrewd majority leader of the Senate. But on the first ballot Kennedy's carefully organized campaign and months of hard talking paid off. He was nominated before the balloting was completed. In an astute move to unite the party and secure southern support in the election, Kennedy asked Johnson, who had won the votes of a third of the convention delegates, to run for Vice-President, which he agreed to do—much to the surprise of the public and the Kennedys.

The Democratic platform promised a continuation of the Fair and New Deals—the liberal program which had brought the party to power in so many previous elections through its appeals to organized labor, ethnic groups, farmers, and the disadvantaged. It called for an increase in the minimum wage, a return to inflexible price supports for farm goods, a revision of immigration laws in order to eliminate discrimination against southern and eastern Europeans, a program of medical aid for the aged, and the ending of segregation in all school districts by 1963. The Republican platform was a defense of Eisenhower's administration, as it had to be under the circumstances. The emphasis was on the peace and plenty which the country had enjoyed during the previous eight years. Both parties were united in their opposition to the admission of Communist China to the United Nations.

The campaign was vigorous and strenuous, in keeping with the youth of the two candidates (Kennedy was forty-three and Nixon forty-six). An innovation of the campaign was a series of four television confrontations between the candidates. Although called debates they hardly fitted the usual format, for neither man made any attempt to answer his opponent's arguments. But the millions of voters who watched the encounters got a close view of how each man responded to the unrehearsed questions directed to him by a panel of newsmen. The consensus was that Kennedy, who was not so well known nationally as the Vice-President, gained more from participation in the series. After the election Kennedy conceded to reporters that without the debates he could not have won the election.

Throughout the campaign Kennedy emphasized his desire to "get the country moving again," to bring idealism, energy, and new ideas into politics and government. The image of a youthful, vigorous, and imaginative leader that came to characterize his later administration began in the campaign of 1960. Vague as his prescriptions may have been, there was no denying the sense of excitement and purpose he injected into a national politics long dulled and slowed by Eisenhower's avuncular personality.

Kennedy's biggest handicap was his religion. In nominating him the Democrats decided that, despite their experience with Al Smith in 1928, a Roman Catholic could be elected President. Soon after his nomination, however, public and covert objections to a Roman Catholic President began to circulate. But unlike Smith, Kennedy from the outset attempted to meet the opposition directly. Even in his primary fight in West Virginia, a state almost entirely old-line Protestant, Kennedy frankly raised the religious issue, saying plainly that religion under the Constitution and in the American tradition should not be a factor in any election. Simultaneously he made clear his own firm adherence to the traditional American conception of separation of church and state. His trouncing of Hubert Humphrey in West Virginia on May 10 gave the Democrats and the country good reason to believe that religion might not be an issue in the coming campaign. (Actually, as it turned out, that was not quite true.) Always Kennedy insisted upon meeting the objections to his religion from the high ground of principle. On September 12 at Houston, Texas, he addressed a group of Protestant ministers on the subject of his Catholicism, which had aroused much anxiety in the heavily Protestant South, just as Smith's candidacy had done thirty-two years earlier. "I believe," Kennedy told the assembled minsters, "in an America where separation of church and state is absolute . . . where no public official either requests or accepts instructions on public policy from . . . any . . . ecclesiastical source."

For the most part, the Republicans refused to use the issue of his religion against Kennedy. Nixon steadfastly adhered to his declaration made at the beginning of the campaign that religion was not an issue.

A Close Election. On election day there was little confidence among pollsters or professional politicians as to the outcome. That night, as the polls closed across the nation, the early returns were equally indecisive. Not until early the next morning was the result definite, and even then the vote was so close that the final count was not clear for days. Kennedy's margin of victory turned out to be 113,057 out of 69 million votes cast. It was the closest election in the popular vote since 1884. The electoral college vote was more decisive, however: 303 to 219. (Even so, a switch of 12,000 votes in five states would have given Nixon a majority in the electoral college.) Although some Republicans held out for several days before conceding, Nixon himself conceded to Kennedy the day after the polling.

Analysis of the returns showed that Kennedy scored heavily in the industrial states that ran from Maine to Maryland, all of which had large Catholic populations. Yet it is not certain that his religion won him many votes he would not have secured anyway. Surveys showed, for example, that his percentage of the vote in Catholic districts like Boston and elsewhere was not substantially higher than Truman's had been in 1948 (or than Johnson's would be in 1964). On the other hand, reliable surveys revealed that he lost as many as 4.5 million Protestant votes that were ordinarily Democratic. As political scientist V. O. Key put it, he won "in spite of his religion." Except for New Mexico, Nevada, and the new state of Hawaii, the only western states Kennedy carried were Michigan, Illinois, Minnesota, and Missouri. In general his strength was centered in the industrial cities—the heartland of the Democratic party—where Jewish and Negro voters, mainly urban-dwellers, strongly supported him. Indeed, the blacks saved South Carolina for Kennedy, since Nixon came within 10,000 votes of capturing that once dependable stronghold of the Democratic party in the South.

The usual black support of the Democratic party was increased greatly by an incident which occurred during the closing week of the campaign. When the Negro leader Martin Luther King, Jr., was sentenced to four months in prison for a traffic violation in Georgia, Kennedy's brother Robert successfully intervened to secure his release. John Kennedy's courtesy call to Mrs. King was

THE ELECTION OF 1960

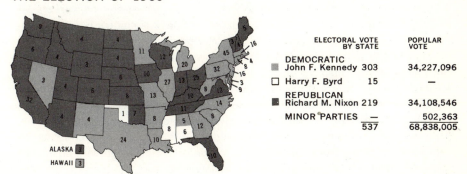

	ELECTORAL VOTE BY STATE	POPULAR VOTE
DEMOCRATIC		
John F. Kennedy	303	34,227,096
Harry F. Byrd	15	—
REPUBLICAN		
Richard M. Nixon	219	34,108,546
MINOR PARTIES	—	502,363
	537	68,838,005

ALASKA 3
HAWAII 3

publicized to blacks in 2 million pamphlets distributed at Negro churches throughout the country the Sunday before the election.

The slimness of Kennedy's victory was not reflected in the elections for Congress. The Democrats came in with huge majorities, counting 65 Democrats to 35 Republicans in the Senate and 262 to 174 in the House. But the avowedly reform-minded new President could not be sure that he would receive congressional support for his program, since conservatives of both parties dominated the councils and the organization of both houses. Indeed, if anything the election had returned more conservatives to Congress. This conservative domination would make the first two years of the new administration both a difficult period and one without much legislative achievement.

Yet it was clear from the election that the country was still—almost thirty years after the advent of the New Deal—strongly Democratic. It remained to be seen whether, without a vote-getter like Dwight Eisenhower, the Republicans could recapture the White House in the future and, even if they did, whether they could ever hope for a Congress controlled by their party.

A New Generation in Office

During his campaign John F. Kennedy called for a new, youthful spirit in government and in the country at large; he never said it explicitly, but the fact was that Eisenhower was the oldest man ever to serve as President and Kennedy would be the youngest ever elected. There was a decided emphasis on youth and vigor in the new President's short, pithy inaugural address: "Let the word go forth from this time and place, to friend and foe alike, that the torch has been passed to a new generation of Americans, born in this century, tempered by war, disciplined by a hard and bitter peace, proud of our ancient heritage. . . ."

Kennedy's emphasis upon youth was apparent in his selection of Cabinet officers. Although many of the new appointees were young and far removed from the business background of the Eisenhower Cabinet, the new President was not doctrinaire on either ground. He selected as Secretary of Commerce Luther Hodges, who was a former business executive in his sixties—"the administration's only link with the nineteenth century," as Hodges phrased it. Kennedy broke boldly with precedent in the appointment of his brother Robert, even younger than himself, as Attorney General. Perhaps the most impressive Cabinet member was the Secretary of Defense, Robert McNamara, president of the Ford Motor Company and a former professor. Kennedy and McNamara hit it off immediately, becoming good friends socially as well as mutually respected co-workers—a rare combination within the Kennedy administration. Also indicative of the new President's willingness to break with the usual practice was his appointment of Douglas Dillon as Secretary of the Treasury, even though Dillon was a Republican and a former member of Eisenhower's Cabinet. For Secretary of State Kennedy passed over Adlai Stevenson to appoint Dean Rusk, a former State Department official and, at the time, head of the Rockefeller Foundation.

One of the striking facts about Kennedy's appointments on all levels was his dependence upon foundations and universities. Of the top 200 appointments, 18 per cent were drawn from educational institutions, as contrasted with 6 per cent in the previous administration. Newspaper columnists joked about the preponderance of Harvard men in the upper levels of the new administration, but they might just as well have talked of the many Rhodes scholars. Businessmen had made up 42 per cent of the top appointments under Eisenhower, but they constituted only 6 per cent under Kennedy.

An Uncommon Man. Although John F. Kennedy liked to think of himself as the representative of the generation born in the twentieth century, in most ways he was far from typical of his contemporaries. Born in 1917 into a newly wealthy Irish Catholic family, he was educated at exclusive private schools and graduated from Harvard just as Europe was descending into the night of World War II. His considerable talent as a writer and observer was displayed in 1939 by the publication of his senior thesis as the book *Why England Slept,* a study of the reasons for England's refusal to oppose the threat of Hitler during the 1930s. During the war Kennedy served as a lieutenant in command of a PT boat in the southwestern Pacific. When his boat was rammed and sunk by a Japanese destroyer, his devotion to his men and the hardships he incurred in order to get them back alive made him a minor hero. After the war his election to the House of Representatives from Massachusetts in 1946 brought him into national politics. In 1952 he was elected to the United States Senate after a hard, close fight against a favored Republican incumbent. Although the Senate suited his tastes better than the House, Kennedy's ambition did not rest there. In 1956 he unsuccessfully competed for the Democratic vice-presidential nomination. After the defeat he began his campaign for the top place in 1960.

Both the youthfulness of John F. Kennedy and the magnetic attraction he had for people are caught in this picture taken during the 1960 campaign. *Photo: Cornell Capa—Magnum*

The ambition was one side of him. Another was his wit, which he turned against himself as well as against Republicans. "I understand that President McKinley and I are the only two Presidents of the United States to ever address such an occasion," he told the Republican-dominated National Association of Manufacturers in 1961. "I suppose that President McKinley and I are the only two that are regarded as fiscally sound enough to be qualified for admission to this organization on an occasion such as this." At another time, as he and his staff relaxed on the rear balcony of the White House after making the harrowing decision to establish the Cuban quarantine, he lightened the gloom with the remark, "I hope you realize that there's not enough room for everybody in the White House bomb shelter."

There was also his pragmatism, his refusal to be tied down by theory or preconceived ideas, including those of his liberal supporters. In fact, he distrusted people who called themselves liberals, and when he himself was denominated a liberal, he quickly qualified the description to "practical liberal" or "pragmatic liberal." He never joined the liberal organization Americans for Democratic Action, for example, or even the American Veterans Committee, a liberal veterans group formed at the close of the Second World War. As a member of Congress he had revealed a conservative streak when he refused to vote for the repeal of the Taft-Hartley Act (though he had opposed it originally) and when he supported the Twenty-Second Amendment. (His much-commented-upon refusal to speak out against the actions of Senator McCarthy was dictated not by conservatism but by his concern for the opinion of his Irish Catholic constituents, who idolized the Wisconsin senator.) Even before he became President, then, Kennedy evidenced the detachment that characterized his White House years. As one of his biographers, James M. Burns, has suggested, this detachment was a reflection of his divided origins. Although an Irish Catholic, born of conservative parents, he displayed the manners, the education, and the intellectual outlook of a member of the eastern establishment. One Massachusetts Democratic politician put it well: "Jack is the first of the Irish Brahmins."

As President, Kennedy obviously enjoyed his job; it never seemed too big for him, as it did in the beginning for Truman, or boring, as it appeared to be for Eisenhower. Kennedy seemed to thrive on the pressures of the presidency and welcomed its opportunities for leadership. In that way he was like F.D.R. But unlike Roosevelt, Kennedy tended to make much of the history and grandeur of the office, using the presidency as a way of giving Americans a sense of purpose and unity; in the process, however, the office began to be less down-to-earth, more pretentious, a trend that reached its culmination during the presidency of Richard M. Nixon.

The most spectacular example of Kennedy's use of the office for setting aspirations for the people, and one which some unfriendly historians think was his only positive achievement as President, was his announcement in 1961 of the Apollo space program. "I believe that this nation should commit itself," he told Congress in characteristic rhetoric, "to achieving the goal, before this decade is out, of landing a man on the moon and returning him safely to earth." (At the time of his announcement 58 per cent of Americans opposed the venture. The goal was actually achieved in July 1969, when Neil Armstrong and Edwin Aldrin, Jr., walked on the surface of the moon, their gambolings in cumbersome space suits witnessed on television by an estimated one billion people.) Despite the high-flown rhetoric that he was wont to use in seeking to arouse Americans to new achievements in rivalry with the Russians, Kennedy exhibited none of F.D.R.'s simple nineteenth-century certitude about life. A realistic pessimism and sense of the true ambiguities of life were characteristic of his thinking. Once after a successful press conference on television he wistfully remarked to his assistant, "We couldn't survive without TV."

The Domestic Achievements of the Kennedy Years

Getting the Country Moving. During the campaign Kennedy had attacked the Eisenhower administration for failing to achieve a rate of economic growth commensurate with those attained by the industrial nations of Europe. As he pointed out, one of the social consequences of a relatively low rate of growth was high unemployment, which reached almost 6 million in the first months of the new administration. He proposed a number of measures to stimulate economic growth, but perhaps his most significant innovation was to call attention to the gap between the views of the new Keynesian economists on the proper and central role of government in the economy and the myths that businessmen and the public accepted as economic truths. Ever the pragmatist who scorned ideology because he thought it interfered with understanding reality, Kennedy insisted upon educating the country in economics as no President before him had ever done. Like Theodore Roosevelt, he used "the bully pulpit" of the presidency to the fullest. His most notable effort in this connection was the commencement address he gave at Yale University in June 1962. His text was, "How can we look at things as they are, not through party labels or through position labels, but as they are—and figure out how we can maintain this economy so that it moves ahead?" His answer was: "What we need is not labels and clichés but more basic discussion of the sophisticated and technical issues involved in keeping a great economic machine moving ahead." The specific targets of his remarks were those members of Congress and the business community who thought balancing the budget was the most pressing fiscal task of government. To such people he pointed out that the national debt was actually a smaller proportion of the gross national product in 1962 than it had been in 1945, and consequently a much reduced burden. He also denied that business confidence in government was a necessary condition of prosperity, observing that the downturns of 1929, 1954, 1958, and 1960 came when Republicans, who were traditionally friendly to business, occupied the presidential office.

Early in his administration Kennedy took steps to stimulate the economy. In September 1961, for example, the minimum wage was increased to $1.15 an hour, with a further increase to $1.25 to go into effect two years later. The Housing Act of 1961 provided funds for urban renewal, low-income housing, and farm housing, thereby creating almost half a million jobs in the construction industry alone. But these and other economic measures taken in 1962 were palliatives rather than remedies for unemployment. The principal measure for stimulating the economy enacted under Kennedy's administration and, indeed, the major domestic legislative achievement of his first two years in office was the Trade Expansion Act of 1962. Kennedy recognized that the success of the European Economic Community, or Common Market, as it is usually called (then made up of France, Italy, West Germany, and the Benelux countries), threatened to cut into American markets abroad. As a countermeasure he proposed a drastic revision of the Reciprocal Trade Act, which expired that year. The Trade Expansion Act marked an even greater departure from protectionism than had the Reciprocal Trade Act of 1934. It gave the President new powers to cut tariff rates, an area in which Congress had always heretofore guarded its prerogative. It also provided for federal aid to those businesses and workers adversely affected by the resulting competition from abroad. Kennedy envisioned the act as a means of stimulating American economic growth by opening foreign markets. By permitting the importation of certain foreign goods, particularly from the Common Market, the administration hoped to secure in return wider markets for American goods, while increasing, through foreign competition, the efficiency of industry in the United States.

Kennedy's most successful recipe for stimulating the economy—a by-product of his acceptance of Keynesian economics—was the reduction of personal and corporation income taxes. He recognized that, despite an unbalanced budget, a cut in taxes would leave consumers with more money, the spending of which would act as a massive stimulant to growth. And with growth, total government revenues, despite the cut in tax rates, would actually increase. The President advocated a tax cut in the summer of 1962 and repeated the proposal three times in 1963, but conservative legislators, led by Democratic Senator Harry F. Byrd of Virginia, would not vote a cut while federal expenditures were larger than revenues. Only under the Johnson administration was the cut enacted, and it then produced the precise effect Kennedy had predicted. Not only did federal revenues rise, but soon thereafter the country enjoyed the longest boom in its history, during which the economic growth rate was 6 per cent or more.

A Short Honeymoon with Business. Ever since the 1930s the business community had been wary of, when not actively hostile toward, Democratic administrations. Unlike Eisenhower, Kennedy was no advocate of businessmen in government, but he did hope to avoid the hostility businessmen had felt toward Truman and Roosevelt. His hopes were dashed in the spring of 1962, however, when business hostility reached a new high as a result of the President's handling of a dispute over wages between steel industry executives and the steelworkers' union.

During March and early April the administration had worked closely with management and labor in the steel industry to avoid a strike and an inflationary wage increase that everyone recognized would set back the slowly growing economy. Responding to government pressure, the steelworkers' union agreed to sign a new contract with the companies without receiving the usual wage increases for the first year; the tacit understanding was that the steel manufacturers would not raise their prices. Ten days after the strike had been averted, the president of United States Steel announced that his company was raising its prices. Kennedy and his advisers were incensed, convinced that they had been betrayed. At a press conference the next day he lashed out: "Some time ago I asked each American to consider what he would do for his country and I asked the steel companies. In the last twenty-four hours we had their answer."

Characteristically, the President did not confine his anger to words. Suddenly the antitrust division of the Justice Department began to investigate signs of monopoly in the steel industry, and the Defense Department announced it would be awarding new contracts only to those steel companies that did not raise prices. Presidential indignation and the resultant threats had their desired effect: other steel companies failed to follow the lead of United States Steel, which soon rescinded its increase. The business community, however, was up in arms over the incident.

Thus, like his Democratic predecessors Truman and Roosevelt, Kennedy found himself at odds with business. And a sharp and deep drop in the stock market the following month did nothing to enhance his standing in business circles.

Kennedy and Negro Rights. In 1966 a public opinion poll revealed that John F. Kennedy was remembered by blacks as having done more for them than even Lyndon Johnson, under whose administration more civil rights legislation had been enacted than during any administration in the previous ninety years. Yet there was justice in putting John F. Kennedy in first place. He was the first President in the twentieth century to make the cause of Negro equality his own and the nation's.

Kennedy's involvement in the Negro revolution came late, as it did for most white Americans in the twentieth century. It seems to have been aroused first by political needs. Despite the gesture of concern for Martin Luther King during the campaign, in his first days in office he appointed no task force on civil rights, though many other subjects received such attention. He did appoint blacks to important jobs in government, however, and, as occasions arose in the course of the civil rights struggle in the South, the President supported his brother Robert's keen interest as Attorney General in the rights of blacks. One instance of such support occurred in the spring of 1961 when blacks and whites protesting segregation in interstate travel (Freedom Riders) were attacked by mobs in Alabama. The President saw to it that soon thereafter the Interstate Commerce Commission ordered the immediate desegregation of all waiting rooms in bus, plane, and railroad terminals.

The federal government's protection of Negro equality was not so easily extended to Mississippi. In the early fall of 1962 Kennedy was compelled to intervene with military force in that state just as Eisenhower had been compelled to do at Little Rock, Arkansas, five years before. When the state and the University of Mississippi refused to honor a federal court order to admit James Meredith as the first black student to Ole Miss, the President dispatched 300 U.S. marshals to protect his rights. The marshals were met by a barrage of rocks, bottles, and bullets from a howling mob of students and townspeople; the riot, in which two persons were killed and scores injured, lasted fifteen hours before 5000 United States troops brought order to the university town of Oxford. Meredith was admitted when order had been restored and graduated in 1963. His enrollment was the first break in the heretofore solid resistance to desegregation in Mississippi; it was followed by the admission of blacks to all levels of education in the state.

In May 1963 when police in Birmingham, Alabama, brutally used dogs, clubs, and fire hoses to break up black demonstrations, the resulting violence caused the President to send federal troops into that city to restore order. Such acts of intimidation against blacks moved him in June to advocate, in a nationwide address, additional federal legislation to carry forward the black revolution. His appeal was frankly ethical. Carefully he pointed out that equal rights for blacks "is not a sectional issue . . . [nor] a partisan issue. . . . We are confronted primarily with a moral issue. It is as old as the Scriptures and as clear as the American Constitution." His address was given added, if unnecessary, point that same night by the ambush killing of Medgar Evers, the black leader of civil rights workers in Mississippi. On June 19 Kennedy sent his civil rights bill to Congress. He did not live to see it enacted, but it became law under the Johnson administration after a three-month filibuster in the Senate.

In recent years Kennedy's achievements on behalf of Negro rights have been criticized for being too little and for being tainted with a pragmatic concern for votes. The black historian John Hope Franklin, writing in 1973, perhaps best summed up the disillusion that has dimmed some of the brilliance that once surrounded the Kennedy name among blacks. "There are only three Presidents since the Civil War who have been important in the area of civil rights—Truman, Kennedy, and Johnson," Professor Franklin wrote. "Truman broke through the thick crust of indifference. Kennedy set the stage for action. Johnson applied the action. If I had to rank them in importance, Kennedy would be third."

The Blighting of the Promise. Toward the close of 1962 the President and his administration were looking forward to the second half of his term. The broad program of economic reform announced in 1961 had not gone very well, for despite the large Democratic majorities in both houses, many parts of the program had run into considerable resistance in Congress. Twice in those first two years Congress had rejected programs for medical care for the aged—despite two major public addresses in favor of them by the President. Similarly, Kennedy's plea for federal aid to education had fallen on deaf ears, and his recommendation for a Department of Urban Affairs, which recognized the need for help to the cities, had also failed to pass. A similar fate overtook his further request for half a billion dollars in federal grants to those cities working out long-range plans for mass public transportation. Even in foreign affairs, where his record of achievement was brighter, Kennedy stumbled over congressional resistance, particularly when conservative southern Democrats in the House joined with Republicans in 1962 to cut the President's foreign aid program. Until the end of 1962 the only major achievement of the administration had been the Trade Expansion Act. Then in November the administration received strong support from the country. Instead of losing thirty to forty seats as was normal in an off-year congressional election, the Democrats lost only a handful in the House and held their large majority in the Senate. For that reason, and because of the large amount of important legislation that was working its way through the congressional mill, 1963–1964 was full of promise. The tax bill, the aid-to-education bill, and the civil rights bill aroused expectations of a commendable achievement for the first Kennedy administration.

That promise, however, was killed by an assassin's bullet. On November 22, 1963, John F. Kennedy was shot to death while riding in an open car through the streets of Dallas. The motive for the shooting will probably never be known, since his alleged assassin, while in the hands of the police, was himself shot to death by a local resident said to be incensed by the President's murder.

The assassin's bullet killed more than the hopes of the Kennedy administration; it murdered a man who had won the admiration and deep affection of large numbers of his countrymen and of people throughout the world. A decade after his death one is struck by the emotional response his name still triggers in ordinary people in Africa, Asia, and Europe. His death stunned the nation and the world with its suddenness and irrationality. His youth, his wit, his eloquence had symbolized that which was hopeful, vibrant, and fresh in his generation and now he was gone. "Like a great green cedar," one eulogist said, "he came crashing down, still in full vigor and strength."

His death left most of his work unfinished; its completion would be the task of his successor, Lyndon B. Johnson, a quite different personality and President.

SUGGESTED READING

The Eisenhower years have not produced much scholarly literature on politics, but two journalistic accounts are important for understanding the political trends and issues of the early 1950s: Samuel Lubell, *The Revolt of the Moderates* (1956) and Louis Harris, *Is There a Republican Majority?* (1954). Both books are especially valuable on the election of 1952. The speeches of Adlai Stevenson, which did so much to win support for him among intellectuals, can conveniently be read in Adlai Stevenson, *Call to Greatness* * (1962). Kenneth S. Davis, *A Prophet in His Own Country* (1957) is a favorable biography of Stevenson by a journalist; Herbert J. Muller, *Adlai Stevenson: A Study in Values* (1967) eulogizes the man and his ideals. One of the earliest and more critical biographies of Eisenhower is Marquis Childs, *Eisenhower: Captive Hero* (1958), written by a knowing journalist. More recently two long, critical studies of the general have appeared, drawing upon private as well as public papers. Peter Lyon, *Eisenhower, Portrait of the Hero* (1974) is a full-length biography, with over half of the almost 900 pages devoted to his prepresidential years; somewhat less critical is Herbert S. Parmet, *Eisenhower and the American Crusades* (1972). Arthur Larson, *Eisenhower, the President Nobody Knows* (1968) is favorable. A sympathetic portrait of the leader of the conservative Republicans is by a newspaperman, William S. White, *The Taft Story* (1954); more balanced and full is the readable James T. Patterson, *Mr. Republican* (1972).

The story of the Eisenhower administrations is conveniently available in Robert L. Branyan and Lawrence H. Larsen, eds., *The Eisenhower Administrations, 1953–1961; A Documentary History,* 2 vols. (1971). James L. Sundquist, *Politics and Policy* (1968) compares the Eisenhower administrations with those that preceded and followed. Merlo J. Pusey, *Eisenhower the President* (1956) is favorable, while Dean Albertson, ed., *Eisenhower as President* * (1963) is a collection of published articles, most of which are rather hard on the President and his administrations. Perhaps the best analytical study so far of the President is contained in a general work, Richard E. Neustadt, *Presidential Power: The Politics of Leadership* * (1960), which also covers the Truman presidency. The book has value and interest also because of the influence it exerted upon John F. Kennedy.

The most rewarding sources are the reminiscences of friends or members of the

* Available in a paperback edition.

administration. Excellent is Robert J. Donovan, *Eisenhower: The Inside Story* (1956), which is drawn from Cabinet minutes and other confidential documents. Sherman Adams, *First Hand Report* (1961) is an account by the President's closest adviser in the White House; unfortunately it is not very revealing or candid, tending to defend the President. Quite the opposite is Emmet John Hughes, *The Ordeal of Power* (1963), also written from inside the administration but with a caustic pen and much disenchantment. Dwight D. Eisenhower, *The White House Years,* 2 vols. (1963, 1965), is the President's own memoirs; it is pedestrian and concedes no failures, but cannot be overlooked.

The changing situation in education during Eisenhower's administrations can be followed in Paul Woodring, *A Fourth of a Nation* (1957), James B. Conant, *The American High School Today** (1959), and Martin Mayer, *The Schools** (1961). Both Conant and Mayer were influential in bringing about reforms in school curricula. The controversy over public power is examined in a scholarly monograph, Aaron Wildavsky, *Dixon-Yates* (1962), in which the administration is absolved of any wrongdoing, but found culpable of serious ineptitude in handling the matter.

The early years and the mood of the black revolt can be glimpsed in Anthony Lewis, *Portrait of a Decade* (1964). It draws upon the columns of *The New York Times* to describe the upheaval for civil rights beginning in 1954. Louis E. Lomax, *The Negro Revolt** (1962) is a straightforward, sympathetic account by a prominent black author. The outstanding black leader of the decade has told his story of the Montgomery bus boycott of 1955 in Martin Luther King, Jr., *Stride Toward Freedom** (1958).

Something of the conservative flavor of the Eisenhower years can be gleaned from William F. Buckley, Jr., *Up From Liberalism* (1959), a polemic by a then young, truculent conservative, indicting the New Deal-Fair Deal liberals.

The election of 1960 is covered in dramatic prose and astutely analyzed in Theodore H. White, *The Making of the President** (1960); see too Schlesinger and Israel, *History of American Presidential Elections,* vol. 4, already cited in Chapter 1.

The impact of the Kennedy administration on intellectuals, the country, and the world can be measured in the large number of books that have appeared on the President and his few years in the White House. Undoubtedly the best book on the prepresidential years is still James MacGregor Burns, *John Kennedy: A Political Profile** (1959). It is written by a skilled political scientist and draws upon Kennedy's private papers. Hugh Sidey, *John F. Kennedy, President* (1964) is by a journalist and less critical than Burns' study. Several people who were close to the President have written books, sometimes very lengthy ones, detailing the years in the White House. A dramatically written, but partisan account is by a trained historian, Arthur M. Schlesinger, Jr., *A Thousand Days* (1965); Kennedy's closest assistant and adviser, Theodore Sorenson, has written a more straightforward though equally laudatory account of the same White House years, *Kennedy** (1965). More personal and less weighty accounts of the Kennedy administration are Pierre Salinger, *With Kennedy** (1966), a memoir by his friend and press secretary, and Evelyn Lincoln, *My Twelve Years with John F. Kennedy* (1965) by the President's private secretary.

More recently a reevaluation of the Kennedy years has begun. Representative of it is a critical study by an English journalist, Henry Fairlie, *The Kennedy Promise: The Politics of Expectation* (1973). In a comparison with Eisenhower the general comes out more reasonable and balanced than the overly rhetorical and "imperial" Kennedy. Jim F. Heath, *John F. Kennedy and the Business Community* (1969) is a good, brief scholarly analysis of one aspect of Kennedy's administration. Herbert Stein, *The Fiscal Revolution in America* (1969) surveys the changes in governmental attitudes toward financial and tax policy that Kennedy initiated.

The official version of the assassination of the President is contained in the *Report of the Warren Commission** (1964). That report and the assassination have been the subject of a good bit of controversy. Perhaps the most temperate of the several critiques of the report is Edward Jay Epstein, *Inquest: The Warren Commission and the Establishment of Truth* (1966). The story of the events leading up to Kennedy's assassination and its immediate aftermath is told in great detail in William Manchester, *The Death of a President* (1967).

CHAPTER FOUR

ACTIVISM TRIUMPHANT

V ICE-PRESIDENT JOHNSON was riding in the same motorcade as Kennedy when the President was killed in Dallas. Johnson's first act when the President's death was confirmed was to insist that he be sworn into office even before his plane carried him back to Washington. This swift, decisive action was to be characteristic of his presidency. For though there had been a Johnson in the White House before him and even a previous President who had been born in Texas, events would soon show that Lyndon Baines Johnson was a quite different President from either Andrew Johnson or Dwight Eisenhower.

Johnson Takes Over

The New President. Immediately the new President plunged into the job of mastering the office that had eluded him in 1960. The contrast could not have been greater between the young, eastern-born and urban-bred Kennedy, who had inherited his wealth, and Lyndon Johnson. Born on a farm in semiarid southcentral Texas in 1908, Johnson grew up in straitened circumstances, working his way through school and college by a variety of jobs, including teaching. As many of his speeches were later to attest, the wastefulness and emptiness of the Great Depression never faded from his memory; at the signing of almost every welfare measure he alluded to his experiences as a child and young man in the depressed ranchlands of Texas and across the country during the 1920s and 1930s. His rearing in the agricultural South remained in evidence in his drawling speech and rural metaphors. His sentimental and effusive rhetoric, reminiscent of his father's Populism, contrasted sharply with the low-keyed, taut personal manner of Kennedy. A large man, possessed of enormous energy and will, Lyndon Johnson as President ignored the fact that he had almost died of a heart attack in 1955.

Johnson began his public career as an officer of the National Youth Administration and came to Congress for the first time in 1937, where he was a loyal supporter of the New Deal and a fervent admirer of Franklin Roosevelt. Running for election to the United States Senate in 1948, he won his nomination to the Democratic ticket by fewer than a hundred votes. Yet within four years he was Democratic floor leader of the Senate. There he displayed an ability to dominate that individualistic body unequaled since the days of Senator Nelson Aldrich at the beginning of the century. As his central role in the enactment of the Civil Rights Act of 1957 demonstrated, Lyndon Johnson during the Eisenhower administration was the effective legislative leader of the government. Later events would show that this was only the beginning of the momentous impact that this first southern-reared President since Woodrow Wilson would have on the advancement of blacks to equality.

A Firm Assumption of Power. As President, Johnson proved to be different from Kennedy in more than background and style; he was also able to move legislation through Congress at remarkable speed. The first hundred days of the new administration witnessed the passage of several important bills that previously had been stalled in legislative committees for months. Within those first hundred days the reduction in personal and corporate income taxes that Kennedy had been advocating for over a year was enacted (February 1964). In the same period the foreign aid bill and the Higher Education Facilities Act (December 1963) became law. During the remainder of his first year in the White House,

President Lyndon Johnson's first State of the Union address. *Photo: UPI*

Johnson went on to make a record of legislative achievements that astonished a country accustomed to seeing a liberal President hamstrung by a conservative and tight-fisted Congress. At Johnson's request Congress raised the salaries of government employees again, passed a new low-rent housing act, and enacted a new National Defense Education Act. Most significant of all was the passage of the Civil Rights Act of 1964, after a three-month filibuster in the Senate.

The Civil Rights Act of 1964 was the most ambitious and comprehensive ever placed upon the statute books in the United States. It prohibited racial discrimination in public places, like hotels, theaters, and restaurants; in employment; and in labor unions. Moreover, it provided for the withholding of federal funds from any agency of the state governments in which racial discrimination was practiced. This provision alone carried great persuasive power, since hospitals, schools, and a number of welfare programs, in the South as elsewhere, were recipients of federal funds. The Attorney General was also authorized to institute suits on behalf of individuals who had been discriminated against yet might be too poor to go to court to enforce their rights. Finally, the act prohibited discrimination in the application of voter-registration requirements and established the presumption that any person with a sixth-grade education was literate. In that way literacy requirements, which were often used as a device for disfranchising Negroes in the South, were nullified. The most obvious and immediate effect of the act was the opening of many public accommodations previously closed to blacks. In at least some sections of the Deep South Negroes went to the polls in large numbers for the first time in the twentieth century. For example, in 1964 in Tuskegee, Alabama, a black-belt community, blacks succeeded in electing two members of their race to the city council.

The act was the most sweeping affirmation of the American belief in equality ever enacted. It not only prohibited racial discrimination, but it outlawed discrimination in employment for reasons of sex, nationality, and religion as well. As never before, the federal government committed itself to equality for America's two most visible minorities: Negroes and women.

The War on Poverty. Like all Presidents who have succeeded to the office, Johnson promised to carry on the policies and principles of his predecessor. (He also retained virtually all of the Kennedy Cabinet members through his first year in office.) But almost from the outset of his administration Johnson made it clear that he intended to put his own brand on the liberal Kennedy program. In his first State of the Union message in January 1964, Johnson called for a war against poverty as the keystone to the arch of the policies of his administration. Out of that proposal came the passage of the Economic Opportunity Act, which received his signature in August 1964.

The act was a recognition that most of the poverty in the nation was the result of lack of education, not of lack of jobs or opportunity for work. It appropriated almost a billion dollars for various agencies and projects that would help young people continue their education or receive job training that would enable them to undertake jobs requiring new skills. Under the act a Job Corps was created for training sixteen- to twenty-one-year-old unemployed youths. The act also set up VISTA (Volunteers in Service to America) to mobilize the skills and energies of young Americans on behalf of their poor and disadvantaged countrymen, much as the Peace Corps (see p. 127) was intended to assist in the economic development of foreign countries. Funds were made available to those cities and communities that were working out educational and training programs to help the poor rise out of their cycle of poverty and despair.

Since there had been a Fair Deal and a New Frontier, it followed that there must be a name for the Johnson program. For a while the President seemed able to do no better than "the better deal," a term he and his staff used several times in the early spring of 1964. But in a speech at the University of Michigan in May, he hit upon the title he would stick by. The Great Society, he said at Ann Arbor, was "a place where leisure is a welcome chance to build and reflect, not a feared cause of boredom and restlessness. It is a place where the city of man serves not only the needs of the body and the demands of commerce, but the desire for beauty and the hunger of community. . . . It is a place where men are more concerned with the quality of their goals than the quantity of their goods."

Not everything the President sought in that first year was vouchsafed him. His efforts to fulfill Kennedy's commitment to medical care for the aged and to an increase in social security benefits did not pass Congress. Nor was he successful in pushing through an otherwise remarkably compliant Congress his bill to relieve poverty and arrest economic decay in Appalachia. But within a single year in office Lyndon Johnson had established himself as a strong and effective President in his own right.

The Landslide

The Rise of Barry Goldwater. While the President was working to build a record on which to base his campaign for a full term in the White House, the Republicans were preparing for their own campaign by subjecting his Great Society to severe criticism. As we have seen in Chapter Three, for over twenty years the party had been split between a conservative or Taft wing and a more liberal wing, which since 1940 had provided all of the party's presidential candidates. From time to time during those two decades, the bitterness of the conservatives over their exclusion from the presidential nomination had burst out, but without any effect.

In 1964 the time of the conservatives had come, and Senator Barry Goldwater of Arizona was their man. Barry M. Goldwater was a genial, earnest, millionaire department store owner. As early as 1960 he was frankly calling himself a conservative in a society where it had long appeared that liberalism was the only acceptable label for a national candidate. Waggish opponents of the Senator suggested that his brand of conservatism was really nineteenth-century liberalism, centering as it did upon principles of laissez faire and states' rights. But in the prosperous atmosphere of the 1960s and in the frustrating age of the perpetual Cold War, Goldwater's references to the verities of the agrarian republic and his highly nationalistic approach to foreign policy evoked a warm response from many Americans. Incomes may have been up, but so were taxes; billions of American dollars had been lent and given to nations around the globe, yet wars still raged and others threatened. The racial issue provoked violence and the overcrowded cities, with their rocketing crime rates and spreading slums, threatened the safety and peace of mind of many who wanted to enjoy untroubled their new prosperity. For these Americans it was comforting to hear Senator Goldwater preach patience to the restless black ghettos, promise a reduced and balanced federal budget, and advocate a tough military stand against Communist Russia and China.

The eastern wing of the Republican party did not recognize the attraction Goldwater's conservatism obviously held for millions of frustrated and bewildered Americans. Nor did it understand that for many Republican politicians the conservative program was a welcome change after a quarter century of accepting the liberal reforms of the Democrats, with only the lame qualification that Republicans could carry them out more effectively. Such, in truth, had been the message of Thomas E. Dewey in 1948, Dwight Eisenhower in 1952 and 1956, and Richard M. Nixon in 1960. Why not, as the Goldwater supporters contended, present the electorate in 1964 with "a choice, not an echo"? Provide a candidate who repudiated the principles common to the reforming Democrats from the New Deal to the Great Society, and the American voters' conservative instincts would produce a conservative Republican victory.

Precisely that conclusion was reached by the Republican convention in San Francisco in the summer of 1964. The convention nominated Goldwater on the first ballot and then proceeded to nominate for second place William Miller of New York, who balanced the ticket geographically but hardly ideologically. Miller, despite his eastern origins, was of the same conservative persuasion as Goldwater, though lacking his genial humor and open manner.

The platform the party adopted in San Francisco reflected the conservative domination of the convention; it called for an end to deficit spending, further tax reduction, enforcement of the Civil Rights Act of 1964, and a stronger foreign policy based on "a dynamic strategy aimed at victory," a reference to the increasingly frustrating war in Vietnam.

No Democratic Fight. The Democratic party's convention had no trouble in selecting its candidate: Lyndon B. Johnson was obviously the champion of the party. But the choice of his running mate created some suspense, if only because the President refused to divulge his preference until the last minute. His choice of Hubert Humphrey, senator from Minnesota, surprised many because of Humphrey's long association with the decidedly liberal wing of the party, but it was accepted by acclamation and interpreted as an earnest by Johnson that organized labor, which had feared his conservatism in 1960, need have no anxiety in 1964. The platform not only promised to carry out the principles laid down by Kennedy and Johnson, but also came out for full support of civil rights for blacks, aid to education, medical insurance for the aged, full employment—and, of all things, a balanced budget! Unlike the Republicans, the Democrats went out of their way specifically to condemn extremism on the right and on the left—meaning the supernationalistic John Birch Society and the Ku Klux Klan (which seemed likely to support Goldwater), as well as the Communist party. The contest between the parties, in short, would not be confused by the customary balancing of philosophies in nominees or platforms.

The Campaign and the Election. Despite the clear ideological differences between the parties, there was no high-level discussion of the issues in the campaign, only platitudes and attacks. Moreover, Goldwater proved to be a rather ineffective campaigner; his forte was clearly not the great mass rally and the frequent speechmaking that modern campaigning demands. Recognizing that

THE ELECTION OF 1964

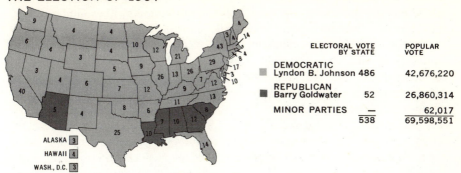

	ELECTORAL VOTE BY STATE	POPULAR VOTE
DEMOCRATIC Lyndon B. Johnson	486	42,676,220
REPUBLICAN Barry Goldwater	52	26,860,314
MINOR PARTIES	—	62,017
	538	69,598,551

ALASKA 3
HAWAII 4
WASH., D.C. 3

some of the impromptu, ill-considered denunciations of New Deal legislation that he had made in the past were now hurting his strength, he tried to qualify his remarks and to assure the country that he was not going to sell TVA to private enterprise or abolish the social security system after all. Johnson was more relaxed and bouyant if only because he was favored in the polls from the beginning. Nevertheless his penchant for folksy phrases and rural figures of speech dismayed many of his more sophisticated, urban supporters, who found his drawl, his lumbering generalizations, and his sentimentality undignified and even embarrassing. He was most effective, however, in charging that Goldwater was too impulsive and belligerent to be trusted with the foreign policy of the nation. Johnson's characterization of the Republican candidate received widespread credence because of Goldwater's refusal to vote for the test ban treaty in 1963 and his well-known advocacy of bombing raids on North Vietnam. The anxiety about the war in Vietnam and the widespread fears that Goldwater would expand the war, that he would "shoot from the hip," as the popular phrase went, undoubtedly turned many voters, including Republicans, against him.

Subsequent analyses of the elections revealed that Goldwater lost millions of Republican votes. Usually safe Republican states like Maine, Vermont, Nebraska, and Kansas went overwhelmingly for Johnson. To put the matter positively, Johnson's victory was the greatest yet in the twentieth century; he received 61 per cent of the vote, or more than F.D.R. in 1936 or Warren Harding in 1920. He carried the District of Columbia and 44 states; while five of the six states Goldwater captured were in the Deep South. Johnson's victory was equally impressive in Congress: 295 seats in the House as compared with 140 for the Republicans; the Senate was also lopsidedly Democratic: 68 to 32.

That the main Republican strength had been in the South showed how completely the traditional political alignments had been reversed. The Deep South, smarting under the Democratic endorsement of Negro equality, turned in desperation to the once-despised Republican party, which under Goldwater ignored blacks when it did not oppose them. Goldwater's emphasis on states' rights also spoke to Dixie. So intense was southern interest in the election that the South was the only region of the country in which the turnout of voters was greater than in 1960. Even more important, the election revealed a 50 per cent increase in Republicans elected to Congress from the states of the former Confederacy, from eleven in 1962 to sixteen in 1964. In 1966 the figure would jump to twenty-three. The decline in the vote throughout the nation resulted from the absentee-ism of many Republicans who were unwilling to vote for either Goldwater or a Democrat. If Johnson's position on civil rights lost him votes in the South, it brought him the overwhelming support of blacks in both the North and the South. (Goldwater had deliberately exposed himself to the opposition of blacks by voting against the Civil Rights Act of 1964.) In no section of the country was Negro support of Johnson less than 95 per cent; in some cities of the North the proportion reached 99 per cent.

Undoubtedly many Negroes voted for Johnson not just because of civil rights, but also because they were poor. For especially in the big cities the low-income groups, a mainstay of the Democrats ever since the New Deal, continued to vote overwhelmingly for the party of Franklin Roosevelt: the proportions hovered around 90 per cent. Old people in retirement areas like St. Petersburg, Florida, who had voted Republican for twenty years deserted the party because Goldwater was believed to be a threat to the social security system. Even many of the well-to-do suburbs deserted their Republican allegiance when confronted with a conservative candidate who seemed to rely heavily upon military solutions to problems of foreign policy. Moreover, since Goldwater's commitment to laissez faire caused him to repudiate farm supports and governmental controls over agriculture, many farmers also abandoned the party on election day. In twenty-three states, later studies showed, the rural vote went more heavily for Johnson that did the state as a whole. The candidate who promised continued price supports, more rural electrification, and more soil conservation payments won the farmer.

On the Road to the Great Society

The Mandate. Johnson's overwhelming victory at the polls, together with his swollen majorities in both houses of Congress, gave him new authority to build the Great Society, the program he set forth in his State of the Union message in January 1965. Bills Congress had turned down in the preceding year now passed with ease. In March, for example, the President signed the Appalachian Regional Development Act, which authorized $1.1 billion for the improvement of the thousand-mile-long mountainous region that runs through eleven states and in which poverty and poor education are endemic. Johnson's war on poverty was further advanced by the Public Works and Economic Development Act of August 1965. That law authorized the spending of $3.3 billion over a period of five years for the economic development of depressed cities and regions.

Two measures introduced originally by Kennedy were enacted into law soon after the new Congress convened. Twice during the Kennedy years the opposition of many Republicans and of the powerful American Medical Association had prevented the passage of bills to provide medical care for persons over sixty-five through the social security system. The new Congress, heavy with liberal Demo-crats and urged on by the President, pushed through a Medicare insurance law, which the President happily signed on July 30, 1965. The act provided that basic hospitalization costs, including nursing home care for all persons over sixty-five, would be paid for out of social security taxes. A supplementary plan, which cost the participant only $36 a year, was set up to help meet additional medical expenses of persons over sixty-five. The President, ever conscious of the historical roots of momentous events, arranged to sign the bill in the presence of the aging former President Harry S. Truman, who in 1945 had first recommended a government health insurance program.

The second piece of Kennedy legislation that Johnson secured from the new Congress was the renovation of the immigration law. Kennedy and the Democratic platform of 1960 had both promised an end to the national origins system of quotas for immigration, but nothing had come of the proposal. The national origins quota system, which first became United States policy in 1924, not only limited the numbers that could enter this country, but also favored certain nationalities over others. For many years the policy had been opposed on the grounds that it discriminated against Asians and southern and eastern Europeans, but the prospect of eliminating the discriminatory policy seemed remote. Truman, for example, had recommended such a change, only to have the McCarran Immigration Act, which reaffirmed the national origins principle, passed over his veto in 1952. Nor had President Kennedy's urging in the same direction been any more effective.

The Immigration and Nationality Act of 1965 provided for the gradual elimination of the quotas based upon national origins, to be completed by June 30, 1968. The total number of immigrants permitted was set at 170,000, with each country outside the Western Hemisphere having a maximum quota of 20,000. Priority of admission was to be given to relatives of citizens, persons with skills, and refugees. In short, the principle of limited immigration, which first went into effect in 1921, was continued. But the practice of basing quotas upon preferences for certain nationalities, which had been in effect since 1929, was now abandoned in favor of a system of priorities based on the dual considerations of national economic need and simple humanity. A significant change from the old law, also, and presumably a concession to proponents of the national origins idea was the establishment for the first time of a quota for immigration from the countries of the Western Hemisphere.

The Education President. In 1964 Johnson predicted that the Eighty-eighth Congress would be known as "the education Congress" because of the important legislation enacted in that field in 1963 and 1964. It seemed much more likely, however, that it would be Johnson himself who would go down in history as the principal advocate of federal aid to education. For, as one of his aides said, "Johnson has a passion for education of the same order of intensity as Kennedy's passion for stopping atomic testing."

In 1964 the old question of whether the federal government should aid the schools or leave the matter to the traditional local authorities ceased to be a live issue. That year a congressional study revealed that the federal government was already spending $2.2 billion a year on education. Congress recognized the new role of the federal government when it passed the Higher Education Facilities Act in December 1963. The act, which originated under Kennedy, marked a new step in federal aid to education. It not only provided grants and loans for the construction of college and university buildings, but for the first time put the federal government into the business of helping develop graduate centers.

As the need for educational facilities mounted in response to the rapidly increasing population and the new prosperity of Americans, the overburdened states and localities turned increasingly to the federal government for aid. The National Defense Education Act of 1964 marked another shift in emphasis that demonstrated anew the expanding federal interest in education. The original NDEA legislation, passed in 1958, had been sparked by the Russian Sputnik, and it appropriately provided loans and grants for the study of mathematics, science, and foreign languages in order to keep up with Russian advances in technology and science. By 1964, however, justifications for aid to education no longer required foreign threats. The NDEA of 1964 provided funds and scholarships in the humanities, too. The Elementary and Secondary Education Act of 1965 authorized the spending of more than a billion dollars over the next three years for grants to the states to raise educational levels in the low-income school districts. The act was a landmark in educational history because it provided aid for the first time to children in private, church-supported schools as well as to those in public schools. Because of the need for improved education in a technically advanced economy, the traditional objections to federal aid to church-supported schools on the grounds that it would violate the constitutional separation of church and state were abandoned. The shift was not unrelated to the fact that in 1960 many Americans had also shed for the first time their historic prejudice against electing a Catholic to the presidency. Fortunately, however, it was a Protestant President who advocated the inclusion of all children enrolled in recognized schools in the first federal program for education below the college level.

President Johnson's oft-stated conviction that all young Americans should have open to them as much education as they could absorb was partly realized in the Higher Education Act of 1965. To the already familiar provisions of loans to students, the new act added federal scholarships of up to $1000 a year for students otherwise unable to attend college. It was a kind of revival on a permanent basis of the program of the National Youth Administration, with which the President had first entered government service in the 1930s. It also continued the long trend toward popularization of higher education begun in the 1920s and further encouraged by the Veterans Readjustment Act of 1944 (the "G.I. Bill"), which gave financial aid to returning veterans who wished to enter colleges and universities after the war. By the end of Johnson's term in 1968 the U.S. was providing 10 per cent of all government expenditures to education, in contrast to only 3 per cent ten years earlier.

A New Departure in Public Housing. In September 1966 the President realized his long-cherished wish to use federal funds to help the poor pay for housing. In 1965 he had urged Congress to pass a bill authorizing the federal government to supplement the rent payments of the poor living in privately owned housing. Only after a long and acrimonious fight was the law enacted, and not until 1966 were adequate funds forthcoming to implement the idea. At the signing of the $22 million appropriation bill Johnson called the program "the single most important breakthrough in the history of public housing. . . . It is a clear-cut but compassionate solution to a pressing national problem." The act permitted the federal government to help pay the rent of those poor who lived outside public housing and who otherwise might not be reached through the usual channels of the poverty program or the public housing laws. In the President's mind it was a part of his larger program to end poverty altogether.

A Southern President Champions Blacks. As a congressman and even as a senator, Johnson had supported the customary segregation practices of the South. But in the late 1950s he began to speak out against the mores of his region, his crucial support of the Civil Rights Act of 1957 being a notable example of this change in attitude. As President his record on Negro rights surpassed that of any President since Lincoln; his public avowal of black equality more than matched that of John F. Kennedy. Undoubtedly Johnson's strongest and most eloquent statement on behalf of equality for blacks was his address at Howard University in June 1964. The goal of complete equality that he set forth in that speech has not yet been achieved anywhere or at any time. Freedom from slavery is not enough, he pointed out, "You do not wipe away the scars of centuries by saying: Now, you are free to go where you want, do as you desire, and choose the leaders you please. You do not take a man who for years has been hobbled by chains, liberate him, bring him to the starting line of the race, saying 'you are free to compete with all the others,' and still justly believe you have been completely fair. Thus it is not enough to open the gates of opportunity. All our citizens must have the ability to walk through those gates. This is the next and more profound stage of the battle for civil rights."

Johnson's actions on behalf of black equality matched his words. As we have seen, he pushed Kennedy's civil rights bill through a reluctant Senate in 1964. In his appointment of Robert Weaver to the Cabinet and Thurgood Marshall to the Supreme Court, Johnson brought blacks into higher levels of the federal government than had any previous President. His principal effort to realize his commitment to black equality was devoted to protecting the franchise for southern blacks. The Civil Rights Acts of 1957 and 1960 had not been effective enough in reducing the barriers to black voting which southern whites had erected, especially in the Deep South.

The Voting Rights Act of 1965. Southern black leaders believed that if blacks could be protected in their right to vote, they would be able to obtain justice from white sheriffs, justices of the peace, legislators, and governors who would then be dependent, in part at least, on Negro votes. As it was, intimidation, local tradition, and ignorance of their rights conspired to keep the number of Negro voters far below the proportion of the population that blacks constituted in many southern states and counties. The voting act, as finally passed in the summer of 1965, provided for federal officials to register black voters in any county in which the Justice Department found that the number of blacks voting in the presidential election of 1964 was less than 50 per cent of those old enough to vote. In this way the often deliberate delays in registration by local officials could be circumvented. Four days after the President signed the bill, federal examiners began to register Negroes in selected counties in Alabama, Mississippi, and Louisiana. The enactment of the 1965 law was a striking gauge in itself of how far the country had come in regard not only to federal action in the political affairs of the state, but also to Negro rights. In 1890 a similar bill had been denounced as a "force bill" and it never reached the Senate. In 1965 the use of federal power on behalf of Negro voters was seen by most citizens as necessary as well as moderate.

The Long Road Ahead. The enactment of the Voting Rights Act, however, did not immediately end the practical disfranchisement of blacks in the South, any more than the passage of the Civil Rights Act the year before had ended racial discrimination in the North or South. Despite the increased registration of blacks in 1966, strong segregationists won the governorships in Alabama and Georgia, though at the same time a Republican moderate on the race question was elected governor in Arkansas as a result of Negro support. All over the country in the middle 1960s it appeared that, as the nation created ever more powerful machinery for achieving the long-neglected goal of equality, both black impatience and white resistance mounted. As some gains were made by Negroes in their pursuit of full equality, they pushed ever more insistently for even greater and quicker improvement in their legal and social position. To many whites the very achievement of any gains at all suggested that the tempo of change ought to slow down, not increase. As ancient social patterns in both North and South were increasingly challenged and broken, whites became more apprehensive and resorted at times to violence. White violence against black demonstrators in Alabama in the spring of 1965 caused President Johnson, like his two predecessors, to send federal troops into his native South to provide the protection that Alabama's segregationist Governor George C. Wallace would not.

Nor was the violence confined to the South or to the initiative of whites. In 1964, in Harlem, Rochester, Los Angeles, Brooklyn, Jersey City, and Philadelphia, as well as other cities in the North, the inhabitants of the black ghettos went on rampages, attacking the police, setting fires, and looting stores and homes. The following summer the eruption into riot of the Los Angeles black ghetto of Watts sent tremors of horror and fear across the nation. The resulting property damage was estimated at $40 million, with almost 4000 arrests, over a thousand wounded, and thirty-four dead from the violence.

White hostility toward black demonstrators in the North now became open. When blacks demonstrated in Chicago in 1966 to influence real estate agents to give up their policy of refusing to sell or rent houses to blacks in white districts, white mobs jostled, hooted at, and stoned them. Martin Luther King, Jr., who led one of the demonstrations, later said that the hatred and violence he encountered on his march through parts of Chicago exceeded anything he had experienced in the Deep South. There were signs in other cities, too, that as the movement for black equality sought to break down the barriers in housing that prevailed in most northern white urban and suburban districts, white resistance would become more, rather than less, adamant. Significantly, a civil rights bill proposed by President Johnson that required open housing failed to pass the Senate in 1966 largely because northern white opposition was so strong. It was the first failure to pass a civil rights bill since the Negro revolution had begun a decade earlier.

The great year of riots was 1967. That spring and summer, outbursts of violence in varying degrees of severity occurred in more than thirty cities. In Detroit and Newark alone sixty-eight persons lost their lives, about 1400 were injured, and almost 7000 arrested. Whole sections of the two cities were burned out. Although at the time whites feared that the violence born of black frustration and discontent would be turned against them, the riots usually were confined to the black sections of the cities. In retrospect these outbursts can only be seen as desperate acts by thousands of blacks whose aspirations had been raised but unrealized.

Widespread and devastating as the riots of 1967 were, the year 1968 saw still more. On April 4, 1968, Dr. Martin Luther King, Jr., perhaps the best known black man in America since Booker T. Washington and the inspired leader of the Montgomery bus strike and numerous other civil rights demonstrations, was assassinated by a white man in Memphis. King had been participating in a protest movement in support of striking Negro garbage collectors in Memphis. In their chagrin and frustration at the news of the death of their champion, thousands of blacks in Washington, D.C., Baltimore, Chicago, and Kansas City, Missouri, along with 120 other cities across the nation, went on a rampage of rage. All told, forty-six persons died, more than 2,600 were injured, and some 22,000 were arrested. Property losses were placed at $45 million.

Open Housing. The only good thing that could be said to have come out of the riots that followed King's assassination was that a bill to outlaw racial discrimination in housing was now pushed through Congress. President Johnson had been seeking such a measure since 1966, but without success. But, as happened with Kennedy's civil rights bill in 1963, an act of violence made Congress receptive. The bill that now came to Johnson's desk outlawed racial discrimination in the sale or rental of about 80 per cent of the housing in the country. Sales of individual or single-family homes, however, were exempt from the law. This act proved to be the last piece of civil rights legislation in the Johnson or Nixon administrations. For by 1968 the great movement for black equality that had begun weakly and slowly under Harry Truman twenty years before, reaching its crest with Kennedy and Johnson, was over. For the moment, at least, white

Dr. Martin Luther King, Jr., leading a march in support of a strike by black sanitation workers in Memphis. A few days later King was assassinated and riots swept the nation. *Photo: Wide World*

Americans had moved as far as they would to compensate for the centuries of deprivation imposed on blacks, first as slaves and then as free people.

The Move Toward Separation. Meanwhile, however, the black revolution had become more than a movement toward integration. It is true that the great mass of blacks looked to equality within the prevailing society. The National Association for the Advancement of Colored People, which had carried on the struggle through the courts, culminating in the Brown decision of 1954, continued its constitutional approach with support from large numbers of blacks. Martin Luther King's Southern Christian Leadership Conference, an organization of the 1950s, emphasized demonstration and public appeals, rather than legal action, but King's own pacifism and commitment to passive resistance meant that violence was no part of this new way. His emphasis on love rather than hatred underscored his commitment to integration as a long-term goal.

But the resistance of many whites to integration moved other black leaders to think in terms of separation as the best avenue for Negro life in America. The Black Muslims, a religious society founded by Elijah Muhammad during the 1930s, attracted national attention in the mid-1950s when the articulate Malcolm X became head of the Muslims in Harlem. The Muslims preached a form of Islam and advocated black separation from whites. After a trip to Africa in 1964, Malcolm X turned away from the narrow black nationalism of Elijah Muhammad. But the great potential for leadership and good suggested in his *Autobiography of Malcolm X* was not realized, for he was assassinated in 1965, presumably by other Black Muslims.

Perhaps the most militant of the nationalist groups was the Black Panther party, which began in the Oakland, California, ghetto in 1966. A former convict of great literary and oratorical talent, Eldridge Cleaver was the best known spokesman of the party; his book *Soul on Ice* became one of the classics of the black revolution in the 1960s, along with *The Autobiography of Malcolm X.* Cleaver fled to Algeria in 1968 after a series of confrontations between police and Panthers. By the 1970s, however, the Panthers were considerably less involved in confrontations with police and more concerned with educational and breakfast programs for black children in the urban ghettos. In 1973 Bobby Seale, another leader of the Panthers in the 1960s, known for his refusal to work within the system, ran for mayor of Oakland and attracted much support from whites as well as blacks for his reformist program.

The figure least influential over the long run in the new black nationalism of the 1960s was Stokely Carmichael, who in 1966, at the age of twenty-four, became head of the Student Nonviolent Coordinating Committee (SNCC). His slogan "Black Power" aroused a new sense of awareness and pride in many young blacks and a sense of identification and cohesion among blacks of all ages. As a leader Carmichael did not survive into the 1970s, but his idea of black power, along with the activities of other nationalist groups, created a new pride in blackness and African origins in dark-skinned Americans.

In retrospect the rise of black nationalism must be seen as a measure of the impatience and even despair of many young blacks. Certainly by the 1970s even many conservative blacks were not sure that integration would be as fully achieved or as rapidly gained as they once had thought. Yet the alteration in the position of blacks, particularly in the South, over the previous quarter of a century was far from negligible, however distant it might have been from full equality. In those years not only was the whole legal basis of segregation dismantled, but the very idea of segregation came under sustained attack. Practices of segregation that went back three generations or more were abandoned. Soon after the passage of the Civil Rights Act of 1964, for example, hotels, restaurants, and theaters in Jackson, Mississippi, in the heart of the old Confederacy, were opened to blacks for the first time in the twentieth century. Blacks also began to appear in northern offices, banks, and other places of work where none had ever been seen before except as cleaning personnel. "I can stand at the entrance to almost any office building in Manhattan today," said Roy Wilkins of the NAACP in 1973, "and watch the office workers come out at 5 o'clock and it's all salt and pepper. Ten years ago they'd all be white." By the end of the 1960s desegregation of schools and universities had begun in every southern state, and by the opening years of the seventies the degree of integration in southern schools was greater than in northern schools, where housing patterns kept schools all white or all black. More blacks were now voting in the South than at any other time since the Reconstruction; by 1970, for example, 67 per cent of the blacks of voting age in the eleven Confederate states were registered as compared with 25 per cent in 1956. That same year Alabama elected 105 black officials—the second highest total in the nation. Indeed, throughout the country in the 1970s blacks figured prominently as elected officials. In 1971 over 1600 blacks were elected to public office throughout the country, of whom eighty-one were urban mayors. In 1975 Atlanta, Newark, Los Angeles, Gary, and Detroit were among the large cities that had black mayors.

Dramatic as the progress was, it was still uneven and short of what black leaders expected or the nation required. For as the seventies opened it was evident that the goals of the 1950s, which had begun the revolution, had been left behind. At one time the aim had been simply to remove from blacks the disabilities of segregation in law and practice. But as that goal began to be realized it became apparent that the problems of blacks were much deeper and would require more profound remedies and much more time than anyone had imagined. Negro poverty, for example, though in part the consequence of a century of segregation, would not be removed simply by eliminating segregation. In fact, the most needed gains on behalf of Negro equality were still to be made; they lay in areas other than legal rights. The struggle for Negro equality and the war against poverty were really two sides of the same problem. Since most blacks were poor, and their poverty was one of their principal disabilities, equality would become a reality in America only when the war against poverty was won. The ending of poverty, however, would be a considerably more difficult job than removing segregation laws. For a while in the late 1960s it seemed as if the antipoverty measures might be slowly but definitely closing the gap between the average incomes of blacks and whites. In 1961–1963, for example, the median income of blacks was about 53 per cent of that of whites, but in 1970 it was 64 per cent. Between 1965 and 1970 the number of blacks in college almost doubled, reaching 7 per cent of total enrollment. Between 1960 and 1970 the proportion of blacks who had purchasing power in excess of $10,000 went from 9 per cent to 24 per cent. But by 1972 the gap was widening again, presumably because the rising unemployment hit blacks first and hardest. Unemployment among blacks in 1972 was still twice that for whites, just as it had been in 1960. Moreover, even though a third of blacks reported incomes of $10,000 in 1972, about 30 per cent were still below the poverty line, while only 10 per cent of whites were.

By the 1970s the black experience of the 1960s made at least two things clear. There was no end to social problems, just as there were no final solutions; no sooner was a problem "solved" or met than it became a different problem. Certainly this was what happened with the problem of segregation and black deprivation. Even in the process of dealing with a problem, of meeting it, new problems were encountered calling for new solutions. The second point flowed from the first, namely, that some problems could not be dealt with in a short period of time, even when enormous amounts of money were expended. Although billions were spent in the war on poverty, no way was found to eradicate poverty, and those ways that were tried were often unable to win the allegiance of the poor. The elimination of poverty and other social ills would have to wait for better solutions.

From New Deal to Great Society. Lyndon Johnson began his political career under the New Deal of Franklin Roosevelt. In a sense his Great Society program was a culmination of the revolution begun by Roosevelt, continued by the Fair Deal, and nurtured by the New Frontier. Johnson's programs for federal aid to education, urban improvement, the war on poverty, and Negro rights certainly went beyond anything contemplated by even the most advanced New Dealer. Yet they could be seen as implicit in the New Deal, especially in its novel use of federal power and revenues. What made the difference was the prosperity of the 1960s. The New Deal's inescapable preoccupation with economic depression was now gone. Moreover, with the economy booming, programs beyond the wildest dreams of New Dealers, such as the war on poverty or the expansion of education, became not only possible but imperative. Even the Negro revolution could be viewed as a product of affluence. Prosperity fired black aspirations and expectations, provided funds for black organizations and demonstrations, and impelled the federal government to take up its long deferred commitment to equality.

In early 1968, as Lyndon Johnson neared the end of his first full term in office, it became evident that his ability to win the support of Congress for his Great Society program was waning. In 1966 the Democrats had lost seats in Congress, so that by 1967 conservatives again dominated both parties. Only a few of the President's antipoverty measures got through Congress, and then only after cuts in appropriations. His request for a tax increase got nowhere at all, though he gave it top priority. Johnson's loss of control over Congress was accompanied by a loss of popular support. By the end of 1967 fewer than 50 per cent of all Americans judged him successful in his handling of his office, though his proportion of the vote in 1964 had been over 60 per cent. By early 1968 his standing in the polls had fallen even lower.

The reasons for Johnson's decline in popularity were several. Part of his difficulty stemmed from the lack of success attending the antipoverty program. Poverty was still evident, the slums remained, and the cities seemed even less attractive or safe than they had before. Moreover, because of his championing of the Negro revolution, many white Americans blamed him for the violence in the cities of the preceding three or four summers. But undoubtedly he was blamed most of all for the continuation of the frustrating and seemingly endless war in

Vietnam. It not only aroused enormous hostility from many young people and intellectuals, but its cost was mounting by leaps and bounds. By the end of 1967, for example, over 15,000 Americans had been killed and the financial bill was reaching $20 billion a year. Indeed, it was the war that destroyed Lyndon Johnson, as we shall see later in this chapter when we canvass its terrible history.

An Activist Foreign Policy: Kennedy and Johnson

When John F. Kennedy entered office in January 1961, the Soviet Union seemed to be at the height of its power and self-confidence. Its annual rate of industrial growth exceeded by a good measure that of the United States, its only rival in economic strength. It possessed not only the hydrogen bomb but the missile capability to deliver that devastating power anywhere in the Northern Hemisphere. Moreover, some of the new underdeveloped countries, like North Vietnam and Castro's Cuba, were already enlisted in the Soviet camp. That January Premier Nikita Khrushchev told his people that "there is no longer any force in the world capable of barring the road to socialism." Boldly he proclaimed Soviet support of "wars of national liberation" wherever they might break out among the underdeveloped nations of the globe.

Because of facts like these, Kennedy during the campaign had charged the Eisenhower administration with losing the initiative in foreign affairs and falling behind in nuclear weapons. His own years in the executive mansion would be devoted to meeting what he considered the challenge of Soviet power. Indeed, Kennedy made his most noteworthy contributions in foreign policy, which had always engaged his interest more deeply than domestic affairs. "The big difference" between domestic and foreign matters, he once said, "is between a bill being defeated and the country being wiped out." Secretary of State Dean Rusk later remarked that when he first met the President-elect to discuss foreign affairs, he was surprised "by the extent to which [Kennedy] wanted to look at everything from the beginning, from the ground up, . . . the origins." Even more than Franklin Roosevelt, John F. Kennedy was to act as his own Secretary of State.

Kennedy recognized that the key to world peace was the relationship between the United States and the Soviet Union. From the beginning of his administration he sought to melt the hard freeze into which those relations had been locked by the U-2 incident. He tried to avoid the clichés of an ideological war against Communism; hence he spoke of "adversary" rather than "enemy." And in his inaugural address he urged that the United States "never fear to negotiate." Yet that same speech bristled with the language of challenge and confrontation, for he also believed that the United States must be prepared to meet challenges to its power, prestige, and interests with resolution and force if necessary. Although genuinely seeking to moderate the Cold War, Kennedy was not prepared to eschew completely the high-flown rhetoric of confrontation, as when he pledged that the United States "shall pay any price, bear any burden, meet any hardship, support any friend, oppose any foe, to assure the survival and success of liberty." Later critics would find in such language the kind of hubris that later mired the nation for a decade in Vietnam. After what Kennedy and his youthful advisers interpreted as the sluggishness and passivity of the Eisenhower administration in foreign affairs, the new government clearly intended to be activist.

For that reason, and especially after the fiasco of the Bay of Pigs in April, Kennedy felt it was essential that he meet with Khrushchev, if only so the two leaders might take each other's measure. It was at their meeting in Vienna in June that the untried President first learned of the Russian leader's determination to expel the Western Allies from their position in divided Berlin. Kennedy was so struck by the seemingly uncompromisable impasse between the two sides that upon his return he expressed his somber reaction in his report to the American people, "We have wholly different views of right and wrong, of what is an internal affair and what is aggression, and above all, we have wholly different concepts of where the world is and where it is going. . . . The question is whether these two systems can ever hope to live in peace, without permitting any loss of security or denial of freedom to our friends. However difficult it may seem to answer this question in the affirmative as we approach so many tests, I think we owe it to all mankind to make every possible effort." Within a matter of weeks one test would be made at Berlin.

Meanwhile two other tests had been inconclusive. As we have seen already in Chapter Three, the attempt to overthrow Castro in Cuba only brought the United States into disrepute. At about the time the Bay of Pigs crisis broke, Kennedy was confronted with Communist expansion in Laos, a new country created out of the former French colony of Indochina. The Laotian situation is properly a part of the later discussion of southeast Asia, but it is mentioned here because it was the first test of the administration in countering Communist expansion. By the end of the first spring Kennedy could count half a success to his credit in Laos, where a compromise was worked out, and a complete failure in Cuba. The real test came in Berlin.

A World at Stake on the Autobahn. Germany was the source and the center of the Cold War. A divided Germany and a divided Berlin, by providing innumerable opportunities for confrontation between the two superpowers, offered the tinder for a global conflagration. In the summer of 1961 it looked as if the final confrontation might be at hand. Khrushchev announced that before the end of the year he would sign a treaty with the Soviet satellite East Germany which would close off all Allied ground and air access to Berlin. When Kennedy had heard of the Russian's intention at Vienna, he had told the Soviet premier that the United States could not abandon its rights, though it would not object to a treaty between East Germany and the U.S.S.R. that did not impair Allied movement in and out of Berlin. Khrushchev, however, was faced with a serious problem. The Communist government in East Germany was extremely unpopular, and ever since the end of the war Germans in the Russian zone had been fleeing to the West, mainly through Berlin, where flight was easiest. By 1961 perhaps as much as a quarter of the total population of East Germany had drained away, usually those persons most valuable to the economy: the young and the skilled. In May 1961 alone 30,000 refugees flocked into West Berlin. At stake was the economic viability, as well as the prestige, of the East German regime.

Kennedy, however, would not abandon the rights which the Allies had won by conquest and agreement in 1945 and which had been further sanctioned by fifteen years of practice. He viewed the Russian intention to sign the treaty with East Germany as more a test of his will than a vital interest of the Russians. Moreover, after his bungle at the Bay of Pigs he apparently felt it imperative that he meet such a challenge with firmness. The difficulty was finding a way to demonstrate his will without seeming to endanger the Russian position in Berlin, for to do so might well precipitate a war. The first part of his problem he met by asking for and receiving from Congress the power to call up 250,000 reservists in the event the Russians should attempt to drive the Western Allies from Berlin. The second part he attempted to meet by publicly acknowledging the Russians' interest in central Europe and vowing that he did not intend to threaten that interest. But clearly the American position was incompatible with the announced Russian intention of signing the treaty with East Germany.

The break in the impasse came on August 13, when the Communists solved the problem of the fleeing Germans by suddenly erecting a concrete-block wall all along the line between East and West Berlin. Although the Western powers, including the United States, were taken completely by surprise, no preventive action could have been taken or was even contemplated. Inhumane and divisive as the ugly wall undoubtedly was, the East Germans and the Russians were within their rights to erect it. The flood of refugees shrank to a trickle and then virtually stopped as the East Germans strengthened and extended the wall and staffed it with sharpshooters. Not sure that the wall was the end rather than the beginning of the Russian action, Kennedy five days later sent 1500 additional troops down the autobahn from West Germany to the Berlin garrison. They would test Russian intentions and be a sign to the apprehensive West Berliners of continuing American support. The convoy was not stopped.

After some inconclusive discussion about Berlin between American and Russian diplomats in the early fall, on October 17 Khrushchev suddenly announced that there was no longer any need to insist on signing a treaty with East Germany. The threat of war was over. Yet at one dramatic moment in Berlin that summer, Russian and American tanks had faced each other in hostility for the first time in the Cold War—indeed, for the first time in history. It was not to be the last confrontation. But, as Kennedy said later, the gradual easing of tensions and the ultimate avoidance of war in Berlin showed the value of endless "jaw, jaw."

Applying the Lessons of Berlin. During the election campaign Kennedy had made much of the "missile gap" that was supposed to exist between American and Soviet military capabilities. In February when Secretary of Defense Robert McNamara had a chance to examine the facts, he admitted that there was indeed a missile gap, but that it was in favor of the United States. More disturbing to McNamara and the administration, however, was his further discovery that, despite the belated efforts of the Eisenhower administration to move away from reliance upon massive retaliation, the military establishment of the United States was ill prepared to fight any war except one involving nuclear weapons. As McNamara wrote in his report to the President, massive retaliation with nuclear weapons was "a strategy believed by few of our friends and by none of our enemies. . . ." The dangers inherent in that approach to defense were forcefully brought home to Kennedy in his talks with Khrushchev in Vienna in June 1961 and during the Berlin crisis. Suddenly the President recognized that in depending upon the nuclear deterrent alone, the United States, in confronting the Russians on the autobahn or any other equally insignificant place, had a choice only between "holocaust or humiliation." A radical expansion of conventional forces would provide additional time in which to deal with a crisis and to decide if a particular issue was worth carrying to the point of nuclear war. The fuse of war, as one adviser put it, could not be removed, but it could be made longer. In May 1961 in a special State of the Union message, Kennedy asked for a massive increase in defense expenditures, all of which was to be used for nonnuclear armaments.

The Kennedy-McNamara strategy of defense made nuclear retaliation a very remote resort; conventional warfare was always preferable to reliance on the ultimate weapon. Kennedy also urged the development of counterinsurgency forces—which later came to be called the Green Berets. He recognized that future confrontations with Communist power might well involve guerrilla warfare and subversion as well as more conventional encounters.

During the three years of the Kennedy administration defense spending rose $17 billion above that of the Eisenhower years, resulting in one of the largest and swiftest buildups of military power in history. Under the dynamic leadership of Secretary of Defense McNamara, military power and the needs of diplomacy were coordinated as never before. With a wide range of military responses now available, diplomacy achieved a degree of flexibility that had long been lacking. (Later critics of American policy in Vietnam would see the origins of that involvement in the efficient and flexible defense establishment of the Kennedy administration, which encouraged the belief that American power could achieve anything it set its mind to.)

Cuba Revisited. After the Bay of Pigs Castro's hostility toward the United States understandably increased. In December 1961, for example, he announced that he was "a Marxist-Leninist and will be to the day I die." In January 1962 Cuba extended its trade pact with the Soviet Union and built up an army of a quarter of a million men. Fearful of subversion by Cuban agents throughout Latin America, the Organization of American States that same month expelled Cuba from membership. During the late spring and summer rumors were rife in the United States that the Russians were setting up missiles in Cuba. Publicly the United States government discounted the stories, but at the same time extremely high-flying U-2 reconnaissance planes periodically swept over the island checking for signs of missile sites. During September and early October only surface-to-air missile sites were discovered, and these, because of their short range, were not considered threatening. On Tuesday, October 16, however, the President was shown pictures of medium-range missile sites under construction in Cuba. Such weapons had a range of 1100 miles, sufficient to reach a large part of the southeastern United States. Kennedy ordered the U-2 flights stepped up to several a day and initiated secret conferences among his closest advisers. Before the week was out sites for intermediate-range missiles were also revealed by the U-2 photos. These missiles, with a range of over 2000 miles, could devastate most of the cities in the eastern half of the United States.

To Kennedy the missiles constituted a dangerous shift in the balance of power in the Cold War, especially since the Soviets had publicly denied the need for, as well as the existence of, such weapons in Cuba. He rejected out of hand the idea that nothing should be done, refusing to equate the Russian missiles in Cuba with the obsolete American missiles in Turkey. He also refused to negotiate the matter privately or publicly with the Soviet Union, as some of his advisers suggested, and despite his own admonition in his inaugural address that the

U.S. should "never fear to negotiate." Actually the presence of missiles in Cuba constituted no greater military threat to the United States than the intercontinental missiles based in the Soviet Union, which were capable of reaching any city in the United States. They did double the Soviet's first-strike capability and were probably emplaced, at least in part, to make up for Russia's serious missile gap. Kennedy, however, envisioned the threat primarily as psychological, as a test of his will to take firm action when challenged by an unnecessarily provocative shift in the balance of forces in the world. Undoubtedly, too, he feared that Castro might gain control of the missiles, though it was known that almost half of the 22,000 Russians in Cuba were assigned to guarding the missile sites. It was the psychological view of the situation, rather than just the military threat, that convinced Britain's Prime Minister Harold Macmillan to support Kennedy's action in the crisis. Kennedy felt certain that if he did not act, the Russian pressure on the United States would increase, the pressure of the Republicans at home would threaten his political strength, and the credibility of America as a great power with responsibilities to protect weaker countries would be shattered.

The discovery of the missile sites was not made public for over a week while the President and some fifteen close advisers met almost constantly to canvass the responses open to the United States. Quick action was necessary, for more missiles were on the high seas and the sites would become operational within a matter of days. Once that occurred the Russian move would be difficult to counter or reverse. A suggestion for a quick, "clean" bombing strike was ruled out as too provocative in view of the large number of Russians at the sites, as well as not entirely effective. Besides it smacked too much, as the President's brother said, of "Pearl Harbor in reverse." Most prominent congressmen who were consulted, including the chairman of the Senate Committee on Foreign Relations, favored the quick airstrike. Gradually, however, the preponderance of opinion among the small group of advisers came to favor a blockade, a "naval quarantine" of Cuba which would stop the Russian ships before they could deliver the missiles.

Recognizing that this was once again a direct confrontation between the two great nuclear powers, Kennedy wanted the most flexible arrangement possible, one that would provide the maximum opportunity for the Russians to back down without humiliation. Always in the minds of the American leaders as they discussed the various responses was the likelihood that the Russians would create a diversion in Berlin or—even more alarming—that the Cuban missiles were themselves only a diversion to mask a new attack on Berlin. No precipitate action must be taken that would provoke war unnecessarily or, alternatively, leave the United States unprepared to meet challenges elsewhere. By quarantining only offensive weapons—permitting even strategic materials like oil and petroleum products through the naval lines—the United States made evident its central concern with the immediate issue. No side issues must be permitted to cloud the naked risk and fundamental interest at stake. By setting up a naval quarantine 500 miles away from Cuban shores the possibility of accidents or causes for war were kept to a minimum, for even if the Russian ships did not stop, the United States Navy ships were under orders to do no more than immobilize them by a shot to the rudder, thereby avoiding unnecessary loss of Russian lives or ships. Thanks to modern electronics the President and his advisers were able to be in direct command of the ships enforcing the quarantine—an unprecedented departure from the usual chain of command in war. Even so, the danger of a provocative act by a trigger-happy naval officer could not be entirely ruled out.

His decisions made, the President spoke soberly to the nation on television on the early evening of October 22, revealing the existence of the Russian missiles and announcing the imposition of the quarantine. He demanded that the Russians remove all offensive weapons from Cuba. One measure of the gravity of the situation was that the Organization of American States, now purged of Cuba, unanimously supported the American intervention, an almost unheard-of degree of agreement where United States intervention in the Western Hemisphere was concerned.

The ensuing week was tense as the Russian freighters with missiles aboard continued to steam toward Cuba, under constant surveillance by American military planes. After three days of watchful waiting, the eighteen Russian ships stopped dead in the water; it was at this point that Secretary of State Dean Rusk remarked, "We're eyeball to eyeball and I think the other fellow just blinked." When the Russian ships turned back the really tough question came to the fore: would the Russians remove the missiles already there and destroy the sites, as Kennedy demanded? Would they abandon their military gain and their first ally in the Western Hemisphere? Personal letters from Khrushchev and Kennedy flew back and forth, the continuation of a private and until then secret correspondence Khrushchev had initiated a year earlier during the Berlin crisis. The rapport that had been built up between the two leaders helped resolve the impasse, but apparently the decisive factor was the explicit threat by the Americans of an invasion of Cuba on Tuesday morning if Khrushchev did not withdraw his missiles. Later McNamara said, "We faced that night [October 27] the possibility of launching nuclear weapons . . . and that is the reason, and the only reason, why he withdrew those weapons." It was also the reason Khrushchev gave to the Supreme Soviet for his retreat. On Sunday, October 29, the Russians agreed to withdraw the missiles in return for a United States promise not to invade Cuba. When the President demanded also that some Russian medium-range bombers be removed, Khrushchev complied.

Even at the time the missile crisis was recognized, as Prime Minister Macmillan said in the House of Commons, as "one of the great turning points of history." Twice the United States had been tested, once in Europe and once in its own backyard, and in both cases the President had acted coolly, cautiously, and above all with regard for the sensibilities and requirements of his opponent, though also with underlying firmness. As Kennedy would say a year later, "Nuclear powers must avoid those confrontations which bring an adversary to a choice of either a humiliating retreat or a nuclear war." Recognizing the need for instant communication in the missile age, the Soviet Union and the United States worked out arrangements for the running of what came to be called the "hot line," that is, a direct private teletype circuit from the White House through Scandinavia to the Kremlin, so that in future confrontations there could be immediate communication to avoid any misunderstanding of intentions on either side. The line's first successful use came during the opening hours of the Israeli-Arab war in June 1967, when the superpowers made it clear to one another that they were not engaging in the fighting. It was used again for the same purpose in the Middle East war of 1973.

At the time, and increasingly since the Cuban missile crisis, some historians have been less impressed with the coolness or the success of Kennedy's handling of the crisis and more impressed by the enormous risk that was taken to assert a point against the Soviets. They argue, in effect, that the strategy was "brinkmanship," not statesmanship. It is true that Kennedy was prepared to risk nuclear war if Khrushchev did not withdraw his missiles, but in a world in which power determines the ultimate relations between nations that risk must sometimes be run. Power in world affairs is psychological as well as physical, and if Kennedy had permitted the surreptitious emplacement of offensive weapons in an area conceded to be an American sphere of influence the ability of the United States to influence other nations would have been severely reduced. Certainly President De Gaulle of France, Prime Minister Macmillan of Britain, and the states of the Americas all recognized this fact when they supported his actions. Domestically, too, failure to stop the missiles would have damaged the President. Indeed, at one point, rather unrealistically it would appear, he told Robert Kennedy that he would have been impeached if he had not acted as he did.

But perhaps the most compelling reason for thinking Kennedy's actions were justified was the marked change thereafter in Russian-American relations. Khrushchev, it is true, soon fell from power, having lost much authority within the Soviet leadership because of his provocative move in Cuba. And the Soviets began rapidly to increase their surface navy, presumably because of their humiliation by the quarantine. They had lacked the flexibility to meet the American challenge on a level below nuclear war. But over the next ten years American-Soviet relations improved steadily and dramatically. The improvement began in the Caribbean almost immediately after the missiles were removed and the naval quarantine lifted. One sign of the return to a less tense atmosphere was the release of a thousand Cuban prisoners who had been captured during the Bay of Pigs invasion. For their release to the United States Castro demanded and received some $50 million worth of medicines.

Détente. After Cuba Kennedy was confident the Russians understood that American power did not threaten genuine Soviet interests and that the United States would not wilt before Russian challenges. As a consequence he worked for further relaxation of tensions. Perhaps his clearest statement of his hope for accommodation was his speech at the American University in June 1963. Pointing out that the Russians had the same fears of us that Americans had of them, he urged Americans to "deal with the world as it is, and not as it might have been had the history of the last eighteen years been different. . . . We must conduct our affairs in such a way that it becomes in the Communists' interest to agree on a genuine peace, . . . to . . . let each nation choose its own future, so long as that choice does not interfere with the choices of others. . . . For in the final analysis our most basic common link is the fact that we all inhabit this planet. We all breathe the same air. We all cherish our children's future. And we are all mortal. . . . The United States, as the world knows, will never start a war."

Although the speech was overshadowed in the United States by the civil rights address given by Kennedy the next night, in Europe, and especially in the Soviet Union, it was hailed as a significant break from the frozen rhetoric of the Cold War. Khrushchev told Averell Harriman that it was the "best speech by any

President since Roosevelt." The Russian newspapers published the speech in full, and thereafter all Western broadcasts to the Soviet Union, even those in Russian, ceased to be jammed.

Clearing the Air. Kennedy's American University speech was delivered in the context of a concrete effort to moderate the Cold War. Ever since 1956, when Adlai Stevenson made the suggestion during his campaign of that year, there had been sporadic talk of halting nuclear testing by the U.S.S.R. and the United States. Such testing released large amounts of radioactive materials which were not only dangerous to the health of those nearby, but which spread around the globe to affect people far beyond the borders of the nuclear powers themselves. Two fears held up American acceptance of a ban on testing. One was that the Russians would continue to test secretly and thereby forge ahead of the United States in the nuclear arms race. The other was that any cessation of tests, even if adequately monitored, was bad because it deprived the United States of the opportunity to acquire the knowledge necessary for improving its weapons systems. The first objection was taken care of by equipment that enabled the United States to detect nuclear tests anywhere in the world, except perhaps those conducted underground. Therefore, if the Russians should cheat, the U.S. would know about it and could resume testing itself. The second point, that continued testing was necessary to improve weapons systems, was answered by the fact that the gains likely to be made by further testing were inconsequential compared with the dangers from continued contamination of the atmosphere. The Russians' primary objection was that their security would be breached by the inspection necessary for monitoring the ban, an argument that stalled the discussions between the United States and the Soviet Union for several months. The President's address at the American University in June broke the log jam. In July, after talks in Moscow, the two nuclear powers signed a treaty agreeing not to test nuclear devices in the air, under the water, in outer space, or in any place that would permit radioactive debris to fall beyond the tester's borders. No inspection was required. (Underground tests were still legal.)

Despite some preliminary opposition in the United States, the treaty was accepted overwhelmingly by the Senate in September 1963. In short order it was signed by ninety-nine other nations, with only France and Communist China, among the major nations, failing to agree to it. Their refusal was presumably dictated by a wish to develop their own nuclear devices; in the next three years both exploded nuclear devices in the atmosphere.

Behind the drive for a test ban treaty there had been a larger objective in Kennedy's mind: limitation of the threat of nuclear war by keeping the number of nuclear powers as few as possible. In May 1963 Kennedy told one of his advisers, "If we don't get an agreement this year . . . I would think the genie is out of the bottle and we will not ever get him back in again. . . . Personally I am haunted by the feeling that by 1970, unless we are successful there may be ten nuclear powers instead of four. . . . I regard that as the greatest possible danger and hazard." Proliferation did not move as fast as Kennedy feared, for in 1974, when India exploded a nuclear device, it became the sixth member of the club. Yet the danger was real and the Johnson administration took up the cause of a nonproliferation treaty with the Russians in 1965. It was not until the Nixon administration that one was signed.

The Peace Corps. During his campaign Kennedy had promised that he would seek ways of tapping young Americans' idealism and sense of service to the world. In March 1961 he acted on his promise by issuing an executive order setting up the Peace Corps. The corps would consist mainly of American youths who would work on various projects for social and economic improvement in the under-developed countries of the world. It was clearly understood that there would be no paternalism in the operation: the Americans would live as the native popula-tion did; they would be paid very little by American standards, and what they were paid would be held for them in the United States. In September Congress approved the corps in a permanent form, appropriating $30 million for the first year. At the conclusion of that year virtually all domestic critics and the foreign countries to which the Americans had gone to work judged the scheme a success, both in promoting friendlier feelings toward the United States and in making solid contributions to the improvement of the economies of the host countries. When, during the height of the Vietnam War, American intentions abroad became suspect among many young people, interest in the Peace Corps fell off. But in the 1970s interest revived, both among Americans and in foreign countries. In 1974, for example, some 6500 young Americans worked in almost seventy coun-tries on projects ranging from teaching English to agricultural renovation.

The Alliance for Progress. America's troubles with Castro's Cuba redoubled Kennedy's resolution to grapple with the economic and political problems of Latin America. After all, the threat of Castro was not his military power, which was negligible when compared with that of the United States, but his example as head of a revolutionary state in a region in which widespread poverty, illiter-acy, and great extremes of income provided fertile soil for subversion and revolu-tion. It was well known that Castro supported Communist subversion wherever he could, if only to end his diplomatic isolation in the hemisphere. On March 13, 1961, in addressing a group of Latin American diplomats, Kennedy suggested a plan "to satisfy the basic needs of the American peoples for homes, work and land, health and schools" through massive economic assistance from the United States. The plan, which soon received the title Alliance for Progress, was intended to be a partnership between the United States and the several Latin American countries, in which the latter would undertake to help themselves through neces-sary tax and land reforms while receiving economic aid and advice from the United States. The idea struck fire among the Latin American countries and was officially supported by the Organization of American States at Punta del Este in Uruguay in August 1961. In the course of the following year the United States provided almost a billion dollars to get the program started.

But progress was slow. In 1965, for example, President Johnson recognized that the orginal span of ten years proposed for the achievement of self-sustained growth was too ambitious. He suggested that the timetable be extended to twenty years. Few of the countries, however, made much progress, if only because they would not make the serious structural renovations in land holding, taxation policies, and distribution of wealth that were necessary. Most Latin American countries remained poverty-stricken, often beset by extremely high rates of infla-tion and some of the highest rates of population growth in the world. The principal exceptions to the pattern, though not in regard to inflation, were Mexico and Brazil, both of which were clearly on the way to becoming industrialized societies. Brazil, for example, in the 1970s had one of the highest rates of economic growth in the world. Significantly, the Alliance for Progress could take little credit for this advance.

A Johnson Doctrine. Most of the threats to or denials of democracy in Latin America originated not on the left, but on the right. One of the worst was the regime of Rafael Trujillo in the Dominican Republic. After an oppressive rule of thirty years, Trujillo was assassinated in the fall of 1961. But the removal of the widely detested dictator did not bring either freedom or political stability to the Dominican Republic. Uprisings and military coups overthrew seven governments in four years. In April 1965 a military-civilian revolt attempted to restore to power a liberal nationalist, Juan Bosch, whom conservatives and the army had forcibly removed nineteen months before. Fearful that the ensuing warfare between the rebels and the conservative military regime would result in a Communist take-over supported by neighboring Cuba, President Johnson on April 28 sent 2,000 United States Marines to the capital. Ostensibly sent to protect American lives and property, the troops, as the President later admitted, were actually intended to forestall a Communist coup. The President's action was attacked vehemently in the United States and throughout Latin America as a violation of past promises against unilateral intervention in the affairs of the American states. To many observers the danger of a Communist take-over seemed remote and unsubstantiated by the evidence given by the State Department. Nevertheless, by early May there were 14,000 troops in Santo Domingo, the capital, and the number eventually reached 30,000. At the United States urging an Organization of American States peace-keeping force was created to join the United States forces in restoring order to the island nation. U.S. troops were not withdrawn until the middle of the summer as preparations were finally getting under way for free elections, and the last did not leave until the summer of 1966.

In Latin America and throughout the world the Santo Domingo affair served to counter much of the good will that the Alliance for Progress had generated in the previous four years. The occupation of the Dominican Republic was the first overt and direct military intervention by the United States in Latin America since the enunciation of the Good Neighbor policy by Franklin Roosevelt over thirty years before. Johnson's action, which he defended in two television addresses to the country, obviously stemmed from his fear of another Cuba. The presence of an established Communist state in the Western Hemisphere had been a basis for Republican criticism of the Kennedy and Johnson administrations; Johnson did not want to give his critics another stick with which to beat him. Where Communism was not involved, the President could reveal his sympathy with Latin American independence, as in his agreement in 1965 to negotiate a new treaty with Panama to recognize that country's sovereignty over the Canal Zone. It was also argued that American intervention in the Dominican Republic had not prevented the Dominican people from finally expressing their political preferences, as they did in the elections held in early 1966.

But more important than the example of Cuba in accounting for Johnson's precipitate intervention in the Dominican Republic was the fact that the United States was already engaged in a costly and expanding war in Vietnam. The

President felt he simply could not afford to allow a triumph for Communism in the Caribbean, however remote that possibility might be. The war in southeast Asia was unquestionably the most significant development in foreign affairs and the greatest threat to world peace since the Cuban missile crisis of 1962.

The Vietnam War

The Growth of a Dubious Commitment. When John F. Kennedy conferred with President Eisenhower preparatory to assuming the presidency, the general admitted that he was leaving behind an important piece of unfinished business: the Communist threat to take over Laos, a small country in Indochina. Kennedy agreed with Eisenhower that there must be no Communist take-over, and he went on television to make his determination public. The difficulty in Laos was that a weak, unstable regime favorable to the Western powers was under attack from the pro-Communist Pathet Lao, an insurgent group supplied by Communist North Vietnam and the Soviet Union. By supporting militarily the Laotian regime, Kennedy managed in 1962 to bring about negotiations that resulted in a coalition government and a temporary end to the civil war.

But Laos was only a sideshow to the main event in southeast Asia. It was Vietnam that came to dominate American foreign policy for almost a decade. No more than a small noise in the wings under Eisenhower, the war in Vietnam came into the spotlight under Kennedy. With Lyndon Johnson and Richard Nixon it filled the stage of foreign policy, directing the action and rewriting the script. Its prosecution alienated major Asian and European friends and allies, though the Philippines, South Korea, and Australia supported the American effort. Increasingly, beginning in 1965, Americans asked themselves how they had become mired in this second frustrating war in Asia that went on and on.

The American involvement in Vietnam grew out of the Asian revolution and the Cold War; what one began, the other reinforced and complicated. As we have seen already in Chapter Two, a part of the Asian revolution was the overthrow of French colonial rule in Indochina. The leader of the insurgents, Ho Chi Minh, and many of his followers were Communists, it is true, but it is equally true that the Vietminh was a genuine nationalist movement, a part of that broad movement of revolt against Europe that swept first Asia and then Africa.

But the fact that the revolt of the Vietminh was led by Communists meant that when mainland China was taken over by Communists, they provided the Vietminh not only moral and political support, but arms and secure places for training and regrouping troops as well. The French soon found that their difficulties in suppressing the Vietminh were correspondingly increased. In 1950, when the Communist North Koreans and then the Chinese Communists invaded South Korea, Vietnam definitely became a part of the Cold War in the eyes of American policymakers. As a result, the first American military advisers were dispatched to Vietnam that year to aid the French in case the Chinese should seek to expand their help to the Vietminh. As the war in Indochina continued, the United States gradually increased its help to the French on the grounds that the Indochinese revolt, which had once been seen by American officials as merely a colonial revolt, was now a part of the larger effort to expand Communist power in Asia, of which the Korean War was considered the spearhead. By the middle of 1952 the United

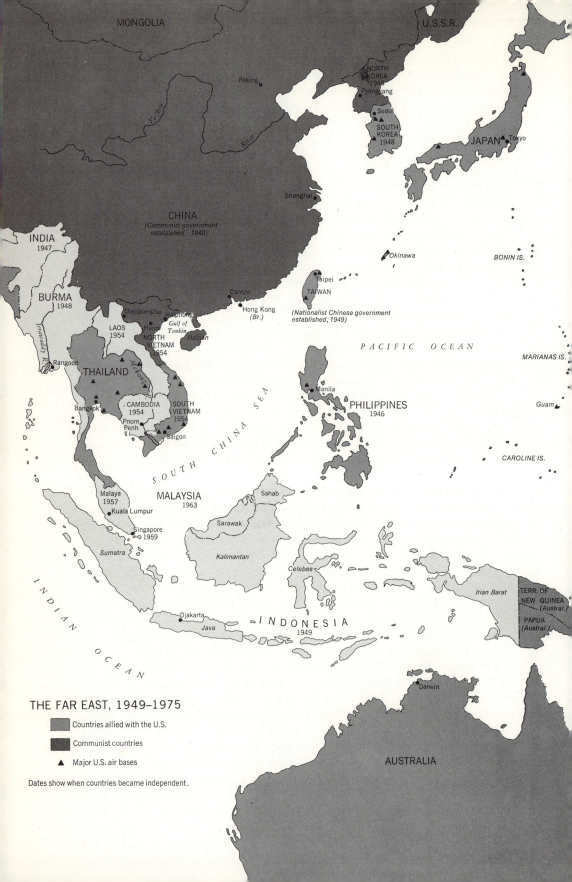

MONGOLIA

U.S.S.R.

Peking

NORTH
KOREA
1948
Pyongyang

Seoul

SOUTH
KOREA
1948

JAPAN

Tokyo

INDIA
1947

CHINA
*(Communist government
established, 1949)*

Shanghai

Okinawa

BONIN IS.

BURMA
1948

Canton

Taipei

Hong Kong
(Br.)

TAIWAN

*(Nationalist Chinese government
established, 1949)*

MARIANAS IS.

Irrawaddy R.

Dienbienphu

Haiphong

*Gulf of
Tonkin*

LAOS
1954

Hanoi

Hainan

NORTH
VIETNAM
1954

PACIFIC OCEAN

Rangoon

THAILAND

Mekong R.

Manila

PHILIPPINES
1946

Guam

Bangkok

CAMBODIA
1954

Pnom
Penh

SOUTH
VIETNAM
1954

Saigon

S O U T H   C H I N A   S E A

CAROLINE IS.

Malaya
1957

Kuala Lumpur

MALAYSIA
1963

Sahab

Singapore
1959

Sumatra

Sarawak

Kalimantan

Celebes

Irian Barat

TERR. OF
NEW GUINEA
(Austral.)

I N D I A N

O C E A N

Djakarta

Java

I N D O N E S I A
1949

PAPUA
(Austral.)

Darwin

THE FAR EAST, 1949–1975

Countries allied with the U.S.

Communist countries

▲ Major U.S. air bases

Dates show when countries became independent.

AUSTRALIA

States was paying for one fifth of the French military effort in Indochina; in 1954 the proportion was up to four fifths. President Eisenhower was so convinced of the need to resist the Vietminh, whom he considered more Communist than nationalist, that he was prepared to commit American troops to Indochina in support of the French if the French would grant unconditional independence to the Vietnamese once the war against the Communists was won. The French, however, were not yet ready to admit that colonialism was at an end.

They admitted it, however, in Vietnam at least, in 1954, after the defeat at Dienbienphu. Later that same year, at a conference in Geneva, the French agreed to withdraw from Vietnam, leaving the area divided temporarily at the seventeenth parallel, with the Vietminh troops withdrawing to the north and the French and their Vietnamese allies and several hundred thousand anti-Communist North Vietnamese collecting south of the line. Elections to determine the form of government and to unify the two parts of the country were scheduled to take place in 1956, but they were never held. Instead, with United States backing, a new republic favorable to the West was created in the South. Its president, Ngo Dinh Diem, was a strong nationalist and for a while he brought a degree of unity to the South, but at the cost of the domestic freedom of his people.

In 1960 the North Vietnamese radio announced the formation of the National Liberation Front (NLF) in the South, dedicated to overthrowing Diem's tyrannical regime. Although the NLF undoubtedly received aid from the North, until 1963 the great majority of the guerrillas fighting against Diem were from the South, and the preponderance of their arms was American equipment captured from the South Vietnamese army. The Vietcong, as the NLF was also called, won recruits to its cause by a combination of persuasion—promising and carrying out land and other reforms—and terror—killing hundreds of officials, teachers, and other representatives of the Saigon government in an effort to destroy its authority in the countryside. The Diem government, despite its nationalist assertions, had dragged its feet in carrying out promised land and other reforms; its command of the peasants' loyalty was correspondingly weak.

For a while the Kennedy administration supported Diem with arms, money, and an increasing number of so-called military advisers; nevertheless, the military situation deteriorated steadily. By 1963 the number of American military personnel in Vietnam was up to 15,500 from 2,000 at the time Kennedy came into office. In the fall of 1963 Diem himself was assassinated in a military coup and an unstable government run by the military followed while the war against the Vietcong faltered. Meanwhile, in an effort to keep the regime in the South afloat, the United States was being drawn ever more deeply into the struggle. In the fall of 1964 President Lyndon Johnson, foreseeing the need for an increased commitment of troops and needing a legal basis for further action, asked Congress for a resolution supporting his authority to "take all necessary measures" to repel any new attacks on American installations and to resist aggression. Congress responded immediately and overwhelmingly by passing the resolution, though it was not told that an expansion of the war was contemplated. It was popularly called the Tonkin Gulf resolution because the administration used an encounter between American and North Vietnamese naval vessels off the shore of North Vietnam to justify asking for the expanded authority.

The Point of No Return. In February 1965 the administration drew upon its new authority. For the first time President Johnson ordered American air forces in South Vietnam to bomb and strafe military sites and supply depots in North Vietnam—the very policy he had derided and warned against during the campaign of 1964 when his Republican opponent, Barry Goldwater, had advocated it. Actually the policy had been quite seriously considered within the administration even before the election, as the secret Pentagon Papers later revealed. The initial attacks were announced as merely retaliation against some particularly effective North Vietnamese rocket assaults on American bases, rather than as new policy—a practice of deception by the administration which would become a habit and which, when exposed later, reduced its credibility with the public. At the same time that he announced the air strikes, the President ordered a stepping up of American ground troops in Vietnam. Throughout the remainder of the year American troop levels rose dramatically, reaching 150,000 by the end of the year.

Vietnam was the longest and one of the bloodiest wars in American history. Here a paratrooper guides a medical helicopter into a clearing to pick up casualties. *Photo: Wide World*

Before the implementation of the buildup Johnson called upon the North Vietnamese to negotiate, offering as a carrot the promise of the investment of a billion dollars of American aid in the development of the Mekong valley, which ran the length of the peninsula of southeast Asia. In emulation of George Marshall's famous Harvard address of 1947, Johnson included North Vietnam in the offer of aid if negotiations could begin. But the North would not respond to the bait, countering simply with its own requirements for peace. Within the administration some advisers, like Undersecretary of State George Ball, suggested that the U.S. "cut its losses" and withdraw. But the die had been cast; the United States under President Lyndon Johnson had committed itself to the defeat of the North regardless of the cost.

The next three years saw many public efforts by the President to bring the Vietnamese to the conference table. Sometimes it involved expanding the bombing of the North, sometimes it took the form of stopping or restricting the bombing for a while, but all of the time it meant expanding the American involvement. By the beginning of 1968 over half a million American troops were in Vietnam, not to mention the airmen on Guam who flew and serviced the giant B-52s that since April 1966 had regularly bombed the Vietcong hideouts in the South, or the large number of Navy men who patrolled the waters along the coast. The history of the Cold War may account for the American involvement in Vietnam, but it cannot account for the heavy commitment of men, money, and prestige. An explanation of that involves the personality of Lyndon Johnson.

The Tragedy of Lyndon Johnson. Johnson's commitment of the United States to the most traumatic and detested war of its history was tied up with his enormous ambitions as President, his powerful wish to leave the mark of unrelieved success upon his presidency. As President he saw himself carrying on, as he said, the policies of two previous administrations in southeast Asia. But the fact was that Johnson was never happy dealing with foreign policy. As a senator he had had little to do with such matters; his habit was simply to support the President, whether a Republican, as with Eisenhower, or a Democrat, as with Franklin Roosevelt, Truman, and Kennedy. As his wife, Lady Bird, put it in 1965, "I just hope that foreign problems do not keep mounting; they do not represent Lyndon's kind of presidency."

Relying upon many of the same advisers as Kennedy, Johnson pushed the same policy, only he pushed it harder, for that was the way he operated in domestic politics. Moreover, he was a strong nationalist, without much subtlety in his thinking about relations between nations. Like most Americans, including his opponent in 1964, Johnson defined a war as something that resulted in victory or defeat; he was not, as he said again and again, going to be the first American President to lose a war. Thus when his military and diplomatic advisers, themselves committed to forcing the North Vietnamese to stop fighting in the South, urged yet another fresh commitment of troops, Johnson might hesitate, as the Pentagon Papers made clear that he did, but in the end he gave in, hoping each time that this would be the final commitment that would bring the North Vietnamese to their knees. Instead, the continuation of the war, rather than defeating North Vietnam, destroyed him.

The war did more than remove a President from politics; it also corrupted the processes of government along the way. The most striking example was the

Tonkin Gulf resolution that Johnson asked Congress to pass in early August 1964, when American destroyers were allegedly attacked by North Vietnamese torpedo boats. Subsequently it was revealed that the American naval units were actually attacking North Vietnamese territory and thus could rightly have expected reprisals. But in order to gain blanket congressional support for the war, the administration concealed that fact. Indeed, as later revelations would make clear, neither Congress nor the public was honestly informed about the war though both were expected to support it with blood and money. Inside the administration in 1965 and 1966 the war was seen as unwinnable. (The Pentagon Papers quoted Johnson as telling his wife in 1965, "I can't get out. I can't finish it with what I have got. So what the hell can I do?") But the public face was always one of optimism, and the public result was increased military and financial involvement.

The tendency of the administration to dissimulate and lie about the nature of the war and its prospects only strengthened as the war became increasingly unpopular. Mass demonstrations against the war began as early as the fall of 1965, as large numbers of drafted troops were being sent to Vietnam. The center of the demonstrations were often college and university campuses, where, in "teach-ins," students and professors debated the merits of the American involvement. One of the ugliest demonstrations occurred in the fall of 1967 when some 35,000 persons marched on the Pentagon outside of Washington, clashing with the police and the Army. Almost 650 persons were arrested, but the President the next week announced his continued resolve to stay in Vietnam as long as necessary to defeat the Vietcong.

Some of the opposition to the war stemmed from radical and Communist support for the rebels, but the vast majority of the demonstrators were people unconvinced that the nation should be heavily involved in a war in southeast Asia. Many were simply appalled at the destruction which the war entailed and which could be seen on television each night. Some simply disliked the prospect of being drafted for war. A few thought the war was worse than death; several young people, in emulation of Buddhists in South Vietnam earlier, set themselves on fire to demonstrate their hostility toward the war. Even those who had no sympathy with the rebels or the North Vietnamese could find reason for opposing the administration on the war. They thought the administration was not pushing the war hard enough; they called for attacks on targets throughout North Vietnam, perhaps even a land invasion, contending that, contrary to administration fears, no wider war would result. In short, the war deeply divided the country.

Yet the more the domestic resistance to or dissatisfaction with the war mounted, the more determined the President became that he would not be deflected from his goal of victory over the North Vietnamese and the Vietcong. Privately and publicly he denounced what he called the "nervous Nellies" and sometimes he came close to considering opponents of the war as traitors. Ironically, he could not see that his own determined resistance to domestic opposition was no different in kind from the North Vietnamese refusal to surrender in the face of his bombers.

Johnson could no more control the domestic opposition to the war than he could bomb the North Vietnamese to the peace table. Throughout the remainder of his term in office he suffered a humiliation that no other President since Lincoln

Young antiwar protestors confront military police outside the Pentagon in October 1967. Mounting opposition to the Vietnam War was one factor in President Johnson's decision not to seek reelection. *Photo: Bernie Boston—Washington Evening Star*

had been put through: he was unable to travel where he wanted to and to speak to his countrymen. Demonstrators, usually young people, appeared to shout him down or otherwise silence him when he appeared in public. By 1967–1968 he could visit no public place outside military bases with impunity. As an adviser to President Nixon wrote privately in 1969, Johnson "was the first American president to be toppled by a mob." In 1968, he wrote, Johnson even had to slip "into the back door of St. Patrick's Cathedral like a medieval felon seeking sanctuary" when attending Cardinal Spellman's funeral.

The most telling manifestation of popular opposition to Johnson came in November 1967 when Eugene McCarthy, a liberal Democratic senator from Minnesota, announced that he would run in the upcoming primaries against the President to provide an alternative on the question of the war. Despite the opposition to the war, no one in either party thought McCarthy could be a serious threat to Johnson, who had been elected by an overwhelming majority and who was the indisputable commander of the party machinery.

On January 29, 1968, at the beginning of Tet, the Vietnamese lunar New Year, the Vietcong and the North Vietnamese launched a major offensive against thirty provincial capitals held by the South Vietnamese forces. The force of the attack took the Americans and Vietnamese allies by surprise. At one point fighting was going on within the American embassy in Saigon itself. Although a severely shaken administration bravely announced the Tet offensive a complete failure, few believed it.

As it turned out, the offensive proved to be the end of the line for Lyndon Johnson. He turned down a request for additional troops, though once again he had been assured they would bring the victory for which he had waited so long. Then, in March, Senator McCarthy received almost as many votes in the New Hampshire Democratic primary as the President himself. To the months of harrassment and perhaps even danger to his life, the election added a new measure of popular repudiation of his policies in Vietnam and, ultimately, of him. He could now either abandon war—a course he had publicly and privately refused to adopt—or abandon the presidency. In a surprise television announcement at the end of March, Johnson irrevocably removed himself from consideration for renomination, announcing at the same time a partial cessation of the bombing of North Vietnam. Although the war had already killed hundreds of thousands of Vietnamese and thousands of Americans, the political career of Lyndon Johnson was its most spectacular casualty. The question of Vietnam would be left for still another President to wrestle with, just as Johnson had inherited it from his predecessor. And even then the war in southeast Asia that had been entered into so confidently would require yet another four years before it could be removed from the center of American and world politics.

SUGGESTED READING

The history of the Johnson administration has barely begun to be studied by scholars. The story of Johnson as Vice-President is told sympathetically by a journalist in Leonard Baker, *The Johnson Eclipse* (1966). Another journalistic study of Johnson's career, William S. White, *The Professional: Lyndon B. Johnson* (1964) is by a personal friend, and is extremely laudatory. More critical and yet understanding is Rowland Evans and Robert D. Novak, *Lyndon B. Johnson: The Exercise of Power* (1966). Eric F. Goldman, *The Tragedy of Lyndon Johnson* * (1969), though by a professional historian, does not purport to be a scholarly study; it relates, revealingly, the author's experiences in the Johnson White House. George E. Reedy, *The Twilight of the Presidency* (1970), though by Johnson's press secretary, is highly critical. The delineation of the expansion of presidential power that Johnson did so much to augment is put into some historical, if partisan, perspective in Arthur M. Schlesinger, Jr., *The Imperial Presidency* (1973). The election of 1964 is reported in loving detail and analyzed in Theodore H. White, *The Making of the President, 1964* * (1965). The ideas of the losing candidate in that election can be examined in Barry M. Goldwater, *The Conscience of a Conservative* * (1960).

The literature on the Negro revolution after the 1950s is enormous. The best general study is Benjamin Muse, *The American Negro Revolution: From Nonviolence to Black Power, 1963–1967* * (1968). David L. Lewis, *King: A Critical Biography* * (1970) is undoubtedly the best study of Martin Luther King, Jr., and his ideas. Robert E. Conot, *Rivers of Blood, Years of Darkness* * (1967) is an exciting narrative of the Watts riot of 1966. A scholarly analysis of the riots of the 1960s is Robert Fogelson, *Violence as Protest* * (1971). An effort to re-create an aspect of life in the black ghetto is Elliott Liebow, *Tally's Corner: A Study of Negro Streetcorner Men* * (1967). A critical introduction to black separatism is Theodore Draper, *The Rediscovery of Black Nationalism* * (1970). Stokely Carmichael and Charles V. Hamilton, *Black Power* * (1970) is by advocates. Harold Cruse, *The Crisis of the Black Intellectual* * (1967) is an important study of black self-conscious-

---

* Available in a paperback edition.

ness as well as an example of how one black intellectual reacted to the 1960s. An insight into ghetto life as well as an understanding of Malcolm X is provided in Malcolm X and Alex Haley, *Autobiography of Malcolm X* * (1965). A good study of Malcolm's thought as well as his shift in ideas after his break with the Muslims in 1964 can be found in Archie Epps, ed., *The Speeches of Malcolm X at Harvard* * (1968). Eldridge Cleaver, *Soul on Ice* * (1968) is a classic of the Negro revolution of the 1960s.

The foreign policies of the Kennedy administration can be studied in some of the literature already mentioned at the end of Chapter Three, but that must be supplemented by Roger Hilsman, *To Move a Nation,* written by a foreign policy official in the Kennedy administration. The very dramatic and awesome confrontation with the Soviet Union over Cuba has naturally evoked a good deal of writing. Elie Abel, *Missile Crisis* * (1966) is reliable as far as it goes and is by a knowing newsman. The best scholarly work is Graham T. Allison, *Essence of Decision* * (1971). The diversity of views on the confrontation can be readily examined in Robert A. Divine, ed., *The Cuban Missile Crisis* * (1971). Kennedy's handling of this and other foreign policy matters has come in for increasing criticism over the years. Two such critical books, though of a popular nature, are Louise Fitz-Simons, *The Kennedy Doctrine* (1972) and Richard J. Walton, *Cold War and Counter Revolution: The Foreign Policy of John F. Kennedy* (1972). An expert on Communism has realistically dissected the Cuban revolution in two books, Theodore Draper, *Castro's Revolution: Myths and Realities* * (1962) and *Castroism: Theory and Practice* * (1965).

No aspect of recent foreign policy has produced more books than the Vietnam War. A balanced discussion of the background of the war can be found in Bernard Fall, *The Two Vietnams: A Political and Military Analysis* (rev. ed., 1965). Ellen Hammer, *Vietnam Yesterday and Today* * (1966) is by a historian of southeast Asia. The best introduction to the American involvement is G. M. Kahin and John Lewis, *The United States in Vietnam* * (1967). John T. McAlister, Jr., *Viet Nam: The Origins of Revolution* (1969) is scholarly and historical. A book that succeeds in putting the war into the context of Vietnam is Frances Fitzgerald, *Fire in the Lake* (1972). Townsend Hoopes, *The Limits of Intervention* (1969) is an insider's report on his disillusionment with Johnson in Vietnam. David Halberstam, *The Best and the Brightest* (1972) is a biting and fascinating account, by a knowing journalist, of how American leaders got mired in Vietnam. The administration's secret history of the Vietnam involvement is available in one-volume and four-volume paperbacks: *The Pentagon Papers* * (1971), which painfully reveal the deceptions of the administration. Something of the domestic impact of Vietnam can be learned from Norman Mailer, *Armies of the Night* * (1968), a novelist-participant's account of the great confrontation between dissidents and the Army in front of the Pentagon in 1967, and from I. F. Stone, *In a Time of Torment* (1967), the articles of a liberal journalist. W. W. Rostow, *The Diffusion of Power* (1972) is a defense of U.S. foreign policy from 1957 to 1972, by a former foreign policy adviser to Johnson, in which almost no concession to critics is made.

Even before the American involvement in Vietnam ended, prominent political figures as well as scholars and radicals were denouncing American overextension around the world. J. William Fulbright, *The Arrogance of Power* * (1967) and Eugene McCarthy, *The Limits of Power* * (1967) are books by liberal Democratic senators voicing that concern. Two historical studies of the problems of economic development are Robert Heilbroner, *The Great Ascent* * (1963), a short introduction to the subject emphasizing the difficulties, and Cyril E. Black, *The Dynamics of Modernization* * (1966), delineating the different routes toward development in the last two centuries.

CHAPTER FIVE

THE RETREAT
FROM ACTIVISM

*J*OHNSON'S WITHDRAWAL was only the first and the least severe of the blows under which the nation staggered in the spring of 1968. On April 4 Martin Luther King, Jr., the civil rights leader and Nobel Peace Prize winner, was assassinated on a motel balcony in Memphis, Tennessee. As we have seen already, his death set off violence in a hundred cities across the nation. The third shock of that spring came in connection with the Democratic campaign for the presidency.

The Campaign of 1968

The real contest for the Democratic nomination started even before Johnson withdrew from the race. It began on March 15, three days after Eugene McCarthy's large vote in the New Hampshire primary humiliated the President, for on that day Senator Robert Kennedy, a brother of the late President, announced his candidacy for the Democratic nomination. Once Johnson was out of the race the battle was between Kennedy and McCarthy, both liberal, both opposed to the Vietnam War, and both Roman Catholic. But whereas Kennedy was an activist like his brother, though less humorous and more mystical, McCarthy was scholarly, dry-witted, worldly, and a poet. Rarely did he permit himself to be enthusiastic about anything. Moreover, he was not at all sure he really wanted the nomination, though he did want to offer a choice to Democrats and Americans on the conduct of the war. He did not conceal his resentment of Kennedy's late arrival in the antiwar camp once the political power of the antiwar sentiment had been established by his own victory in New Hampshire. Both Kennedy and McCarthy ran in several state primaries, but it was not until Kennedy's victory in the California primary on June 4 that it became obvious McCarthy was falling behind. On the evening of his triumph, as Kennedy was walking away from a victory speech to his supporters in Los Angeles, he was shot by a fanatical anti-Zionist. He died the next morning.

Robert Kennedy had attracted around him a more intensely loyal and emotional following than even his brother had. Young people, Chicanos, Indians, blacks, as well as antiwar people, flocked to his cause. To many more Americans he represented the continuation of John F. Kennedy's dedication to social reform and to concern for the disadvantaged. The deaths of Kennedy and King in the same spring shriveled hope in many American breasts.

The Conventions. Despite the assassinations and the despair that followed in their wake, politics ground on. The Republican convention met first because the Democrats, expecting Johnson to be their candidate, had scheduled their convention for the very end of August. The favored Republican candidate was Richard M. Nixon, despite his defeat in 1960 and a subsequent defeat in 1962 when he ran for the governorship of California. Since those setbacks he had worked hard to gain support in the party and to keep in the public eye through trips abroad to meet world leaders. Two liberal Republicans who were once considered likely candidates for the nomination dropped out of the running before the convention opened, and a more conservative contender, California's Governor Ronald Reagan, entered the contest too late to make a strong stand. As a result, Nixon was nominated on the first ballot. It was a measure of his command of the party's center that he accepted the convention's nomination surrounded by his defeated

President and Mrs. Nixon at the Forbidden City in Peking, China. *Photo: UPI* opponents. Goldwater could not have done that in 1964. For his Vice-Presidential candidate Nixon chose a virtual unknown, Spiro T. Agnew, the first-term governor of Maryland. Agnew was a newcomer to politics, having risen from a county official to governor in one leap. Once a partisan of Rockefeller, Agnew was thought to be a little more liberal than Nixon. In office, however, he showed himself to be even less liberal and more doctrinaire.

After the death of Robert Kennedy there was no serious doubt that Vice-President Hubert Humphrey would be nominated by the Democratic convention in Chicago that August. But the convention did not proceed as smoothly as had been expected, reflecting instead the distressed mood of a country tormented by assassinations and a long war. Reformers within the party, for example, insisted on democratizing the process for selecting delegates. Early in the convention they succeeded in having a committee appointed, headed by Senator George McGovern of South Dakota, to draw up rules for the 1972 convention to insure the adequate representation of women, young people, and ethnic minorities, all of whom had been underrepresented in past conventions. These rules, when applied in 1972, were to have a devastating effect upon the party, but in 1968 they merely portended the more significant fight that erupted over the party's stand on the war, especially over whether to stop the bombing of North Vietnam.

While the convention bitterly debated the issue, in Grant Park some 10,000 demonstrators, many of whom were college students, chanted their demand for an end to the bombing. The police who were guarding the convention hotels across the street from the park were veterans of previous clashes with some of the demonstrators. Without warning the police charged. The sight of police beating unarmed and frequently bleeding demonstrators was instantly transmitted by TV cameras to a shocked convention and nation. A national commission investigating the encounter later described it as a "police riot." Tear gas not only hung over the park, but seeped into the Hilton Hotel across the street, where candidates Humphrey and McCarthy were headquartered. At the convention itself, some six miles away, the news of the riot led to bitter charges and counter-charges by delegates.

In the end Humphrey was nominated, with Senator Edward Muskie of Maine as his running mate. The platform offered no significant alternative to the Johnson policy on the war, and Humphrey himself was, of course, a member of the administration. Thus the Democrats provided no rallying point for those who opposed the war and neither did the more conservative Republican party, in whose ranks were relatively few opponents of the bombing of North Vietnam, much less of the war itself.

The campaign was complicated by the candidacy of George C. Wallace of Alabama, who ran on the American Independent party ticket. A folksy speaker, not yet fifty years old, Wallace had first come to national prominence in 1962 when he promised to stop desegregation in Alabama, even if he had to "stand in the schoolhouse door." He did stand in the door when federal authorities came to Alabama to back up federal court orders, but he soon stepped aside when pressed. In 1964 he ran in several presidential primaries and received as much as 40 per cent of the vote in northern states, suggesting that his resistance to desegregation of schools did not go unappreciated in the North. His own third party in 1968 had no chance of winning, of course, but it was a serious threat to Humphrey in the traditionally Democratic South, and the enthusiasm Wallace stirred in some northern states suggested that he might draw away from Humphrey many of the normally Democratic blue-collar voters. Indeed, some observers thought he would cut into the electoral votes of both parties sufficiently to deny a clear majority to any candidate and throw the choice of President into the House of Representatives.

The Republican Comeback. The campaign revolved around the war in southeast Asia and the social problems at home. Nixon stressed the alarming increase in violence in the cities, especially the summer riots of the previous four years, and the rise in street crime. He attributed these evils to the leniency of the Democratic administrations toward demonstrators and rioters and to the permissive attitude of the Supreme Court toward criminals. Among other things Nixon promised to fill vacancies on the court, if elected, with judges who were "strict constructionists," as he phrased it, and who were prepared to strengthen the hand of "the peace forces as against the criminal forces." Playing upon the widespread public fear of crime in the cities, he promised to end the permissiveness that he insisted lay at the root of lawlessness. Although he had long supported the aims of the war against Communism in southeast Asia, Nixon promised to bring the conflict in Vietnam to an honorable close, though he declined to say how. In the television appearances on which he heavily relied, in contrast to his whirlwind and physically exhausting personal campaign in 1960, he shunned the issue of integration, which had become increasingly unpopular among whites, particularly those living in northern suburbs. "Our schools," he said early in the campaign, "are for education, not integration." He concentrated instead upon the issue of "law and order," about which there could be little controversy. Generally Nixon portrayed himself as a leader dedicated to bringing the people together again after the divisions of the 1960s.

After the disastrous beginning in Chicago, Humphrey's campaign was slow in getting started and disorganized as well. From the beginning the public opinion polls showed him behind Nixon, and campaign contributions came in slowly. When Humphrey tried to talk about the possible return of some American troops, he was undercut by administration denials that such a move was likely. Edmund Muskie, however, proved to be a godsend to the campaign, for he could talk convincingly with students and other opponents of the war. Then President Johnson came forth with a firm endorsement of the candidates and Texas seemed to be swinging into line. (Texas would be the only southern state Humphrey carried.) Organized labor mounted a major campaign on Humphrey's behalf, an effort that wooed a good number of blue-collar workers back from Wallace, who had begun the campaign only 10 percentage points behind Humphrey in the polls. Finally, in a speech at Salt Lake City in late September, when he was still well behind Nixon, Humphrey cut himself free from Johnson's policies by pledging to stop the bombing of North Vietnam if elected. During October Humphrey gained on Nixon noticeably; blue-collar workers who deserted Wallace went not to Nixon but to Humphrey. Meanwhile behind-the-scenes discussions between the U.S. and the Vietnamese suggested that Johnson might stop the bombing himself, for the President was now working hard for Humphrey. The final word of a halt to the bombing and the setting up of a conference in Paris did not come until October 31—only three days before the election. The opinion polls predicted

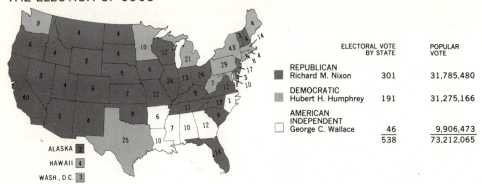

	ELECTORAL VOTE BY STATE	POPULAR VOTE
REPUBLICAN Richard M. Nixon	301	31,785,480
DEMOCRATIC Hubert H. Humphrey	191	31,275,166
AMERICAN INDEPENDENT George C. Wallace	46	9,906,473
	538	73,212,065

ALASKA 3
HAWAII 4
WASH., D.C. 3

a close race, suggesting to some that Humphrey was rapidly overtaking Nixon in the last days. But there were not enough days left.

Although Nixon won by only half a million votes out of 73 million cast, he carried thirty-two states to Humphrey's fourteen. The only southern state Humphrey carried was Texas; Wallace won five, Nixon seven. But outside the South the old Democratic coalition held: Catholics, Jews, blacks, the young, union members, and people with grade-school educations lined up as usual behind the Democratic candidate. But if Nixon and Wallace voters were combined, some commentators noted, they seemed to constitute a new conservative coalition, one that marked an end to the liberalism that had dominated American politics for almost thirty years. A team of English reporters spelled out the elements of the coalition: "Nixon owes his election to the votes of the middle-class, old stock, Protestants of the West, the Middle West, and the Southern Border, and in general to the business class, and its allies. He won those votes because he bade for them. And he is more exclusively the choice of those classes than any President since Herbert Hoover."

Disengagement and Détente

A Man of Images. In several ways Richard Milhous Nixon was the quintessential public man of the postwar years. Born in 1913 in a small town outside Los Angeles, of lower-middle-class Quaker parents, Nixon graduated from Whittier College and then Duke Law School, where he distinguished himself by his hard work. After service in the Navy, he began his political career in 1946 in southern California as a vigorous anti-Communist. California was then not only a center of anxiety about domestic Communism, but also the state in which the new aerospace and petrochemical industries of the postwar era flourished, providing the wealth for the sprawling suburbs and new materialistic life-styles of an increasingly affluent America. Nixon's greatest appeal as a politician was always to those who feared they might lose or have to share their new material gains. Rarely did he set higher aspirations for Americans, but he often provided them with reasons for self-satisfaction.

No previous statesman, with the possible exceptions of Henry Clay and William Jennings Bryan, was at the center of public life for as long as Richard

Nixon. His career in national politics spanned almost thirty years, beginning with his entrance into the House of Representatives in 1947. He became nationally known through his central role in the exposure of Alger Hiss. Thereafter he moved swiftly onto the anti-Communist track, winning election to the Senate in 1950 by falsely portraying his opponent, liberal Democrat Helen Gahagan Douglas, as a supporter of Communist causes. As Eisenhower's Vice-President during the 1950s Nixon stood close to the moderates of the Republican party, but he was careful not to rupture his ties with the right wing, as his strong support of Goldwater in 1964 demonstrated. His own election to the presidency in 1968, after the defeat in 1960, must have been particularly welcome since it confirmed his conviction that hard work and determination paid off.

Although Nixon's entire adult life had been spent in politics, in personality he exhibited few of the attributes usually associated with successful politicians. One English observer referred to his "ineradicable charmlessness"; almost everyone acknowledged his wooden speaking gestures and undistinguished voice. Unlike John F. Kennedy or Lyndon Johnson, who loved to "press the flesh" on the hustings, Nixon did not enjoy physical contact with people. Rather, as his close associate Henry Kissinger said, "the essence of this man is loneliness." To his intimate friends and family Nixon was humorous, even witty, but most Americans knew him best as overly serious, often sentimental, and embarrassingly self-righteous. While millions undoubtedly admired him, few apparently loved him.

His rigid personality did not help with the press. Nixon's almost lifelong battle with the media was more painful even than Johnson's conflicts during the Vietnam War. A man who believed a proper image to be more important than substance, Nixon found the press and television essential to his political life. But that emphasis upon image caused him to try to manipulate or control those he could not win by persuasion. In one sense, it was his emphasis upon images that was his undoing, for his presidency ended when the difference between his carefully cultivated image and the real Nixon became public knowledge.

Winding Down the War. During the campaign Nixon had refused to divulge the details of his plan to end the war so he could "keep his options open," as he liked to say, and keep the enemy off balance. His critics contended that in fact he had no plan. But Johnson's political destruction, the mood of the country, and the interminable war itself made clear that Nixon had to extricate the United States from Vietnam. Withdrawal became a part of a larger policy of giving a new "low profile" to America in the world. At Guam in November 1969, in a statement that came to be known as the "Nixon Doctrine," the new President said that in the future the obligations of the United States in defending its allies in Asia would be carefully defined, rather than unlimited; Asians would be expected to assume a larger share of their own defense.

The previous spring he had announced that he would withdraw 25,000 troops from Vietnam over the next ninety days. Thus began the policy of gradual withdrawal that was to continue for four years before final disengagement was achieved. Critics contended that the process was deliberately slow in order to perpetuate the administration and its party in power through the next presidential election. The administration argued, on the other hand, that the withdrawal was paced by the need to protect American troops still exposed to attack and to make sure that the removal of United States troops would not leave the South Vietnamese ready victims to renewed military assaults from the Vietcong and North Vietnamese. Billions of dollars in equipment and training were expended in the South to build up the army there so it could defend the country once the American forces were finally gone. This policy Nixon called Vietnamization.

The President was willing to take great risks to insure that the regime in the South would not collapse after the completion of the American withdrawal. In the spring of 1970 he ordered American forces to support a South Vietnamese invasion of neighboring Cambodia (and eventually of Laos, too) in an effort to destroy enemy supplies and disrupt the buildup of enemy troops. Cambodia had long been used as a sanctuary by North Vietnamese troops and the Vietcong, since it was too weak to counter effectively violations of its neutral territory. The immediate effect of the invasion was to widen the war and to overthrow the government of Cambodia's Prince Sihanouk, who had long been critical of the American presence in Vietnam.

To many Americans the Cambodian invasion came as an even greater shock than the assassinations of two years before, for most had believed the war was being ended. The same week in which the President announced his act of brinkmanship in foreign policy, four white students were killed by jittery national guardsmen during an antiwar demonstration at Kent State University in Ohio and two black students were killed by police at Jackson State College in Mississippi during another demonstration. The shootings were widely recognized as indicative of the deep divisions and even hatred that the war had spawned among Americans. Subsequent investigations of the Kent State killings revealed that the soldiers had been only too willing to use bullets against students protesting the war. The popular reaction was measured by a veritable explosion of strikes by angry students at almost 300 colleges and universities. Delegations of teachers and students descended on Washington to plead with the President to change his policy in Vietnam, but he only reiterated his original promise to withdraw American troops from Cambodia within a matter of weeks. The American troops were indeed withdrawn on schedule, but both Cambodia and Laos continued to be devastated by war. There was little evidence that the expansion of the fighting and bombing had brought the end of the war any closer or hastened the withdrawal of American troops from Indochina. But there could be no doubt that it had increased sharply the number of refugees throughout Indochina and widened the destruction in the already war-wracked society.

As the gradual removal of American ground troops from Vietnam continued, the administration proceeded with the negotiations in Paris that President Johnson had agreed to in the fall of 1968. For some time neither side would accept the other's proposals. Then in the early spring of 1972, North Vietnamese troops launched a powerful assault across the demilitarized zone in the north and the Cambodian border in the west. For a while it looked as if a repetition of the devastating Tet offensive of 1968, which had toppled Johnson, was in the making. "An American defeat in Vietnam would encourage . . . aggression all over the world," President Nixon contended as he announced a further widening of the war. To support the reeling South Vietnamese troops, he ordered stepped-up bombing raids against North Vietnam, including the capital, Hanoi, and the major port, Haiphong, neither of which had been bombed since 1968, and the rail lines from China. He also directed the Navy to mine Haiphong harbor. His intention was to cut off the military supplies from the Soviet Union and China that made such offensives possible. Although Russian ships were in Haiphong harbor and Chinese workers and soldiers may have been deployed along the rail lines, neither China nor Russia took any action; they confined their responses to denunciations of American "aggression." The renewed pressure upon the North was possible because Nixon had worked out new relationships with China and Russia the year before (see pp. 146–48). And in the absence of any reversal of the troop withdrawal program, both Communist countries apparently were convinced that Nixon did intend to end the American involvement in Vietnam, even if at his own slow pace.

But an end to the fighting was agonizingly slow, consuming all of 1972. Henry Kissinger, a former Harvard University professor of political science and now the President's foreign affairs adviser and indefatigable traveling diplomat, carried on secret negotiations in Paris and Saigon. Several times in the summer and fall, as the election neared, Kissinger announced the closeness of a cease-fire, only to have some kind of hitch prevent it. Meanwhile the military forces of the United States in Vietnam had dwindled to fewer than 75,000 troops. American airpower, however, was not reduced. During Nixon's four years of winding down the war more bombs were dropped on Indochina than during all of Johnson's years. Although President Nixon undoubtedly wanted to announce a cease-fire agreement before the election, he was not able to do so. Indeed, during November and December negotiations almost broke down entirely; Kissinger charged Hanoi with procrastinating while its army moved equipment and supplies into the South in anticipation of a cease-fire agreement. In the week before Christmas the President ordered renewed bombing attacks on Hanoi and Haiphong. After twelve days of heavy bombing by B-52 planes, the bombing north of the twentieth parallel was halted. Later Nixon asserted that his decision to bomb at such a rate had led directly to the cease-fire agreement which was announced finally in January 1973.

The Cost of the War. Fought in a part of the world remote from American shores, the war in Vietnam was the longest in American history. Not even the War for American Independence had lasted so long. Measured by American lives lost, it ranked as the third most costly, though the medical services were the most proficient and advanced of any war's and the enemy was without airpower. The pounding that American explosives gave to the enemy was almost beyond comparison. Between February 1965 and August 1972 the United States dropped three and one half times as many bombs and shells on Vietnam as all the allies dropped on Germany and Japan during the Second World War. The price of this punishment was the disruption of the lives of the people of Vietnam, North and South, but especially in the South, where all the ground fighting took place. Although it will never be known precisely how many people were forced to flee this punishment, estimates of some 10 million refugees in South Vietnam, Cambodia, and Laos are probably not far wrong. And those figures do not include the hundreds of thousands who had to flee the aerial bombings in North Vietnam. Civilian deaths reached almost half a million in the South, with another million wounded. Official figures for the dead among the South Vietnamese military were 185,000.

Even these astronomical figures cannot reveal the social and psychological destruction wrought by the war upon the society of Vietnam. Large stretches of the countryside were denuded of vegetation or bombed into a maze of holes and ruts; whole villages were reduced to ruins, some completely obliterated by bombs and fire. Saigon itself swelled with refugee shacks and hovels while new buildings rose upon the wealth gained from the profits of war and the American presence. The comparative wealth of American soldiers and bureaucrats enriched even as it corrupted the Vietnamese peasants, tradesmen, and young women with whom they came in contact. Inflation soared, destroying many while making others rich, and tearing irreparably the old fabric of Vietnamese society. In return for the great cost, was anything of importance gained? Only time would tell, for two years after the American withdrawal of troops Vietnamese were still dying in war. The regime in the South for which so much had been spent still survived, but it was neither a democratic government nor a particularly successful one. The possibility that it would fall to the North remained.

The war had its impact on Americans in Vietnam, too. American soldiers were sometimes driven to excesses that disgraced their uniforms. The most sensational example of the corruption the war could work became known just as the fighting was slowing down. It was the massacre, in March 1968, of over a hundred defenseless Vietnamese at the village of My Lai by a patrol of American soldiers under the command of Lieutenant William Calley. The atrocity was hushed up for over a year by an Army command innured to such barbarities, but its revelation in November 1969 brought out once again how deeply the war divided Americans. Some defended the action as inevitable and understandable in a guerrilla war, while others denounced it as the natural consequence of a society's being too long involved in a war without point.

Diplomatic Breakthroughs. One reason President Nixon was able to put pressure upon the North Vietnamese in 1972 without undue fear of Chinese or Russian reprisals—a fear the Johnson administration was never free of—was that in the previous year he had moved to a new level of diplomacy with both Communist China and Communist Russia. The opening to China came first. In the summer of 1971 the President announced that he had accepted an invitation to visit the People's Republic of China—the result of secret negotiations between Chinese officials and Henry Kissinger. The President visited China in February 1972.

The implications of the presidential trip were far-reaching. At the very least the visit marked the end of twenty years of hostility between the United States and China, a period that had included armed conflict between the two countries. At most it marked a turning point in the constellation of forces in world politics. China was now joining the comity of nations, evidently willing to bear responsibilities toward maintaining an orderly world of diplomatic intercourse. Now that the United States had withdrawn its objection to the seating of the People's Republic in the United Nations in place of Chiang Kai-shek's government, the Communist Chinese took a more restrained attitude toward Taiwan. China still claimed Taiwan, occupied by Chiang, as an integral part of its territory, but it ceased pressing the issue.

One of the less desirable aspects of Nixon's breakthrough on China was that it was undertaken without consulting the Japanese, though they were vitally interested in any new relationship with China. Only a year before, the Japanese had loyally followed the American lead in opposing the seating of Communist China in the United Nations. After the Nixon visit to China Japanese foreign policy began to place less dependence on and less faith in American reliability in the future. In 1972 Japan, China's old enemy, opened commercial and diplomatic negotiations which culminated in Japanese recognition of the People's Republic as the sole sovereignty in China and Taiwan and in the resumption of diplomatic relations. In October of the same year a new trade agreement was signed between the two countries.

Nixon's visit and its aftermath did not make China and the United States allies, of course, nor did diplomatic recognition immediately follow, for there was still the delicate question of breaking off the long-time association with Chiang Kai-shek's regime on Taiwan. After the visit, the United States pledged to maintain its treaty commitment to Taiwan. The new diplomacy with China was followed within two months by Nixon's visit to Moscow for talks aimed at easing tensions between the two countries and arriving at some agreement on the mutual reduction of nuclear arms. During the remainder of his first term Nixon also visited Communist Yugoslavia, Romania, and Poland, adding impressively to his cherished collection of "firsts" for American Presidents and demonstrating the lessening of hostility between capitalist West and Communist East. Even in the midst of the Watergate revelations in the fall of 1973, the London *Times* editorialized that "on the record to date, Mr. Nixon's Administration's achievements in the field of foreign affairs are the greatest since those of President Truman and General Marshall."

Behind this dramatic about-face by the veteran anti-Communist Richard Nixon and the leaders of the two largest Communist states lay the growing hostility between the Russians and the Chinese. Ever since 1960, at least, the two giants of Communism had been growing apart, partly for ideological reasons peculiar to Communist doctrine, but principally because of competing nationalisms. By the early 1970s the hostility between them had resulted in the massing of troops along both sides of their common 4000-mile border. Occasionally the world heard of actual armed clashes between them along the Ussuri river in eastern Siberia, and Western visitors to China reported that the Chinese genuinely feared a Russian invasion. As the acknowledged weaker of the two Communist states, China needed a counterweight in the form of better relations with the United States, and Richard Nixon was sufficiently flexible in his own thinking about foreign affairs to seize the opportunity. This need for a counterweight was apparently also in the minds of Chinese leaders when they pointedly deplored in 1974 any disruption or weakening of the European Common Market. For a strong, united Europe, allied to a friendly United States, was clearly China's best defense against Russian domination.

The Russians, on the other hand, feared that the United States and China might combine against it. Hence throughout 1972–1974 the Russians were more receptive than ever to moderating the Cold War. In May 1972 the first Strategic Arms Limitation Treaty (SALT) was signed, in which the United States and the U.S.S.R. agreed to limit themselves to a specified number of missiles and other nuclear weapons. In June 1973 Leonid Brezhnev, the head of the Communist Party and therefore the actual head of the Soviet Union, visited President Nixon at Camp David for a series of talks. The meeting resulted in nine agreements, some important, some minor, but all evidencing better relations between the only two nations that could bring the world into a nuclear holocaust. Four other countries had a nuclear capability, but none could withstand the power of either the United States or the Soviet Union.

After the withdrawal of the United States from active participation in the war in Indochina, the principal source of serious conflict between the United States and the Soviet Union was the Middle East. There the United States was closely identified with beleaguered but defiant Israel, while the Soviet Union was the supplier of arms and advice to Jordan, Syria, and Egypt, the Arab states surrounding Israel. It was the United States support of Israel that permitted the Israelis to defend themselves successfully against the surprise attack by Egypt and Syria in October 1973. After the Israelis had rallied to such an extent that they almost brought Cairo and Damascus under ground attack, the United States compelled them to halt their drive. It took over six months for a cease-fire to be worked out in the tense region. Thanks to indefatigable shuttling between capitals by Henry Kissinger, now Secretary of State, the diplomatic miracle was achieved. The Arab states and Israel signed an agreement in Geneva early in 1974.

Although it was doubtful that ending the fighting and charting new boundaries in the Middle East would bring a final resolution of the deep-seated animosities in the region between Arabs and Israelis, it was clear that the Soviet Union and the United States, at least temporarily, had drawn the fire from the last remaining spot of serious irritation in the global relations of the two superpowers. The achievement was clearly the work of Henry Kissinger, whose conception it seems to have been and whose untiring efforts brought it about. Again, however, the deeper explanation for the accommodation between the powers was not simply goodwill. The Russians had a strong interest in improving their trading agreements with the United States for they wanted to increase their production of consumer goods by importing the most recent American technology. The United States also had an interest in détente, for Russia would provide a new market, and peace in the Middle East would be valuable to America's European allies, who depended heavily on that region for their oil.

On balance, by the end of 1974 it looked as if the Cold War was indeed over, though there would still be problems between states. But the old hostility, suspicion, and lack of communication, which Kennedy in the early 1960s had only begun to break down, by the 1970s had reached a level at which traditional diplomacy was once again the primary basis of international relations. No major state was outside the international order, as both Russia and China had been for so long. The significance of the achievements of Secretary of State Kissinger's diplomacy was well summed up by the London *Sunday Times* on June 9, 1974. "Kissinger has a certain star quality," wrote the newspaper. "The astonishing diplomatic equestrianism which enables him, so far successfully, simultaneously to ride the unpredictable Russian stallion and the nervous Chinese mare, must evoke the praise of all but the most jaundiced critic. The foreign policy aim of the Nixon administration used to be presented as a partial disengagement of the United States from its world role. In fact, Kissinger's activities in the Far East and now the Middle East have increased rather than diminished that role, at least in its diplomatic sense."

Nixon's Domestic Policies

In his first State of the Union message President Nixon said that, whatever achievements in economic growth there may have been during the 1960s, that had also been a period when "we witnessed the greatest growth of crime, the greatest increase in inflation, and the greatest social unrest in America in a hundred years. Never has a nation seemed to have had more and enjoyed it less." His answer to these defects of the 1960s, he made clear, was to reduce the role of the federal government in the economy and in the functioning of the society. Parodying John F. Kennedy, he said that Americans should not ask what the government could do for them, but rather what they could do for themselves. In line with his promise to end deficit spending, the first Nixon budget showed a surplus which was achieved by almost $3 billion in cuts in domestic spending. Even when inflation seemed a serious threat to prosperity, Nixon resolutely promised not to impose government controls on prices and wages. As part of his effort to shift the emphasis in government from Washington to the states, he advocated the sharing of federal revenues with the states and cities. Congress did not act immediately on these measures, but it did agree in 1969 to a cut in taxes, which the President had also recommended.

Flexibility at Home. Events, however, soon interfered with Nixon's efforts to keep the government's role minimal; in the process he revealed that he could be as flexible in domestic matters as he was in foreign affairs. In 1970, for the first time in nine years, inflation wiped out the gain in median income for a family of four. In less than two years unemployment rose from 3.5 per cent in 1969 to 4.9 per cent of the work force in 1970. Not surprisingly, in 1970 the government reported that the number of families below the poverty line had risen for the first time since the figures began to be collected ten years before. That autumn both the President and Vice-President Spiro Agnew campaigned for a Republican Congress, but the rising inflation and unemployment proved to be powerful opponents. The Democrats not only made gains in the House, which in itself was not unusual, but they also won eleven governorships from the Republicans. In the face of the pressure for action, the President announced "an expansionary but not inflationary budget" for 1971 which included a $11.6 billion deficit, the largest in American history. (The deficit in his next budget broke even that record.)

But the inflation and stagnation of the economy could not be remedied by deficits alone, so the President displayed a flexibility in economics as surprising as his reversal on Red China. In August 1971 he announced a ninety-day freeze on wages, prices, and rents in an effort to control inflation, and three months later he set up agencies to police new federal economic guidelines. Thus, after years of describing himself as an opponent of the "New Economics," Nixon embraced Keynesian theory and the well-known Democratic conviction that government had a responsibility to regulate the economy. The controls he instituted, however, proved inadequate to the task. Although new guidelines were promulgated, in 1973 prices continued to rise at an ominously rapid rate—as they did in all the major industrial countries of the world. The principal answer of the administration to inflation remained greater production—a remedy that not only would take time but, more important, was of dubious effectiveness.

Nixon also demonstrated his flexibility by recommending that the federal government provide a minimum income of $1600 for every family of four on welfare. Since the idea had been advocated by liberals years earlier, many Democrats supported it in principle, but liberal Senators rejected the figure of $1600 as inadequate. No agreement was reached and so no new welfare program was enacted during the Nixon years, despite what looked at one time like a significant breakthrough in national thinking about dealing with poverty. Virtually everyone agreed that the current welfare programs were confused, often counterproductive, as well as enormously expensive, yet Congress and the President could not agree on the details, however much in agreement they were on the principle. Liberals charged that the administration was not truly interested in meeting the problem or reaching an agreement; the administration countered by accusing the liberals of being overly generous with public funds for welfare.

Nixon further showed his flexibility when he adopted an earlier Democratic idea of sharing federal revenues with the states as a part of what he called his "New American Revolution." And at the very end of the 1972 session of Congress a bill to give $5.3 billion to the states and cities was enacted into law. Not since the Jackson administration, 140 years before, had the federal government contributed revenues to the states. This time, however, the motive was not to relieve the government of a surplus—it in fact had none, only a deficit and a huge debt—but to help the beleaguered cities and states cope with their mounting problems of poverty, slums, inadequate transportation, and pollution. The implementation was conservative in that cities and states received federal money in proportion to their federal tax payments, not in proportion to their social or economic need.

Some Wins, Some Losses. In June 1972 President Nixon signed a landmark bill providing some federal money for nearly every college and university, thus carrying on the lavish participation of the federal government in higher education begun by Lyndon Johnson. The act also provided that any student needing money to attend college could obtain a loan up to $1400 a year. Public colleges and graduate schools were prohibited from discriminating against women students on pain of loss of federal funds, a response to the growing interest in women's rights throughout the country.

Nixon and Congress also agreed on a tax cut in 1969 to stimulate the economy and on the President's recommendation to make the Postal Service an independent agency. Agreement was more reluctant on measures that cost money. Nixon only grudgingly signed a 20 per cent increase in Social Security payments in July 1972, for he thought it inflationary, but he also anticipated it would be passed over a veto. The President did exercise his veto in the case of a mammoth sewage-treatment bill passed at the same time, only to have the $24.6 billion measure passed over his veto. He claimed that only $6 billion was permissible if inflation was to be controlled, yet early in his administration he had promised to give high priority to cleaning the nation's air and water. The administration also supported the development of a supersonic transport airplane (SST), which many environmentalists opposed because of its excessive noise and its threat to the upper atmosphere. But Congress refused to appropriate funds for its development and construction. This was probably the first time in the history of the industrial revolution that a machine capable of being built was deliberately not constructed because of its threat to the environment.

A Conservative Administration, Too. If in new areas like revenue sharing or family welfare assistance, Nixon showed himself to be less conservative than many Americans had expected, in most of his actions he was far from liberal. Certainly this was true in regard to the civil rights of blacks. In an educational act in 1972 Congress interfered for the first time in the school desegregation issue; it prohibited any new court-ordered school busing for purposes of racial balance until June 1974. This in itself was evidence that the country had become more conservative on the issue, but still not so conservative as the President, who angrily denounced the provision for failing to prohibit present as well as future court-ordered busing on any grounds. The administration's lack of enthusiasm for school integration had caused one official of the NAACP to denounce it in 1970 as the most "anti-Negro" administration since the 1920s. Significantly, in the election of 1972 blacks were the only ethnic group that failed to increase their vote for Nixon over 1968.

The conservatism of the administration was demonstrated most obviously in the speeches of Vice-President Agnew, who went out of his way to castigate liberals in the press and in public life as dangerous to American values. Again and again he raised his voice against youthful war protestors, denouncing them for their lack of discipline, patriotism, or intelligence. It was doubly shocking, therefore, when the self-righteous Agnew was forced to resign in October 1973 for accepting bribes while governor of Maryland and defrauding the federal government on his income taxes. He was replaced in office, in accordance with the newly ratified Twenty-fifth Amendment to the Constitution, by Gerald Ford, an equally conservative, but honest Republican congressman from Michigan.

Nixon showed his own conservative colors by speaking out against laws making abortions easier to obtain—even taking sides in an election on the issue in New York State—and vetoing a bill that would have provided federally supported child-care centers for working mothers, arguing that such measures weakened traditional family ties. (He conveniently ignored the fact that millions of mothers were already working and needed such assistance.) The record of the administration on civil liberties was similarly conservative. Nixon's first Attorney General, John Mitchell, considered the Supreme Court's decisions protecting the rights of accused persons too lenient. He contended that the national government could tap telephone wires without court permission in the name of national security, but the Supreme Court later rejected his argument. Like his chief, Mitchell frequently invoked the need for law and order, and was a principal supporter of the Crime Control Act of 1970, which provided federal funds for strengthening local police forces as well as broadening the activities of the FBI.

Also in line with his efforts to move the country away from what he considered undue judicial "permissiveness" were Nixon's recommendations to fill vacancies on the Supreme Court. His first appointment in 1969, of Chief Justice Warren Burger to replace Earl Warren, was widely approved, even though it was expected Burger would be more conservative than Warren. But Nixon's next two nominees—southern "strict constructionists," to use the President's own words—were rejected by the Senate on the grounds that, while they may have possessed the required ideological outlook, they were not professionally qualified. Before his first term was completed, however, Nixon had had the opportunity to appoint three justices, in addition to Burger, all with records that reflected conservative legal views. They soon made their conservatism felt. In June 1972, for example, the Court for the first time in eighteen years was unable to render a unanimous decision on a school desegregation case because two of the new justices voted against the majority.

A New Kind of Presidency. Although the Democrats controlled Congress throughout the first Nixon administration, about 44 per cent of the President's measures were passed. Furthermore, since the President was more interested in holding down spending than in funding new programs of his own, he had little need to seek congressional approval for extraordinary appropriations. And if Congress insisted on spending more money than he approved he could always fall back on the veto. Indeed, in 1972 his vetoes killed some $30 billion worth of appropriations for welfare and labor programs. When the Senate refused in 1972 to pass his recommendations for limiting spending to no more than $250 billion a year, Nixon announced that he would "impound" funds if necessary (that is, not spend them, even if appropriated). In this way, he said, he could avoid breaking "my promise to the American people" to avoid a tax increase. In 1973 some $15 billion appropriated by Congress for a hundred programs were impounded by the President. (Later the courts would declare impoundment illegal.)

In short, the administration's record in dealing with Congress was one few Presidents, considering the division of the parties, would have found unsatisfactory. But apparently it represented more congressional opposition than Nixon and his top advisers could tolerate. By the end of his first term they were moving toward a new kind of presidency, one in which the dependence on Congress would be minimized, if not eliminated.

The future that the administration had in store for Congress was evident in the plan for the reorganization of the Executive Office begun at the end of 1972 and announced by the President on January 5, 1973. The plan would permit the Executive Office to run the government with virtually no need to justify its actions to Congress. The Cabinet and the federal bureaucracy were to be effectively bypassed by a streamlined White House staff and super Cabinet, which would be the actual executive. Central to the whole operation were the President's two top staff men, H. R. Haldeman and John Ehrlichman, neither of whom had ever been elected to office or had more than cursory contact with national politics. Both were, events would show, arrogant, ruthless, and preeminently loyal to Richard Nixon. Behind the top officials was an enlarged White House staff, which in 1971 numbered 5400 as compared with 1670 in 1963. All on this staff were appointees of the President and without accountability to Congress or to the permanent officials of the various departments of the government. Indeed, the size of the White House staff allowed the executive branch to bypass almost entirely the federal bureaucracy in formulating plans and running the government. None of these White House officials could be summoned before Congress, nor were any subject to senatorial confirmation. The plan, which was withdrawn in the first month of the second administration in the face of revelations about the Watergate scandal, would have virtually removed the presidential office from accountability to Congress or even to the voters, except once every four years during a presidential election. The President would have had courtiers as well as enormous power.

Richard Nixon, it should be said, did not initiate the movement toward a presidential "court"—a monarch surrounded by his courtiers. George Reedy, Lyndon Johnson's press secretary, had already described its essential lineaments in the previous administration and there had been clear signs of its development under John F. Kennedy as well. A large part of the increase in personnel attached to the presidential office actually took place under Johnson. But with Nixon, partly because of his own "loner" personality that required his insulation from public scrutiny, and partly because of the intensely loyal advisers he surrounded himself with, this trend reached a frightening climax. A landslide victory in the election of 1972 was to be the final step in the move to institutionalize power without accountability, to establish a kind of Gaullist, plebiscitary presidency in the United States.

The Avalanche of 1972. There never seems to have been any doubt that Richard Nixon would seek reelection, and before the Republican convention met in August he had also made clear that he wanted his controversial and outspoken Vice-President, Spiro Agnew, to be his running mate again. The Democrats, however, could not settle so easily upon Nixon's opponent. Hubert Humphrey, who had long aspired to the presidency and who had been only narrowly defeated in 1968, wanted to try once more. But before the Democratic convention met in July in Miami Beach, George McGovern, a senator from South Dakota and long a vigorous opponent of the war in Vietnam, had shown that he was a strong favorite in various state primaries. The McGovern supporters were highly organized and they worked hard to win as many primaries as possible, capitalizing on the strong vocal opposition to the war and on the demand for domestic reform from many Democrats across the country. The strength and momentum built up in the primary campaigns won McGovern the nomination on the first ballot. (How much his nomination was helped by the various "dirty tricks" carried out by the Nixon forces to embarrass or discredit McGovern's opponents for the nomination is hard to say. Later revelations in the Watergate investigations made clear that McGovern was the favorite candidate of the Nixon supporters because he was correctly thought to be easy to defeat.)

McGovern's drive toward the nomination also benefited from the novel constitution of the Democratic convention in 1972. Its members were selected by a new procedure which had been worked out since the Chicago convention four years before, and which guaranteed representation to racial and ethnic minorities, women, and young people. This deliberately broad representation resulted in a convention not only favorable to the candidacy of George McGovern, but also more serious and more dedicated to the political issues of the time than any since the Progressives' in 1912. The platform promised a quick end to the war, a deep cut in military expenditures, tax revision on behalf of low-income people, and increased expenditures for social services.

The vice-presidential candidate that the convention named, with McGovern's approval, was Thomas Eagleton, senator from Missouri, who was compelled to resign after he admitted having undergone psychological treatment in recent years. Sargent Shriver, a brother-in-law of John F. Kennedy, was named in Eagleton's place. This unexpected change gave a setback to the hitherto highly successful McGovern organization from which it never recovered. As the weeks of the campaign passed, it became clear that McGovern was really the nominee

THE ELECTION OF 1972

	ELECTORAL VOTE BY STATE	POPULAR VOTE
REPUBLICAN Richard M. Nixon	520	47,169,911
DEMOCRATIC George S. McGovern	17	29,170,383
MINOR PARTIES	1	1,378,260
	538	77,718,554

ALASKA 3
HAWAII 4
WASH., D.C. 3

of only a minority of his party and that his very liberal positions on tax reform, welfare, and particularly reductions in military spending were frightening many traditional Democrats into the Nixon camp. Many Roman Catholics, white Southerners, blue-collar workers, and ethnic groups were clearly distrustful of McGovern. As one Democrat said, McGovern had in his acceptance speech opposed what he thought was wrong with American society by calling, "Come Home, America" but he never said, "Come Home, Democrats."

Rather than putting Nixon on the defensive for having failed to terminate the war in Vietnam after four years in office, McGovern found himself on the defensive for having been less than candid in his handling of the resignation of Eagleton. Just before asking Eagleton to resign he had publicly said he was "one thousand per cent for Tom Eagleton and I have no intention of dropping him from the ticket." He also showed himself as less than informed in proposing welfare and tax reforms, which he later had to withdraw under questioning. McGovern's assertions of a connection between the break-in at the Democratic headquarters at the Watergate complex and the White House were largely ignored by the electorate.

Moreover, when George Wallace was definitively removed from the campaign in May because of permanent paralysis to his legs caused by an attempt on his life, the Wallace supporters moved to Nixon, not McGovern, though most of them lived in the traditionally Democratic South. Wallace country became Nixon country. The President's stand against busing in school integration and "hard line" on urban crime and welfare won the support of traditional Democrats in northern cities as well as in the white South.

The enormous lead that the polls showed for Nixon from the outset of the campaign continued to election day. As a result, the President left the actual campaigning to Vice-President Agnew and other subordinates. Nixon probably made fewer campaign speeches than Franklin Roosevelt did in 1944 in the midst of the Second World War. Yet the Committee to Reelect the President worked overtime to drive up the President's majority as high as possible. Nixon fund raisers, for example, gathered over $60 million, a record for any campaign in history. Indeed, as the Watergate investigations would later show, the very surfeit of money was an irresistible temptation to criminal action on behalf of the President's reelection. Henry Kissinger worked incessantly, as we have seen, to bring the war in Vietnam to a conclusion before election day, but that final feather in Nixon's cap was denied him.

The results of the election make evident that the President did not need an end to the war to win one of the biggest popular votes and the highest electoral college victory in American history: 61 per cent of the popular vote and forty-nine states. McGovern, by capturing only Massachusetts and the District of Columbia, was as badly defeated as Alfred Landon in 1936. Those who had contended that McGovern would be the "Democratic Goldwater"—too far out of the mainstream of either party to win—proved to be right, since Goldwater had done better than McGovern. Subsequent analyses of the election showed that as many as 39 per cent of the people who usually thought of themselves as Democrats voted for Nixon. Fifty-four per cent of trade union families said they had voted for Nixon, a defection from Democratic allegiance unknown since the first administration of Franklin Roosevelt. Over half of the Catholics voted for Nixon, though in 1968 only 38 per cent had. Even the Jewish vote, which usually was heavily Democratic, went 37 per cent to Nixon. Only Negroes, among racial and ethnic groups, remained true to their traditional Democratic allegiance, but many blacks simply did not vote at all.

Nixon's victory completed the breakup of the Democratic solid South which Harding had begun in 1920. Nixon captured, with huge majorities, every one of the former states of the Confederacy, a feat never before achieved by a Republican candidate. Significantly, too, for the future of southern politics below the level of presidential elections, three white Republican congressmen were elected from Mississippi and Louisiana for the first time.

Nevertheless, it would be a mistake to see Nixon's victory as a Republican resurgence. His campaign had concentrated on "reelecting the President" rather than on winning a Republican majority. In his few campaign speeches the President rarely mentioned his party and in some southern states Nixon campaigners refused to help Republican candidates who were running against conservative Democrats and supporters of the President. His reelection was intended to be, and in fact was, a personal victory, even though Nixon had little personal appeal for the electorate. His overwhelming majority was actually a measure of the fear of what George McGovern and his liberal followers would do in power, rather than an indication of positive support for Richard Nixon. One sign of this was the fact that only 55 per cent of those eligible bothered to vote—the lowest proportion in a presidential election since 1948 and down from 61 per cent only four years before. Another indication was that the Democrats continued to control both houses of Congress by substantial majorities, as they had since 1957.

The Debacle of Watergate

Both the tendencies and the intentions of the first Nixon administration had been to increase the prestige, power, and insulation of the President. His overwhelming victory at the polls reinforced this movement, for now he and his advisers could claim that he was free from obligations to party and beyond the control of Congress. The arrogance of his personal White House staff in dealing with individual congressmen, even Republicans, and with congressional committees suggested that the second term would see the new plebiscitary presidency in practice. It would be remote, unaccountable to Congress, and subject only to popular election once in four years. Professor Herbert Nicholas, an astute English observer, pointed out even before Watergate the dimensions and the dangers inherent in the new presidency: "Since he [the President] is a monarch his critics can rarely meet him as equals; since he lives outside the legislature he does not have to engage in debate; since he is supra-party he does not have to defer to the demands which such [a] living political organism would make on him; since he is surrounded by a court of his own choosing he cannot guarantee that he will be told unpleasant truths; since he is himself an image and depends on images he is exposed to constant and insidious pressures to confuse appearance and reality. It is bad enough if he deceives the people, but it is far worse if the President deceives himself." Watergate, however, would suggest that self-deception was not the principal danger from the new presidency.

The tendency toward plebiscitary government was stopped in its tracks, rudely and definitively, by a series of events in the first months of the new administration. These events also revealed how deliberate the growth of presidential power and insulation had been and, above all, how dangerous the lack of accountability in the presidential office had become. For the Watergate scandal was a striking example of what could happen when a few men whose first loyalty was to a man and not to the office he held were free to exercise the enormous power of the presidential office without accounting to anyone except themselves and the man they served.

The Watergate Scandal. On June 17, 1972, as the Democratic convention was approaching, five men were arrested while breaking into the Democratic National Headquarters at the Watergate complex in Washington. They were caught attempting to install electronic spying devices to listen in on Democratic plans. It was the fifth attempt to "bug" the headquarters and the second that actually got inside the offices. The Democrats naturally tried to make political capital out of the news, but were unable to establish links between the burglars and the Republican party or the White House. Soon after the burglars were convicted in January 1973, however, the involvement of White House officials in the Watergate break-in became known. Throughout the spring and early summer millions of Americans watched the televised hearings held before Senator Sam Ervin's special Watergate Committee investigating the ramifications of the break-in, particularly as they touched the White House. The connections to the White House inner office were exposed by the confessions of leading figures in the Committee to Reelect the President and by the President's own counsel, John Dean, who admitted to perjury and the obstruction of justice in trying to prevent the connection between the White House and the break-in from becoming public knowledge.

As the hearings proceeded, the dimensions of the illegal activities widened shockingly, though the central question of how involved the President was in the break-in and subsequent cover-up was difficult to answer since the President fought to protect what he called the confidentiality of his official activities. His two closest advisers in the White House, H. R. Haldeman and John D. Ehrlichman, were compelled to resign because of the accusations against them and both his former and present Attorneys General, John Mitchell and Richard Kleindienst, were implicated in illegal actions. Kleindienst pleaded guilty to lying to a Senate Committee, but Mitchell was cleared of the charge of having improperly

The testimony of John Dean, former chief counsel to President Nixon, before the Senate Watergate Committee was vigorously denied by the President, but later confirmed by the White House tapes. *Photo: Fred Ward—Black Star*

handled campaign funds. In 1974 Mitchell was again indicted, and this time convicted, along with Ehrlichman and Haldeman, on charges of obstructing justice in covering up the break-in at the Watergate. All told, by the spring of 1974 thirty-three former members of the White House staff or the Cabinet had been indicted or convicted, or had pleaded guilty to various criminal acts. By February 1975 eight had already been found guilty; in addition, Nixon's personal lawyer had pleaded guilty to criminal charges and been sentenced to jail, along with four others from the staff of the Committee to Reelect the President.

Even agencies usually above politics were shown to have been tainted by the drive to reelect the President or by the cover-up. Both the FBI and the CIA had helped carry out what John Mitchell later referred to as "the White House horrors." The acting director of the FBI, L. Patrick Gray, confessed that he had destroyed evidence because he thought that was what the White House wanted. Later it was revealed that the Internal Revenue Service had been called upon illegally to provide confidential information to use against political opponents. (The misuse of these agencies would later figure in the House Judiciary Committee's impeachment charge of abuse of power by President Nixon.)

The hearings also revealed that the group of men who broke into the Watergate had been organized by the White House as an undercover unit to "plug leaks" of government secrets. One of the leaks that precipitated the formation of what came to be called the "plumbers" had been the publication in 1971 by the *New York Times* of a long, highly confidential government study of the growth of American involvement in Vietnam, called the Pentagon Papers. The papers had been stolen and publicly released by Dr. Daniel Ellsberg, a researcher temporarily in government employ. In 1971, in an effort to obtain incriminating or embarrassing evidence on Ellsberg, the "plumbers" had broken into and ransacked Ellsberg's psychiatrist's office. When this "White House horror" became publicly known in 1973, Ellsberg's own trial for having leaked confidential information was quashed by the presiding judge.

Perhaps the most sensational revelation that came out of the Senate hearings was the information that ever since 1970 the President had "bugged" his own offices. This news opened up the way toward establishing the President's own possible involvement. The struggle to obtain access to the presidential tapes, first by the Senate Watergate Committee and later by the Watergate Special Prosecutor and the courts, occupied the President's staff for the rest of 1973 and much of 1974. Nixon invoked "executive privilege" and the separation of powers to prevent the confidential conversations from becoming public; he released tapes only when confronted with court orders.

The Watergate scandal dwarfed in scope and differed in kind from any other scandal in American governmental history. Unlike the Star Routes frauds of the Grant administration or the Teapot Dome bribery of the Harding years, Watergate did not involve financial corruption or bribery. It was more sinister than that for it concerned people who, having been intrusted with government authority, used that authority not only to break the law, but to hide those illegal acts from public knowledge and the processes of the law. This degradation of American institutions of government was largely redeemed by the fact that the press and the courts functioned as they were supposed to. It was through these institutions, particularly as represented by the *Washington Post* and Judge John Sirica, that the cover-up was ferreted out and exposed, and thorough investigations and prosecutions set in motion.

The President Resists. Nixon's handling of the Watergate revelations from the outset was self-defeating, though he always insisted he was innocent of any wrongdoing. The first of several major miscalculations by the President of the mood of the country was his firing of the Special Prosecutor, Archibald Cox, who had been appointed in May 1973, when it became clear that an investigation of the Watergate affair, free from the tainted Department of Justice, was imperative. On Saturday, October 20, 1973, Nixon ordered Cox to cease asking for more tapes and files, though when Cox was appointed he had been promised a free hand to investigate illegalities wherever the evidence led and to have access to any evidence he needed. Cox insisted on obtaining the evidence and, when he refused to resign, Nixon asked the Attorney General to fire him. That official refused to do so, as did his deputy; both officials then resigned. A more compliant Acting Attorney General fired Cox and abolished the office of Special Prosecutor.

The reaction from the country was explosive. By Monday morning some 200,000 telegrams had been sent to Washington, virtually all of them condemning the President's actions. For the first time impeachment proceedings seemed a possibility. On October 22 the House Democratic leaders agreed to ask the Judiciary Committee to begin an inquiry into whether or not a bill of impeachment ought to be presented to the House. Thus began the first serious consideration of the impeachment of a President since 1868. Across the nation newspapers called for Nixon's resignation or impeachment. *Time* in its first editorial in fifty years counseled resignation.

As a result of the uproar, Nixon abandoned his attempt to stop the independent investigation begun by Cox. He appointed a new independent prosecutor, who exacted ironclad promises of full cooperation, though subsequent months would show that the President did not have the same definition of full cooperation as the Special Prosecutor or Congress.

Yet the President remained defiant. At an extraordinary press conference in Florida he impassionately proclaimed, "The people have to know whether or not their President is a crook. Well, I am not a crook. I have earned everything I've got." His emphasis on the lack of financial gain in the various Watergate crimes exhibited a strange insensitivity toward law breaking. Even so, it was shown later that he had in fact padded his income tax deductions while President so as to underpay his taxes by almost $450,000.

For a while, at least, Nixon's defiance paid off. His veto of a bill to curb the President's power to send troops abroad without congressional approval was upheld in the House just four days after the explosion over Cox's dismissal. The House was still far from willing to consider impeachment or censure.

During 1973 and early 1974 Nixon's popular support continued to fall, though most Americans, in or out of public life, clearly were not ready to face the issue of impeaching a President; they preferred he resign. The President played upon the fears of impeachment by saying he was defending the presidency from partisan assault and from attempts to weaken the office.

The President's last-ditch resistance to giving more evidence or tapes, as well as his inability to gauge the impact that the widening scandal was having on public opinion, were demonstrated once again in April 1974. In a bold move to counter all the demands from investigators, courts, and congressional committees for more tapes, he announced on a special television broadcast that he was issuing some 1300 pages of transcripts from the tapes. His critics immediately discounted the act as self-serving since the transcripts would be those that showed him in the most favorable possible light. But once the transcripts were available for wide reading, the reaction was another explosion of disbelief and outrage. Once again Nixon had misjudged the temper of the country. As one columnist put it, the conversations in the Oval Room of the White House read like a dialogue in a locker room among small-town cronies discussing the horse races or fixing a deal. For neither the level of the language—many "expletives deleted" punctuated the text—nor the conspicuous lack of ethical considerations was what most Americans, in public life and out, expected at the highest level of their government.

Even Nixon's hitherto most loyal supporters in Congress could not conceal their disenchantment. Senate Republican leader Hugh Scott spoke of the "deplorable, disgusting, shabby, immoral performances." The staunchly conservative *Chicago Tribune* called for Nixon's removal from office.

A Truncated Second Term. The first two years of the second term were dominated by Watergate; several times Nixon pleaded with Congress and the press "to get Watergate behind us and get on with the business of America." The prestige and influence of the President, despite his enormous majority in 1972, were clearly diminished, his White House staff dispersed by resignations under fire, his bureaucracy alienated or ignored, and his relations with Congress under the cloud of impeachment proceedings.

Under the circumstances Nixon's efforts to control mounting inflation were no more effective than they were novel. In his first budget in 1973 he tried to reduce government spending by calling for more than a hundred cutbacks or outright terminations of welfare programs, but with revenues falling in a stagnant economy he had to announce a deficit of $12 billion. In March and June of 1973 he temporarily imposed price controls, first on meat and then on a number of other goods, in an effort to stop the spiraling prices, but the rate of inflation continued to rise in 1974. Between June 1973 and June 1974 the increase in prices was just short of 10 per cent, an annual rate unknown in the United States since the Civil War. Food prices went up even faster, rising 18 per cent in one year. If inflation in general was still at a lower rate than in most European countries, the rise in food prices exceeded that of any country in the Common Market. For the principal and most successful agricultural producer in the world that fact was indeed a cause for concern. For many people the rapid increase in prices, which was cutting seriously into the vaunted prosperity of America, was a more powerful reason for removing Richard Nixon from office than Watergate. Politicians certainly felt that, between Watergate and the continuing inflation, Republican chances in the future were reduced enormously, even in those areas like the South and Middle West where Watergate aroused less concern.

When the Arab-Israeli war in the fall of 1973 brought home to all Americans the growing shortage of oil and other sources of energy throughout the world, the Nixon administration came in for further criticism for failing to anticipate the shortage and then for allowing the oil companies to reap large profits from the subsequent rise in petroleum prices. As a result of the Arab countries' temporary but frightening cutback in oil deliveries to Europe and the United States to prevent aid to Israel, the President announced the goal of making the United States self-sufficient in energy. Considering that less than 30 per cent of American oil came from Arab countries, the goal was not impractical, but it would mean further increases in the cost of fuel and energy in general at a time when inflation was already the greatest threat to the well-being of Americans.

The elevation of Henry Kissinger to Secretary of State in the fall of 1973 ensured that the President and the country would continue to have the services of the highly successful "Super K," as the newsmagazines called him. Yet there was evidence that Nixon's precarious position within the country may have been weakening his influence in foreign affairs. In the spring of 1973, for example, he asked Congress to grant him authority to lower, raise, or eliminate tariffs to ease world trade. Russia in particular was anxious to conclude a favorable trade agreement with the United States, which the House passed in December 1973 at Nixon's request. But the Senate was reluctant to accord a "most favored nation" status to Soviet trade because of Russia's hostility toward Israel and the Soviet refusal to permit dissident Jews to leave the Soviet Union. The rapidity with which the Soviets came to an agreement on the number of strategic missiles with President Ford in November 1974 strongly suggested that the Russians had been having serious doubts that the Nixon administration in its last months could get an agreement accepted by an increasingly hostile Congress and public.

Another Nixon "First." The summer of 1974 saw the climax of two years of Watergate. The sequence of events was swift and fatal. In July the Supreme Court in a unanimous decision ordered the President to turn over to federal trial Judge John Sirica all the tapes of his conversations that had been asked for by the Special Prosecutor. The President's argument that he was beyond the reach of the courts, even in a criminal procedure, was rejected, though the Court conceded for the first time that a President had the right to the privacy of his conversations when criminality was not at issue.

A few weeks later the Judiciary Committee of the House, which for months had been considering in closed sessions the evidence for impeachment, began to hold public televised meetings during which the evidence was thoroughly debated. In addition to the Democrats, who constituted a majority of the committee and who almost unanimously supported impeachment, seven out of seventeen Republicans on the committee voted for two articles of impeachment against the President, and two Republicans voted for a third charge. The first charge cited Nixon for obstruction of justice, the second for abuse of power, and the third for contempt of Congress. Unlike the impeachment proceedings against Andrew Johnson over a hundred years before, these were carefully and fairly conducted; not even Republican partisans could sustain allegations of improper procedures or railroading of the President.

Within days after the committee's vote for impeachment and before it could submit a report to the House, which everyone conceded would impeach the President, Nixon, complying with the Supreme Court decision, released the contents of a taped conversation in his office on June 23, 1972, only five days after the Watergate break-in. The revelations were devastating. The transcript clearly showed that the President had not only been informed of the burglary, but had gone on to participate in the cover-up. No longer could there be any question that the President had been lying all along about his involvement. Nixon also revealed that he had not told his defense attorneys of this tape, nor had he informed the Republicans on the House Judiciary Committee who had so vigorously defended his name during the impeachment debates. To a man, his supporters on the committee now called for his impeachment.

But before the House could take any action on impeachment, the President, under intense pressure from chagrined party leaders, resigned on August 9. In his speech to the nation the night before his resignation, Nixon characteristically omitted any reference to having done anything illegal, nor did he allude to the widespread belief that he would have been impeached by the House and convicted by the Senate. Instead, he explained his resignation on the grounds that "I no longer have a strong enough political base in the Congress" to remain in office.

In short, he blamed his resignation on his party in Congress for deserting him.

The transition of power from Richard Nixon to Gerald R. Ford, the first man to be appointed Vice-President under the Twenty-fifth Amendment and the first President to accede to the office without popular election, was greeted with relief by the nation. Although Ford had publicly defended the President's probity around the country for months, upon taking office he made clear he believed, as he said in his brief inaugural address, that "honesty is always the best policy" and that "truth is the glue that holds governments together."

The Public Response. The new President, however, was not able to escape the public revulsion against Republicans. In fact, he encouraged it by granting Nixon in September 1974 a full pardon for any possible crimes committed while President. Seeking, he said, to close the wounds of Watergate, Ford actually opened them wider. His clearly unpopular act certainly made the Democratic sweep in the November elections more devastating for his party. As a result of the elections the Democrats commanded three quarters of the seats in the House, three fifths in the Senate, and almost three quarters of the state governors' chairs. For the first time since the Johnson landslide of 1964, the suburbs voted strongly Democratic. Ford's old seat in Michigan, despite his personal intervention in the campaign, went to a Democrat. The impact of Watergate could be measured even more directly in the defeat of four Republicans in the House Judiciary Committee who had defended Nixon against impeachment; only one Republican who had supported impeachment lost his seat.

The elections represented a repudiation of Nixon's conservatism as well as his criminality. Many of the newly elected members of Congress were young and known for their liberal views on public issues. This was true of Republicans as well as Democrats. Some thirty regular Republicans lost their House seats, while only one out of thirty-six members of a liberal Republican House study group lost his seat. Another measure of the voters' rejection of conservatism was the widespread success of black candidates, even in the South. Almost one hundred state or national offices were now held by Negroes; blacks won lieutenant governorships, in Colorado and California, for the first time since Reconstruction.

But this quite proper response of voters to political actions of which they disapproved was not as promising as it might seem. The fact that only 38 per cent of the eligible voters bothered to go to the polls suggested a deep, popular disenchantment with politics and government. As recently as 1970 the proportion had been 45 per cent; and the campaign of 1972 had brought out 55 per cent. Nor did the certain conflict between the liberalism of the new Congress and the acknowledged conservatism of President Ford promise quick or easy solutions to the mounting social and economic problems the distracted Nixon administration had been unable to confront, much less solve. The nation, it is true, had weathered the unprecedented storms of Watergate, the resignation of a corrupt Vice-President, and the resignation of a criminal President, but every week, as inflation and unemployment mounted, the need for solutions and action grew. All that could be said with confidence about the future was that the new government was not under the cloud of Watergate and that the Nixon administration's threat to constitutional government had been turned back.

SUGGESTED READING

There are few scholarly works on the Nixon administrations, though the Watergate issue promises an outpouring of books within a few years. For Nixon himself, the best friendly biography does not deal with his presidency at all: Earl Mazo, *Nixon* (1968). The best study of Nixon is undoubtedly Garry Wills, *Nixon Agonistes: The Crisis of the Self-Made Man* * (1970). Bruce Mazlish, *In Search of Nixon: A Psychohistorical Inquiry* * (1972) overemphasizes psychological determinants in his character. Nixon's own story, *Six Crises* (1962) is indispensable to anyone seeking to understand him, for it is much more revealing than any presidential autobiography—and was intended to be so. For the early years in the White House, Rowland Evans, Jr., and Robert D. Novak, *Nixon in the White House: The Frustration of Power* (1971) helps explain the move to a new kind of presidency. Friendly to Nixon yet providing some insights into the character of the man is Allen Drury, *Courage and Hesitation: Inside the Nixon Administration* (1972). William Safire, *Before the Fall: An Inside View of the Pre-Watergate White House* (1975) is a favorable, but not uncritical, view by a former speechwriter and intellectual supporter of Nixon.

The campaign and election of 1968 is covered with his usual attention to detail by Theodore White, *The Making of the President, 1968* (1969). A group of English journalists did a better job in Lewis Chester, et al., *An American Melodrama: The Presidential Campaign of 1968* (1969). For a cutting, but revealing study of Nixon's view of campaigning see Joe McGinniss, *The Selling of the President* * (1969). The appeal of Robert Kennedy is made evident in Jack Newfield, *Robert Kennedy: A Memoir* (1969), by a supporter. A thorough study of the Kent State shooting, which was so crucial in the Nixon administration, is Peter Davies, *The Truth About Kent State: A Challenge to the American Conscience* (1973). It contains a number of dramatic and horrifying photographs of the shooting.

The campaign and election of 1972 and the Watergate scandal have already produced some revealing books. Theodore White, *The Making of the President, 1972* (1974) is weakened by his isolation of Watergate from the story of the campaign and candidates. Bob Woodward and Carl Bernstein, *All the President's Men* (1974) is a fascinating report by the *Washington Post* reporters of how they uncovered the story of the century. Jeb Stuart Magruder, *An American Life: One Man's Road to Watergate* (1974) is the first and highly informative memoir by a convicted participant in the cover-up. *The White House Transcripts* * (1974) contains the full text of the presidential tape recordings issued by Nixon in April 1974. It needs to be read to understand the popular revulsion against the President three months before his resignation. A brief but incomplete story of the Watergate story, replete with pictures, is William V. Shannon, *They Could Not Trust the King* (1974). Reporters Dan Rather and Gary Gates have tried to pinpoint the responsibility for Watergate in *The Palace Guard* (1974). Watergate conspirator and erstwhile mystery writer and CIA agent E. Howard Hunt tells his version, with some omissions, in *Under Cover* (1974).

* Available in a paperback edition.

CHAPTER SIX

THE CULTURE OF AFFLUENCE AND ANXIETY

I N 1928, OBVIOUSLY impressed by the ability of a machine civilization to produce enormous quantities of goods, Herbert Hoover optimistically spoke of the possibility of abolishing poverty in the United States. After the crash of the next year and the ensuing Great Depression, his words became ashes in his mouth. Yet in the years that followed World War II, Hoover's prophecy seemed close to realization. For the first time the great majority of Americans were living in a society of plenty.

The Shape of the Postwar Economy

In 1945, after four years of wartime prosperity, the total value of all the goods and services produced in America—called by economists the Gross National Product (GNP)—was $212 billion; by 1960 that figure had more than doubled and by 1971 the United States had reached a GNP of over one trillion dollars. No other people in the world had ever achieved such a high level of production. That was the first big fact of the postwar economy.

The second was full employment. After the ordeal of the Depression no industrial country, and certainly not the wealthy United States, would accept anything less than a job for anyone who wanted to work. During the 1930s the realization of the goal of full employment, which the New Deal had courageously proclaimed, eluded Americans. Throughout the Depression decade between 15 and 25 per cent of the civilian labor force was without work. After 1945, however, unemployment was reduced to minimal proportions. During the 1950s, for example, the average annual rate was 4.6 per cent; during the 1960s it fluctuated around 5 per cent, and in 1972 the rate was still below 6 per cent. This figure meant, to be sure, that millions of men and women who wished to work could not find jobs, but the spectre of large-scale unemployment that had haunted workers since the beginning of industrial America over a century before did not recur after World War II.

The third characteristic was really an aspect of the first two, but it was so important psychologically and historically that it deserves to be mentioned explicitly. In the thirty years after 1945, the United States did not experience a major depression. During no other thirty-year span in the history of the Republic had that been true. There were three serious recessions, to be sure—those of 1949, 1953–1954, and 1958—but all were shallow and short-lived when compared with the depressions of 1893–1897 and the 1930s. Moreover, the period from 1961 to 1969 constituted the longest period of uninterrupted prosperity in the history of the nation. (The recession that began in 1973, however, promised to exceed those of the 1950s.)

Finally, a fourth characteristic of the American economy marked a new stage in the history of the United States. During the 1950s the United States became a major importer of industrial and consumer goods, thereby reversing a trend that had begun in the 1870s, when the nation first began industrializing. In the 1950s the United States passed the United Kingdom as the greatest importer. The large increase in industrial imports was yet another measure of the high rate of consumption among Americans, for with their new wealth they demanded more and more foreign goods, as the large number of Volkswagen autos, Sony televisions, and Minolta cameras testified.

Tract housing in California. *Photo: Joe Munroe—Photo Researchers*

In the years after 1945, in short, the prominent reality of American social life was the enormous wealth being produced by the economy. To the emerging countries of Africa, Asia, and South America, the economy of the United States appeared fabulous; and even industrial countries like the U.S.S.R. and Great Britain saw the consumer plenty of the U.S. as a distant goal. It was not that the American economy was growing so rapidly, for other industrial societies, like Japan, Germany, and the U.S.S.R., had higher annual rates of economic growth. It was the sheer amount of production, even when counted on a per capita basis, that set the United States apart from the rest of the world. For Americans the burgeoning economy, despite some ups and downs in the business cycle, was the underlying pulse of their culture. As we shall see, abundance affected not only the goods and services Americans bought, but also the values by which they lived. But before we look at some of the cultural consequences of prosperity—as well as some of its dark spots—let us examine the changing shape of the economy and the causes of its growth.

The Roots of American Economic Growth. One underlying cause of the boom of the postwar years was the growth of population. In the years after 1945 the birth rate climbed until it reached a high of 25.2 births per 1000 population in 1956–1957. At the same time the death rate fell and, owing to improvements in medicine, life expectancy at birth lengthened. One of the surprises for demographers was the increase in family size that took place during the 1950s, especially among the middle-income groups. Heretofore rising income and increasing urbanization, both of which were characteristic of the postwar years, had been accompanied by smaller families. The baby boom and the longer life expectancy of Americans were sources of prosperity; together they meant a rising demand for housing, food, manufactured goods, and services. Part of the increase in the size of families during the 1950s was due to the postponement of children during the war and part was due to the prosperity that encouraged parents to enlarge their families. In that sense the new prosperity perpetuated itself. (By the 1970s, however, the birth rate was lower than at any time since the Depression.)

The rapidly expanding economy of the 1950s and 1960s was highly institutionalized. The individual entrepreneur so celebrated in national myth was still in evidence, but he or she was no longer a significant figure in the functioning of the economy. In 1958, for example, there were some 5 million individually owned businesses outside of farming, mining, and fishing, but even when all of these were taken into account, 85 per cent of all employed persons were working for someone else. In 1900, by way of comparison, 36 per cent of all members of the working force had been self-employed.

The largest businesses were corporations and of these only a small fraction dominated the economy. In 1958, for instance, one tenth of the almost 600,000 corporations received over half of the net income of corporate enterprises. In 1968 less than 3 per cent of all corporations received almost four fifths of the total income of corporations. The large corporation was one source of the nation's economic growth. As we shall see a little later, one requirement for economic growth was the constant flow of new products and techniques, which came primarily from scientific and technological research. Corporations with the facilities and large amounts of capital and income necessary for research were therefore an important cause of that growth.

The large corporations, in turn, were encouraged by the prosperity. With the federal government now acknowledging its responsibility to prevent or at least to mitigate a depression, corporate businesses could afford to be less cautious in their operations and therefore to invest more in the economy. The enormous military spending, which reached $50 billion annually in the early 1960s and then shot up to $80 billion a year during the Vietnam War, also acted as an incentive to corporate activities and profit accumulation. In the light of these supportive circumstances, it is not surprising that few large manufacturing enterprises failed, though many small businesses did. Out of the 1001 largest manufacturing firms in 1951, all but nine were in existence nine years later.

During the 1960s, too, American corporations began to spread overseas to take advantage of new markets and new sources of labor and raw materials. By the early 1970s several hundred multinational corporations were operating in Europe, Latin America, and Asia, often producing the same goods they produced in the United States, but with local labor and for a local market. It has been estimated that by 1972 the capital invested in international combines had reached at least $80 billion, or almost triple the figure in 1960. Their production of goods and services amounted to $300 billion, which was larger than the GNP of any country except the United States and the Soviet Union. Or, put another way, of the hundred largest economic units in the world, only fifty were nations; the other fifty were multinational corporations.

These giants of the international economy, if they were American in origin, often came in for criticism for being agents of a new kind of American imperialism, though many host countries welcomed them for the capital and expertise they brought and the jobs they provided. At the same time, within the United States they came under attack for using capital, often accumulated in the United States, to provide new jobs for foreign, rather than American, workers. The goods produced abroad, moreover, often competed with American-made commodities, to the chagrin of American labor unions. From a historical point of view the new multinational corporations brought a new, albeit private stability and order to the international economy, a development that resembled the order and stability brought to the American economy in the nineteenth century by big business. The multinational corporations were a measure, too, of how the technological advances of the affluent years since 1945 had tied the United States and the world together in a new global economy.

Although government in the United States had little to do directly with the rapid spread of the multinational corporation, the federal government was certainly a major force in stimulating economic growth at home after 1945. By the 1950s it was much more than a regulator of the economy, as it had become under the New Deal; it was also a very substantial and active participant. Indeed, after 1955 the expenditures of the local, state, and federal governments were so large that they dwarfed those of any other segment of the economy. Their purchases amounted to more than one fifth of all those made in the economy. The federal government's role as purchaser, aside from any of its other economic roles, was so large that the Johnson administration was able to prevent price increases in aluminum in 1965 and copper in 1966 simply by releasing large quantities of these strategic metals from its stockpiles. By the 1970s the expenditures of the federal government alone equalled a quarter of a trillion dollars a year, or roughly a quarter of the GNP.

The federal government was also one of the principal forces sustaining the housing boom of the 1950s and 1960s, which in turn was one of the important causes of the economic growth after 1945. Through agencies like the Federal Housing Administration and the Veterans Administration, the federal government helped finance mortgages for the construction and purchase of millions of one-family homes. During these same years the government poured money into the housing industry through its support of low-income public housing.

Many economists believe that the demand for housing, which had been building up all through the Depression and the war, was the chief cause of the postwar prosperity. Certainly the backlog of demand was enormous. In 1945, one authority has calculated, all the housing in the nation was actually worth 8 per cent *less* than in 1929, despite the inflation during the war years. Very little construction had taken place during the thirties, yet since 1929 the number of households had risen by 8 million, or 26 per cent. When the defeat of the Axis powers released American savings from government restrictions, the housing boom began, lasting into the seventies.

The importance of housing to economic growth can hardly be exaggerated since residential construction usually makes up between 20 and 25 per cent of all private investment. During the 1950s over a million dwelling units were built each year, a number greater than the annual number of new families. During the even more prosperous sixties the number of housing starts averaged 1.5 million a year. As a result, in 1971 two fifths of all the occupied housing units in the country had been built in only the preceding twenty years.

The growth in population, the increased government expenditures, the backlog of consumer savings, and the housing boom were not the only sources of economic growth, important as they were. The large increase in productivity must also be included in the list. Between 1890 and 1914 the advance in the output per man-hour in the United States was 22 per cent; in the years between 1945 and 1959 the increase was between 35 and 40 per cent, almost double the earlier rate.

Mechanization, Automation, and the Computer. What was it that enabled American workers to increase their productivity? Primarily it was a greater use of machines and power. As machines became more sophisticated and versatile, workers became only feeders, supervisors, and operators; the machines did almost all the labor. Efficiency was further enhanced by new integration processes whereby interruptions in the manufacturing of goods were avoided and time saved, as in the so-called continuous-flow processes in many industries. It was possible now to combine a sequence of operations into a single one. For example, in the making of automobiles, one machine now drilled holes in crankshafts, whereas before twenty-nine different machines had been required.

The principal contribution of the 1950s to increased production was the introduction of automation. Automation differs from ordinary machine production in that people are no longer necessary to operate the machines: the machines are self-regulating through the use of electronic devices that work much as a thermostat does when it turns the heat on or off in a room as the temperature changes.

Perhaps the best-known and most sophisticated form in which electronic automation appears is the computer, another innovation of the years immediately after 1945. The computer quickly became a part of virtually every form of enterprise. It became indispensable for the processing of records that once were tediously and expensively handled by innumerable clerks; it is used for all kinds of scientific research projects and it can even be programmed to translate foreign languages or compose music.

The result of the new machines, new processes, and greater use of electrical energy was the continuous reduction in the hours of labor needed to turn out goods. In 1947, for example, it took 310.5 hours to make an automobile; by 1962 the time had been cut by more than half.

Behind the drive for mechanization and automation lay the willingness of business and government to invest ever increasing amounts of money in scientific and technological research for the further improvement of methods and machines. During the 1950s outlays for research and development rose faster than the GNP, reaching $13.7 billion in 1960; during the following decade the figure doubled. The proportion of the GNP devoted to research and development in the U.S. was several times higher than for any western European industrial country. About half of the total was contributed by the federal government, the remainder by private businesses and foundations.

A novel and fruitful relationship developed between business and government on the one hand, and the colleges and universities on the other. Recognizing that research was one source of new products, techniques, and increased productivity, both business and government drew heavily upon the knowledge and skills of the intellectual community through research grants and consulting contracts. Expenditures for education from all sources rose sixfold between 1945 and 1965 while the GNP only tripled. Never before had the university community been so heavily involved with and dependent upon government and private business; some farsighted universities took elaborate precautions to prevent distortion of their commitment to free and untrammeled research and to lessen dependence upon government and business funds. But not enough of them did so to avoid the student protests and confrontations of the late 1960s, which demanded less dependence by universities on a government that was waging an unjustified war in Vietnam. In the inflationary 1970s, however, few institutions of higher learning could function without some direct support from the government.

The Social Consequences of Prosperity

Regional Transformations. One of the most striking changes that followed upon the new prosperity was the improvement in the economy of the South, long the most economically depressed region of the nation. Although the South continued to report a high birth rate and inadequate out-migration to counterbalance it, personal income per capita during the 1950s rose faster there than in the rest of the nation. Moreover, by 1961 the proportion of workers in the South engaged in manufacturing had risen from 18 per cent in 1945 to almost 24 per cent, a proportion that put the region on a par, for the first time since the Civil War, with the Far West. If Texas was not included, the South by the 1970s was still the most rural region of the country, but its cities were growing at a faster rate than those of the nation as a whole.

The beginnings of the alterations in the South went back to the 1930s, with the improvement in cotton prices because of the Agricultural Adjustment Act and the building of the TVA, which not only brought electricity to the rural South but, through its reclamation and conservation programs, helped rehabilitate the heart of the region. During the war the many Army training camps in the South injected large amounts of federal money into the southern economy, helping raise per capita income and thereby providing a firmer and broader market for southern industries. After the war the weakness of organized labor in the South, as well as the mild climate, which cut heating costs, attracted northern industry southward. The continuing migration of blacks out of the South also reduced the downward pressure on wage rates that the South's high birth rate had long exerted. Increased expenditures on education and a determined interest by Southerners in economic growth were instrumental in creating a truly New South in the years after 1945. Yet even in 1968 the average wage of workers in manufacturing in the South ($2.50 per hour) ranked below the national average ($3.01) because the South's principal industries—textiles, lumber, furniture, and apparel—were low-wage industries.

There is no need, though, to qualify the story of Texas' growth, which was spectacular not only for the South, but for the nation as well. Many of the new growth industries which were located in Texas, like chemicals, instruments, and airplane construction, doubled or tripled in output between 1947 and 1960. The proportion of the state's labor force engaged in agriculture fell from 16 to 9 per cent during the 1950s alone. Yet in 1970 Texas' agricultural production surpassed that of California, making it the country's largest producer of farm goods (principally cattle and cotton). The new Texas millionaires and the burgeoning economy of the state, based securely upon its large reserves of oil, became a source of both humor and envy throughout the rest of the nation.

But not even Texas could equal California in growth and prosperity. In the course of the 1960s California became richer than many nations. Actually it was bigger than all but four of the countries of Europe and its population in 1970 was greater than that of all but four countries in Latin America. In short, California was a country in itself, boasting an informal and flamboyant style of life built around its mild, sunny climate, and possessing a remarkably productive economy. Among the states of the Union, California was first in industrial production and second only to Texas in agricultural output. Almost half the vegetables marketed in the nation were grown in that one state. At the same time, the number of workers engaged in manufacturing increased 82 per cent between 1950 and 1960 alone. In the early 1960s Los Angeles surpassed Chicago as a manufacturing center. Aside from its climate, which minimized both heating costs and absenteeism resulting from illness, a principal reason for the state's fabulous growth was the large number of federal defense contracts it received for airplane and missile construction, particularly during the 1960s. In the course of the 1960s California passed New York as the wealthiest and most populous state.

The New Agriculture. One minor miracle of the postwar economy was the revolution in agriculture. During the nineteenth century the expansion of agricultural production had been one base that supported the nation's successful take-off into economic maturity. But between the First and Second World Wars agriculture stood almost still, blighted and depressed. After 1945, however, farmers once again made a major contribution to the creation of an affluent society. Per capita consumption of beef in 1970, for example, was almost double what it had been in 1940. The effort on the land made food cheaper for Americans than for any other people in the world. In western Europe, for instance, workers typically spent about 25 per cent of their income for food; in the Soviet Union the proportion was nearly 50 per cent, in Japan it was 35 per cent, and in Venezuela it was 28 per cent. In the underdeveloped countries almost all of a worker's income went for food. In the United States in the early 1970s about 18 per cent of an average family's income was taken up by purchases of food, even though food prices in the United States were rising at a faster rate than in western Europe.

The relatively low cost of food to Americans was a measure of the high level of productivity of American agriculture, an achievement that was reached only through a social transformation. For though agriculture became efficient, competitive, and scientific, as the above comparisons argue, it was not always so, nor did all farmers in the early 1970s meet that description. During the 1950s farming in the United States entered upon that lengthy transition through which industrial labor had passed during the middle years of the nineteenth century—that is, from small individual enterprise to the highly capitalized business. In the course of the nineteenth century urban workers gradually, if reluctantly, recognized that they could not compete with big business and so they became reconciled to working for others. (It will be recalled that the Knights of Labor as recently as the 1880s were still setting as their goal for workers self-employment in industrial cooperatives.) In the years after 1945 farmers were required to make the same adjustment: become a big business or get out of farming.

Because many small farmers refused to abandon farming, at least one fifth of farm families in 1968 received less than $5000 a year from farming. These people—black and white sharecroppers in the South, farmers on marginal lands in Appalachia and the Middle West—actually were as bad off as the poor of the central cities. Indeed in 1968 it was estimated that 23 per cent of the farm population lived below the poverty line, as compared with 12 per cent of the urban population.

Most of the farm goods of the nation were produced on large efficient units that were, in effect, highly organized and highly capitalized factories in the field. Since the 1930s the agricultural acreage had been gravitating into larger and larger units, from an average of 157 acres in 1930 to 394 acres in 1972. Even in 1962 a mere 800,000 farms contained three quarters of all the land under cultivation. The average amount of capital invested per worker in American farms in 1960 was $21,000, or $5,000 more than the amount per worker in nonagricultural enterprises. It was this amazingly high level of capitalization that explained the tremendous productivity of American agriculture that allowed one farmer in 1971 to feed forty-eight other people. As recently as 1960 a farmer fed only twenty-five others.

The great investment of capital was used in a number of ways to increase productivity. One was the liberal use of machines, such as the 4.6 million tractors on American farms in 1969, or the hundreds of thousands of mechanical cotton pickers, combines, and corn pickers, or the airplanes used for spraying pesticides and fertilizers, and even for planting seeds. Advances in chemicals, which made possible the extensive use of pesticides and fertilizers, were undoubtedly a major cause of the enormous increase in agricultural productivity after 1945. Chemicals were used not only to kill harmful insects, but to hasten crop maturity, kill weeds, remove leaves in order to facilitate harvesting, or inhibit unwanted growth. Newly developed chemical fertilizers used in conjunction with new types of seeds doubled wheat and corn yields. The chemical industry also developed new feeds for chickens, which sped up growth and made it possible to raise broilers from egg to maturity in eight or nine weeks. The large broiler houses—three stories high and 600 feet long, containing as many as 50,000 birds all under the control of one person—were a far cry from the makeshift henhouse of the old family farm.

During the 1960s, and especially after the publication of Rachel Carson's *Silent Spring* in 1962, some of the so-called miracle chemicals, particularly pesticides, came under severe attack because of their adverse, sometimes devastating effects upon wildlife and their possible danger to human life. One of the most effective pesticides, DDT, was banned by government order in 1972 after a decade of declining use because of its detrimental effects upon wild animals. Environmentalists objected to many of the new chemicals, but their use was often vital to the continuation of high production in agriculture, which in turn made food available at a relatively low cost to consumers. Higher food prices would be only one of the costs Americans would have to pay if they wished to safeguard their natural environment.

The principal incentive for the increased productivity in agriculture was the government support of farm prices, a policy that began with the New Deal in the 1930s. Once again the role of government in bringing about the postwar prosperity is illustrated. Since the support prices were set at the level necessary to sustain inefficient producers, the policy offered incentives to efficient producers to invest increasing amounts of capital in production and to adopt ever greater efficiencies. For, with a floor under prices, every reduction in the cost of production became an increase in profits for the farmer. In 1961, for instance, support prices were about double the cost of an efficient farmer's production in the best growing areas; the difference between prices and cost was gross profit.

By the 1970s the increase in domestic and foreign demand for agricultural commodities had altered the situation so that price supports were no longer needed to keep up prices. The great stocks of surplus wheat and corn were gone, having fallen 90 per cent in the middle sixties. By 1974 acreage, marketing, and import quotas were being raised by the government for the first time since World War II in order to meet the new demand from home and abroad. In the early 1970s both Russia and China became heavy purchasers of American grains.

Stagnation in Organized Labor. Prior to the 1920s the pattern of labor organization had been that unions gained members in times of prosperity and lost them in times of depression. But this pattern was reversed after World War I. During the twenties, for example, organized labor lost members, despite the general prosperity; in the Depression years that followed trade unions more than doubled their membership, thanks to the encouragement of the National Labor Relations Act and the friendly attitude of the Roosevelt administration. The prosperity of the years after 1945 also contradicted the nineteenth-century pattern. Although membership did not significantly decline in the 1950s, as it had in the prosperous 1920s, it did not keep pace with the growth in the labor force. In 1956 about a third of nonagricultural workers were organized into labor unions; in 1965 the proportion was down to 29 per cent and by 1970 down to 27 per cent.

POPULATION vs. FOOD, 1972

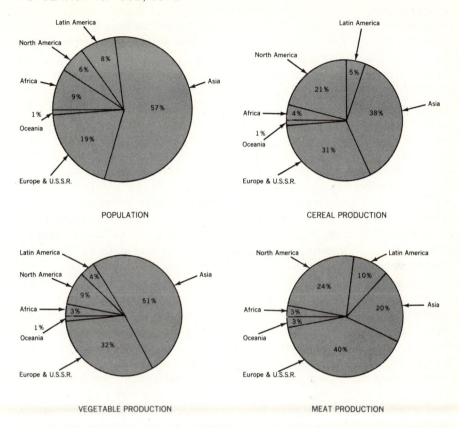

POPULATION

CEREAL PRODUCTION

VEGETABLE PRODUCTION

MEAT PRODUCTION

With only 25 per cent of the world's population, the industrially advanced regions, North America, Europe, and the U.S.S.R., produce 52 per cent of the world's cereal, 41 per cent of the world's vegetables, and 64 per cent of the world's meat. Although Latin America produces more than its share of meat, much of this meat is exported to the countries that can afford it. To make matters worse, the regions of the world that do not produce enough to feed their people have the highest birth rates (from 2.3 to 2.9 per cent annually for the underdeveloped regions, as compared with .9 to 1.2 per cent for the developed regions). *Source:* Food and Agriculture Organization of the United Nations.

This stagnation or even decline in labor organization could be attributed to several causes. One was undoubtedly the stodginess of the labor movement itself. Once militant, enthusiastic, and convinced of its mission, it had become fat and satisfied during the 1950s, resting on the successes of the turbulent thirties. Many of its leaders were old men—the head of the A.F. of L.-C.I.O., George Meany, was born in 1894—veterans, to be sure, of the great organizing drives of the earlier years, but now tired and lacking in imagination. There were few dynamic young men to take their places. Moreover, despite the energy and idealism still evident in a leader like Walter Reuther of the automobile workers, who died in 1970, some of the more energetic new leaders, like James Hoffa of the Teamsters Union, who went to prison for corruption, made organized labor unattractive to outsiders. Many of these new leaders displayed only a narrow conception of labor's role in society. In Germany and Britain, by contrast, many labor unions were demanding, or had already secured, seats on the boards of directors of large corporations to provide workers with a greater voice in management. By the 1950s, too, many large corporations in the United States had learned well the lesson of the 1920s; they gained a favorable public reputation and simultaneously undercut union organizing drives by anticipating some of the demands of their workers for fringe benefits and higher wages. The chemical industry, for example, was able to prevent national unions from organizing its workers simply by accepting independent unaffiliated unions. But undoubtedly the principal reason for the stagnation in trade union membership was the changing shape of the employment structure.

The Dominance of White Collar. In *The Conditions of Economic Progress* (1940), Australian economist Colin Clark pointed out that in a mature industrial society the labor force can be divided into three categories: primary (farming, fishing, and forestry), secondary (manufacturing, construction, and mining), and tertiary (services, trade, and government). One sign of the increasing maturity of an economy, he observed, is the growth of the tertiary category, since such growth is dependent upon the efficiency of the first two. In 1940 about a third of the labor force in the United States fell into the third category; by 1956 half did; by the early 1970s about three fifths of the workers in the United States were rendering services or handling the hard goods which the other two fifths produced. The greatest proportion of the members of this majority were white-collar workers—as distinguished from the so-called blue-collar workers who mined the coal, tilled the soil, and manufactured the goods.

On the one hand, the dominance of the white-collar class testified to the high level of productivity in an economy that could dispense with these workers in fields and factories. On the other hand, it underscored the consumer nature of the modern American economy, for the white-collar class was either distributing the food and goods produced by the blue collars, or providing personal consumer services as physicians, barbers, teachers, TV repairmen, investment counselors, bank tellers, and police officers.

As far as the labor movement is concerned, the importance of the dominance of white-collar workers was the resistance of that class to unionization. Why was this? First of all, by the 1970s about 24 per cent of the work force was composed of professional workers, technicians, or managers, and thus effectively removed from traditional trade union organization. Second, even those many white-collar workers who were less well paid than blue-collar workers did not join unions, principally because they tended to see themselves as having a higher social status than blue-collar workers. Since it was the latter who made up the bulk of unionized workers, many white-collar workers shied away from the institutions and practices associated with blue-collar status. For example, salesclerks, insurance workers, and bank employees, often well organized in Europe, were almost entirely unorganized in the United States. Many white-collar workers in America were quite hostile to labor organizations; for instance, many approved legislation like the Taft-Hartley and Landrum-Griffin Acts, which labor unions strenuously opposed. If the proportion of white-collar workers continues to grow in the advanced American economy, the proportion of workers in unions seems equally destined to shrink unless some breakthrough in organizing workers in the tertiary category of the labor force is achieved.

The Changing Place of Women. A large part of the white-collar class in the early 1970s was made up of women, who after 1940 entered the labor force in ever rising numbers. Between 1940 and 1960, for example, some 9.4 million women joined the ranks of the gainfully employed, as compared with 7.5 million men. In the early 1970s about 44 per cent of women were in the labor force, constituting almost two fifths of the national working force.

For a variety of reasons, the new prosperity made it possible for more married women to work. Employers accepted married women more readily, if only because they needed their skills and labor. Women found jobs in fields like finance and computer programing open to them for the first time as a result of the boom. By the close of the 1950s about one third of all married women were working outside the home, as compared with 17 per cent in 1940. In 1971, for the first time in American history, more than half of all married women worked for money at least part of the year. No longer did one hear the complaint of the Depression years that a working wife deprived a man with a family of a job. It became increasingly commonplace in the prosperous 1960s for young women to continue to work after they married and by the 1970s many young couples began married life with the expectation that both partners would have careers as well as a family. In affluent America marriage ceased to wait on a man's having a good job and a steady income.

Many married women worked, too, simply in order to buy more goods and services for their families. The consumer-oriented nature of American society encouraged the accumulation of goods. Nor should it be forgotten that even in affluent America, most women worked because they had to. Three quarters of all women who worked for pay in 1971 either had no husband at all or had a husband whose income was under $7,000 a year.

Generally the married working woman was a mother. In 1971 out of 18.5 million married working women, 10 million were mothers with children under eighteen. Simply because women were marrying earlier (the median age of marriage in 1971 was 21) and having their children earlier, they have been able to enter or return to the work force after the children had gone off to school. In 1971 almost half of married women with children between six and seventeen (the school years) were in the work force, as compared with only 28 per cent twenty years before. Even women with small preschool children were entering the work force in large numbers. In 1971, for example, 30 per cent of women with children under six years of age were working, as compared with only 12 per cent twenty years earlier. These figures delineated a veritable revolution in the character of the family, the position of women, and the nature of the home during the postwar years, the extent of which is not yet fully evident.

Revolutionary as the large number of working women might be, working has not been especially profitable for women. They continue to be paid less than men: in 1971, for example, women in sales occupations earned an average of $4,485, while men received $10,650; women clerks received, on the average, $5,696, while men in the same general category of work were paid $9,124. Discrimination against women, especially for higher paid jobs and for managerial positions, makes up one third of the charges laid before the Equal Employment Opportunity Commission, created under the Civil Rights Act of 1964.

More women began working outside the home in the 1950s and 1960s, and taking jobs once exclusively reserved for men. Even more significantly, the way women thought about themselves and their place in society began to change in those years. *Photo: Suzanne Arms—Jeroboam*

The continuing discrimination against women and the new job opportunities for women that two decades of prosperity opened up to them combined to produce a women's movement of unusual extent and power. The new feminism of the 1960s and 1970s could be said to have begun with the publication of Betty Friedan's *Feminine Mystique* in 1963. The new movement was both a cause of and a response to the great upsurge in working women, particularly married women. Apparently Friedan's book, which urged women to break out of the home and enter the work force, struck a responsive chord in the minds of many women who were vocationally skilled, yet frustrated with their home-tied lives. Friedan's follow-up organization, the National Organization for Women (NOW), formed in 1966, became a kind of NAACP of the women's movement; it not only attracted the more conservative feminists, but also emphasized the legal approach to breaking down discrimination. More militant groups, often advocating social-ism as the final solution to women's problems, also entered the fray. A national magazine, *Ms.*, devoted to changing the idea of the women's magazine from one concerned primarily with home and children to one pushing women's rights on the job and in politics, became a major new addition to the nation's periodical press.

Thanks to the Civil Rights Act of 1964 and federal executive orders prohibit-ing discrimination on the grounds of sex as well as of race or religion, the federal government forced open new jobs for women in private employments, while insisting that public institutions increase their proportion of women employees, especially in high-level jobs. This new drive to expand opportunities for women opened traditionally male occupations like those of Army general, telephone lineman, jockey, air-traffic controller, and FBI agent to women, either for the first time or in unprecedented numbers. The new women's organizations also mounted a successful campaign to change state laws to make birth control infor-mation and abortions easier to obtain; and they succeeded, too, in arousing a new popular demand—and in some instances, gaining government support—for child-care centers. Child-care centers were not only essential for working moth-ers, but also gave mothers not in the labor force a true choice as to whether or not to seek employment outside the home.

The results of the women's movement were not uniform. As we have seen, the disparity between the wages of women and men still persists, as does the difference in opportunities for advancement on the job. The Equal Rights Amendment to the Constitution, which the women's movement had pushed through Congress in 1972, ran into trouble in many state legislatures. Interest-ingly enough, opposition to the amendment sometimes came from women legisla-tors who preferred protection and privilege in work, rather than equality. But the rising interest of women in politics began to result in new achievements. Women made up 35 per cent of the delegates to the Democratic National Conven-tion in 1972—a hitherto unheard-of proportion—and a black woman, Represen-tative Shirley Chisholm of New York, was placed in nomination for President. The real breakthrough came in 1974 when women won major offices, sometimes for the first time, including the governorship of Connecticut, the Chief Justiceship of North Carolina, the mayoralty of a city of half a million in California, and seventeen seats in Congress. The number of women state legislators jumped 30 per cent. Although the most visible successes have been principally in politics, the change in social attitudes toward women over the preceding thirty years has been highly dramatic. Young women now have before them a much wider range of opportunities and a greater social support for an independent life than at any earlier time in American history.

Chicanos and Amerindians. Women were not the only social group to take a leaf from the Negro revolution's book and seek recognition from the rest of society. One group—the Mexican Americans—were hardly known to most Americans, yet Chicanos, as they often called themselves, made up about 5 per cent of the total population of the United States. Though principally concentrated in the Southwest, hundreds of thousands lived in the Detroit-Chicago area; in short, their disadvantaged social and economic situation—often below that of blacks—was not simply a regional matter. The new Chicano organizations, however, which came into public notice in the 1960s were most active in the South-west and California. In Texas, for example, the Raza Unida party was sometimes successful in local politics. Some of the militant Chicano groups in California went beyond demanding representation in governmental agencies and in private industries and took an active part in the movement against the Vietnam War.

Cesar Chavez was perhaps the best known of the Chicano leaders, principally because of his successful organizing of the California grape pickers, most of whom were Mexican Americans. His grape boycott in 1965–1969 compelled the grape growers to recognize the union and to bargain with it. More Chicanos, too, were now entering the universities and politics, particularly in the Southwest, suggesting that soon they would play a role in the life of the region commensurate with their numbers. Already Congressman Henry Gonzalez of San Antonio was an important figure in Democratic politics in Texas, and Senator Joseph Montoya, also of Mexican-American background, was a leading political figure in New Mexico.

The newest minority group to assert itself in the late 1960s was also the oldest—the Amerindians. Books by militant friends of the Amerindians, like Alvin Josephy's *Red Power* (1971), or by Amerindians themselves, like *Custer Died for Your Sins* (1969) by Vine Deloria, Jr., brought the Amerindian's outlook and resentments to a wider public. Through these books and public protests Amerindians made evident that their objectives for a better deal from American society differed radically from those of blacks, Chicanos, and women. Whereas these latter groups asked for an opportunity to participate more fully and fairly in the comforts of American society, the Amerindians asked to be recognized as different and allowed to keep their separate culture. In effect, of course, that

A member of the American Indian Movement stands guard at Wounded Knee. The occupation ended with the surrender of the protestors and the federal government's promise to discuss AIM charges of broken treaties and demands for compensation. *Photo: UPI*

had been the Amerindians' wish ever since Europeans first arrived in America. Until the Wheeler-Howard Act under the New Deal, however, that wish had not been recognized by the American government. And under President Eisenhower, even that belated recognition had been withdrawn as Amerindians once again were forced off the reservations into society.

In June 1970 the federal government again committed itself to recognizing the special history and place of Amerindians, when President Nixon proclaimed that "the historic relationship between the Federal Government and the Indian communities cannot be abridged without the consent of the Indians." That same year, as a recognition of past injustices to Amerindians, the Nixon administration returned 48,000 acres of land around Blue Lake, New Mexico, which had long been sacred to the Taos Pueblo Indians. Government recognition of the fact that Amerindians did not want to be assimilated into American society, even on an equal basis, was reinforced by public protests. In 1971 a group of Amerindians occupied Alcatraz Island in San Francisco Bay and in 1973 another group occupied the reservation post at Wounded Knee, South Dakota. Although the Bureau of Indian Affairs was headed by an Amerindian for the first time under President Lyndon Johnson, many Amerindians criticized the bureau for being excessively bureaucratic and hostile to the idea of allowing Amerindians to remain separate from the rest of American society if they wished. By 1975 it began to look as if this central aspiration of Amerindians was beginning to be understood, even if not yet fully acted upon by other Americans.

The Limits of Affluence. The significant fact about the high production of the years after 1945 was that the increase in wealth penetrated deeply into the social structure. Other periods in American history, like the 1920s, had been notable for growth and prosperity, but large segments of the population had not been recipients of the new wealth. This was significantly changed in the years after 1945. One measure of the participation of the low- and middle-income people in the prosperity of the postwar years was the 16 per cent increase in the weekly wages of workers in manufacturing between 1947 and 1957, even after changes in prices had been taken into account. Another was the fact that since 1950 the average income of the bottom tenth of the population has gone up about 55 per cent, again taking into consideration price changes. A third measure was the increase in home ownership. In 1940 fewer than 44 per cent of American families, including farmers, lived in homes they had bought; by 1970 the proportion was up to 63 per cent. Moreover, the proportion of Americans who lived below the so-called poverty line steadily declined from 22 per cent in 1959 to 12.2 per cent ten years later. During these same years federal outlays for welfare rose rapidly as the war on poverty advanced. In 1966, for example, federal expenditures on behalf of low-income people amounted to $11.3 billion; by 1971 the figure had more than doubled to $25.5 billion.

Despite the undeniable evidence of the participation of the majority of Americans in the prosperity of the postwar years, the poor and deprived still numbered in the millions. Even when the proportion of the poor was down to 12.2 per cent, that figure still comprised 24 million people, two thirds of whom were white, despite the heavy incidence of poverty among blacks. Moreover, in the early 1970s it became evident that the steady decline in the proportion of Americans below the poverty line was over; in 1970, for the first time in the ten years that figures had been collected on poverty, the proportion increased slightly.

It was also noteworthy that throughout the postwar years, despite the great increase in welfare expenditures under Kennedy and Johnson, the distribution of income barely changed. In 1950 the top 5 per cent of families, in terms of income, received 17 per cent of aggregate income while the lowest 20 per cent received 4.5 per cent. Twenty years later the proportion of total aggregate income received by the top 5 per cent was down to 14.4 per cent, but the proportion received by the lowest 20 per cent was up only to 5.5 per cent. The top 20 per cent of income receivers got about the same share in 1970 as they had in 1950, that is, about twice their proportion of the population. In short, though America in the postwar years was undoubtedly prosperous and most Americans participated in that prosperity, it was hardly egalitarian in income distribution.

The Culture of Affluence in a Nuclear Age

During the 1930s the Depression set the tone and supplied the focus for the culture of the decade; it was the central fact in the lives of Americans. Not surprisingly, a reversal of the economic circumstances of Americans during the years after 1945 brought about a marked alteration in their cultural patterns. The widespread prosperity provided most people with both the money and the time to participate to an unprecedented degree in cultural activities. The new leisure and prosperity also spawned a youth movement whose degree of self-consciousness and activity were unknown in previous American history.

Mass Leisure. The amount of leisure available to the average American worker in the postwar years increased dramatically. The average workweek for the entire labor force, including farmers, was down to 41.5 hours in 1956 from 44 hours in 1940. By 1960 virtually no manufacturing employees worked more than 40 hours regularly, and some highly skilled and therefore powerful unions actually reduced the hours of their members to 35. By the early 1970s some firms were successfully experimenting with the four-day week because they found it reduced absenteeism on Monday morning. Workers, in turn, showed a decided preference for the long three-day weekend. Paid vacations, which had been enjoyed by only about 40 per cent of production workers in 1940, had been extended by the 1960s to almost all employees; moreover, by the 1960s the typical vacation was at least two weeks long, as compared with one week in 1940. Even working hours had become more leisurely in the 1950s. The coffee break, which as recently as 1940 was viewed by most employers as boondoggling, was not only accepted but institutionalized in most offices and factories in the 1950s. Even outdoor construction workers took time off for coffee and doughnuts at a caterer's truck that arrived punctually at the work site each morning.

As might be expected of a people increasingly suburban and property-owning and with more income and more time free from the job, the average American by the 1950s was spending more time outside the home and more money on recreation. Indeed, between 1950 and 1970 the total expenditures for recreation, not including travel, rose more than three times; expenditures on sports supplies and toys rose five and a half times while the amount spent on spectator sports tripled. The number of golfers went up from 3.2 million in 1950 to 10 million in 1970. By 1971 there were over 7 million outboard motorboats in use, an increase of almost 5 million in twenty years. Indicative of the higher incomes Americans were receiving was the fact that the average horsepower of the motorboat engines was five times as great in 1970 as in 1950. The activity of Americans in an age of affluence was also evident in the millions who camped (40 million in 1970) or rode horses (16 million). National park attendance rose steadily from 33 million visitor days in 1950 to over 200 million in 1970.

Foreign travel by Americans reflected their new affluence as well as their restlessness. In 1950 slightly more than 300,000 Americans traveled to Europe or the Mediterranean, but by 1971 the figure was over ten times as great. The statistics also reveal that it was the middle class, rather than the upper class, who were now making trips to Europe. In 1950 the average cost, aside from travel fares, was $742, a sizable amount twenty-five years ago, and the average length of stay was sixty-four days, hardly a period an American with even as much as a month's vacation could manage. But by 1971, despite the increased costs of living abroad, the average expenditure was down to $481 and the stay lasted now only twenty-six days.

Although they enjoyed more free time than ever, Americans in the years after 1945 acted to increase their leisure still further. A great variety of mechanical and electronic contrivances, such as power mowers and cultivators, electric mixers, can openers, shoeshiners, and blenders, were bought to lighten the chores of the home, to use beside the older ones like dishwashers, vacuum cleaners, and washing machines. Prepared foods, which in the 1930s had meant little more than vegetables in a can, now included an amazing range of elaborately processed and packaged foods, from pastry and cake mixes, frozen juices, and prebaked biscuits and breads to frozen fruits, meats, and whole dinners. Even cocktails could be purchased already mixed. The appliances and prepared mixes became so important to a consumption-oriented public that one suspected they were bought for their novelty as much as for the help they provided. Certainly this was true of the electric-powered carving knives, toothbrushes, and can openers. The distribution of some appliances also revealed what Americans were doing with their time. More homes, for example, had televisions in 1970 than had telephones, refrigerators, or washing machines.

There was also a deeper significance to the purchase of mechanical and electronic time-savers. The use of processed foods, along with the widespread distribution of refrigerators, freezers, washing machines, dishwashers, and clothes driers, reflected the steady movement of wives out of the home and into the paid labor force. As we have seen already, during the 1950s and 1960s more women entered the labor force than men; they were principally married women who had never worked before or were resuming work after rearing their children. Even the drudgery connected with baby care was eliminated when possible. Diaper services, disposable diapers, and commercially prepared baby foods were widely used for the first time during the 1950s and 1960s.

Despite the increased interest in outdoor activities, travel, and sports, and the importance of television as the chief evening entertainment of Americans, other cultural activities also flourished in the hothouse of prosperity. Prior to 1939 the paperback book was virtually unknown in the United States. That year Pocketbooks, Inc., brought out its first twenty-five titles. By the middle sixties over 38,000 titles were in print in paper; by 1974 the figure was over 117,000. The number of new books published in all forms increased more than three times between 1950 and 1970, though many Americans remained neither book readers nor book buyers.

The widespread availability of paperbacks, cheap phonograph records, and cheap art meant that Americans were in the paradoxical position of becoming more alike in the midst of a greater variety of cultural forms. The differences in life-styles in the West or the South, which once had been quite distinguishing, were rapidly being eliminated by the mass production of goods, cultural and otherwise. Class differences in dress were similarly being reduced or eliminated by mass production and prosperity. Furthermore, increased mobility within the country continually weakened regional differences, hastening the end of the regional accent, dress, and attitude, while bringing into the homes of all regions a greater array of consumer goods than any other people in world history had enjoyed on such a broad social scale. This dispersion of wealth created mass markets that in turn spawned novel and often unnecessary consumer items, further reinforcing the urge to buy more and own more. The choices open to Americans because of their prosperity were undoubtedly wider than ever before in history, yet ironically the result was a greater homogeneity within the society than ever before. In fact, a reaction against this homogeneity and consumerism— the rise of a self-conscious youth movement—was one of the most significant social developments of the postwar years.

The Young Protest. Young people in America had never been known for their political or social concerns, as, for example, students sometimes had been in continental Europe. But a series of events and circumstances came together in the 1960s to change that once and for all. The upheaval among the young during that decade did not erupt without warning. In the late 1950s, for example, poets like Allen Ginsberg and writers like Jack Kerouac had anticipated in their attacks on materialism, conventionality, and the "straight world" something of what many young people would be asserting loudly in the next decade.

Underlying the great wave of student protest, dissent, and dissatisfaction of the 1960s was prosperity. Because Americans were relatively well off, many became obsessed with material goods, and it was against this, among other things, that many of their children revolted. Ironically, it was prosperity that made the revolt possible.

Because of prosperity many young people could postpone going to work and attend college, where they began to see themselves as a special group, dramatically different in outlook from the adults around them. There they learned to wear a distinctive costume—blue jeans, denim shirts, sneakers or sandals—that set them apart from the rest of society and welded them into a self-conscious group of their own. The new involvement of the federal government in support of higher education helped expand the college population by providing financial assistance to students and to universities seeking to expand their facilities. The advanced, technical economy, too, demanded that many more young people go to college to learn the skills and to gain the knowledge needed to run the economy of the 1960s.

The prosperity of the times also put more money into the hands of young people than ever before, either because there were jobs for the young or because prosperous parents gave their children more money to spend. Many parents who had grown up in the Depression with poor-paying jobs or none at all wanted to make sure that their children lived better than they had. As a result, whole new markets opened up for clothes, records, books, travel, and recreation, all of which were specially directed to young people. This too enhanced that sense of difference and importance that was fundamental to a cult of youth in the 1960s.

The principal catalyst that transformed the new self-consciousness of youth into social protest was the Negro revolution. Although the black protest began in the late 1950s, it gained a special relevance for young people in 1960 with the sit-ins by young black students and then the voter registration movements in the middle sixties. Idealistic white students went South with black students to protest racial discrimination and prejudice, a protest which culminated in 1965 in a huge biracial civil rights march in Alabama from Selma to Montgomery.

As young people discovered the gap between American professions regarding black Americans and reality, they began to discover other failures of adult Americans to live up to the country's ideals. In an affluent society there seemed little or no excuse for the poverty in American cities or in the rural South. As a result radical movements like Students for a Democratic Society (SDS) attracted much wider attention on American college campuses than revolutionary groups usually had in the past. As one former SDS worker later said about the 1962 Port Huron platform of SDS, "It's an idealistic, post-scarcity statement. There is no reason why America, given its resources, given its political development, should be so crass about the needs of poor people."

The new interest in social causes, which contrasted sharply with the complacency of students in the 1950s, was also evident in the enormous popularity of young singer Bob Dylan. Dylan's pilgrimage in 1960 to the bedside of a dying folk singer of the 1940s, Woody Guthrie, symbolized the beginning of the new era. Instead of singing love songs, Dylan wrote and sang about war, bigotry, and nuclear destruction. His songs became a trademark of the early sixties; his audiences were made up of thousands of young people, standing hand in hand, swaying to his songs, his guitar, and his message. It was Dylan's "Blowing in the Wind" that Joan Baez, another of the early pop-folk singers of the sixties, sang to the Berkeley students in 1964 when she urged them to sit in at Sproul Hall, the administration building. Indeed, the upheaval at Berkeley in 1964–1965, before the concern with Vietnam became acute, was another sign of the interaction between affluence, higher education, and the uprising of the young in the 1960s. The University of California at Berkeley, with its 27,000 students, represented the bigness, impersonality, and order that made many young people unhappy about America.

The student demonstrations which punctuated the late 1960s, however, were only partly related to the enormous growth of universities. Sometimes the student disruptions were sparked by a concern for the neighboring community upon which the university was said to be unfairly encroaching. This was the ostensible cause of the student occupation of Columbia University in 1968 and to a certain extent of the student riot at Harvard the next year. Cornell's ordeal came over the issue of the black students' place on the campus, along with other dissatisfactions.

But the most frequent basis for the hundred or more disruptions on American college campuses in those years was the growing student dissatisfaction with the war in Vietnam. Most male students had a direct stake in the war after 1965, when the large scale of American involvement necessitated taking draftees, almost all of whom were college age. Since college students were exempt from the draft as long as they stayed in college, the universities became a natural focal point for those discontented with American society or American policy. Moreover, the rapidly mounting cost of the war dramatized to many students the perverse use American society seemed to be making of its great wealth and productivity. That the protests released forces that could not always be controlled also became evident on some campuses when buildings were burned, guns fired, or bombs exploded.

By 1974 demonstrations were a rarity on American college campuses, though they continued to bedevil European university administrations and faculty. (In 1968–1969 demonstrations and revolts had occurred on university campuses throughout the world, notably at the University of Paris, showing that the war in Vietnam was not the only cause of student discontent.) At some American colleges the uninterrupted academic routines of the early seventies were a novelty after almost half a decade of annual outbursts of protest, disruption of classes, and even violence. Why the demonstrations subsided is not entirely clear, though the end of the draft and the deaths of students, notably the killing of a student at the University of Wisconsin in 1971 by a bomb, undoubtedly played a part. Also, some student demands had been met by granting them a larger role in university governance and in curriculum planning. College administrations, too, had become more adept at handling demonstrations and containing them or heading them off.

The Counterculture. The campus demonstrations were only the physical manifestation of a deeper revolt against the intellectual and social status quo during the 1960s. The intellectual revolt was not confined to the young, either, for many professors and intellectuals helped shape the new outlook. One professor, Theodore Roszak, coined the phrase that came to describe those who found the America of the 1960s wanting. He called the new outlook the Counter Culture. And for many young people, that was what they were seeking: a new way of life that rejected the materialism, hypocrisy, racism, and callousness, as well as the discipline, hard work, and highly organized institutions, that they perceived in America. The informal dress and long hair of many college students not only united them, but symbolized as well the young people's indifference to distinctions of class or race. Individuals, these young people insisted, should be recognized for their human dignity and not for what society said they were. The young's impatience with, if not hostility toward, personal distinctions of dress and manner and their rejection of deference to authority in general were denounced by establishment spokesmen like President Nixon and Vice-President Agnew as the consequences of "permissiveness."

The young people of the counterculture were not content with asking adults to live up to their own ideals; they also began to question some of the adults' values. Perhaps the most profound difference between many young people and their elders—and the most threatening to the latter—was the emphasis the young placed upon feeling. Adults seemed afraid of their feelings, embarrassed by their bodies, and wary of their impulses, while the young gloried in sensation, paradox, and imagination. They were especially interested in mysticism, the occult, Zen

Buddhism, and the writings of existentialist psychiatrist R. D. Laing because all rejected traditional science, logic, and reason.

Actually, the very emphasis the young placed upon emotion and feeling betrayed their new romanticism. For feeling and sensation had also been the interest and the message of the young romantic poets and writers of the early nineteenth century who were in revolt against the reason and reasonableness of the eighteenth-century Enlightenment. Certainly the emphasis upon feeling helps explain the interest in hallucinatory drugs, particularly marijuana, which enhances feelings and imagination while dulling reason and rational thought. It is relevant that nineteenth-century romantics like Samuel Coleridge and Thomas de Quincy, when in search of new experiences and images, had also used drugs.

Another sign of the interest of young people in feeling was the enormous popularity of loud, deeply rhythmic "rock" music, both live and on phonograph records. (By 1974 more money was being spent on recordings than on admission to movies.) Rock music itself was a reflection of the new electronics of the time, for the loudness required the advanced technology of sound amplification, electric guitars, and other electronic equipment that could produce sounds that had literally never been heard before. The character of the music symbolized the values of the counterculture, also, for the very loudness enveloped and involved the listener along with the performer. The music too was new, despite its origins in Negro blues and jazz, for now it was sung by whites to whites, and with new musical twists and increased volume. Even the old-fashioned blues songs became something different when Janis Joplin, one of the white singing stars of the late 1960s, sang "Ball and Chain" to a crowd of white middle-class young people.

Out of the new interest in rock came the discotheque, with its blaring, beating recorded music, its changing-colored strobe lights, and its small dance floor crowded with jerking, jumping dancers. The discotheque was imported from France to Los Angeles in 1961, where it quickly caught on among young people. The new dancing abandoned intricate, precise steps and closely synchronized movements between dance partners. Instead dancers were free to do "their own thing" in time with the strong beat of the ear-splitting music. The vigorous, body-contorting, often erotic dancing of the young made the decorous foxtrot or the graceful ballroom dancing of the previous generation seem like something out of another culture, as, in a sense, it was. As Elmer Valentine, who opened the first discotheque in America, later said, the new dancing of the 1960s epitomized the new attitudes. "Years ago to be a good dancer you had to get ballroom dancing. If a person was a little shy, he went to the dance studios and got taken for a lot of money. Here all you have to do is keep time with the music. You do whatever you want, you ad-lib. You're the creator of your own dance."

Another keynote of the counterculture was the emphasis upon immediate pleasure. It was reason that counseled waiting and preparation before satisfying one's wishes and urges. To this argument of the adult world, the young of the affluent society replied that life was now, not tomorrow. They saw little need to wait until they had a good education, a paying job, or a bank account before they saw the world, lived with their beloved, or followed their other impulses. For them making money or working for a home in the suburbs did not represent the best possible life, as it had for many earlier young people. Worthwhile living meant doing what was interesting rather than what paid well; it meant having satisfying relationships with people rather than competing with them. At its best the counterculture emphasized cooperation rather than competition, or as one of the popular slogans of the time phrased it, "Make Love, Not War."

Like earlier romantics, young people often assumed that men and women were essentially good, that only wrong ideas or institutions were responsible for the evils in an affluent society. As another professor, Charles Reich, the author of the best-selling defense of the counterculture, *The Greening of America* (1971), wrote, "There is nobody whatever on the other side. Nobody wants inadequate housing and medical care—only the machine. Nobody wants war except the machine. And even businessmen, once liberated, would like to roll in the grass and lie in the sun. There is no need, then, to fight any group of people in America. They are all fellow sufferers."

To many adults, particularly those who remembered the Great Depression, the counterculture was based on shockingly impractical philosophy. Some were quick to charge that it would persist only as long as its exponents continued to be subsidized by their parents or at least knew that they could always turn to their parents in time of financial stress. And it is true that within three years after the appearance of Reich's optimistic book on the triumph of the counterculture —or what he called "Consciousness III"—the picture was considerably darker. Contrary to his assertions, there were many opponents of good medical care, better housing, and other reforms needed in America. And only too often those opponents were in positions of great political and social power. But some young people did manage to live by their philosophy of the 1960s without help from parents and though the communes that had sprung up around the country may have dwindled, some survived into the seventies.

The phrase "the generation gap" came into prominence during the 1960s to describe the conflict between the young and adults, but its widespread use obscured the fact that the counterculture and the young who espoused it undoubtedly influenced society. The changes could be seen in the long hair on businessmen and truck drivers as well as on "hippies." Blue denim clothes for adults and the new bright and varied colors of men's dress showed that the counterculture had in part, at least, been co-opted. Marijuana smoking became so fashionable among adult intellectuals and young business people that many college students went back to beer and cheap wine. Some states reduced the penalties for marijuana smoking as the fears about its addictive effects began to dissipate in the face of findings from the many studies interest in the drug had evoked during the 1960s. On a broader level, the nation gave recognition in 1971 to the seriousness and responsibility of the young by quickly passing the Twenty-sixth Amendment, which lowered the voting age to eighteen. Even more significant was the fact that by 1974, forty-one states, including the most populous, California and New York, went on to lower the age of majority from twenty-one to eighteen for almost all legal matters.

"The Straights." Because the young of the counterculture were vocal and because they affected the remainder of society so profoundly, it was easy to mistake them for the majority of young people. That they were a minority of the young does not alter the fact that their influence was significant. But by the same token it would distort the picture of the last decade to ignore the majority of young people who did not attend college, did not participate in antiwar demon-

strations, or did not campaign for Eugene McCarthy, Robert Kennedy, or George McGovern. In fact, most of those who attended college in the 1960s, as earlier, probably did so in order to get a good job and to do better in life economically than their parents. College remained the great social escalator in America in the 1960s, as it has been since the 1920s. Many young people worked for the reelection of Nixon and Agnew; postelection surveys showed that young people did not vote as heavily as adults and that when they did they divided their votes more or less equally between Nixon and McGovern. Furthermore many of the college-age students who did not go to college heartily disliked the counterculture and its denial of traditional American values and standards.

The counterculture and the activities of the young were only one, albeit important, sign of a change in attitudes and outlooks in the postwar years. Among the values the young emphasized was individualism—the right of individuals to run their own lives and to work out their own futures. Although the gap in age, experience, and outlook between young people and the Supreme Court was indeed great, the Court nevertheless displayed a concern for the individual that was not only judicially and constitutionally important, but was an additional measure of the culture of affluence. It is not without relevance, for example, that Richard Nixon criticized the Court as well as the young for "permissiveness."

Individualism in the Law

The New Freedom of the Supreme Court. Prior to 1945 the Supreme Court was best known as the guardian of the established order. But in the 1950s it assumed a new position as the defender of individual rights, even when the accused were Communists. In the case of *Yates* v. *United States* (1957), for example, the Court seriously modified the decision in *Dennis* (1951), which had upheld the conviction of eleven Communist leaders for conspiring to advocate the overthrow of the government by force in violation of the Smith Act (1940). In the *Dennis* decision Chief Justice Vinson had written that the mere existence of "a highly organized conspiracy" to overthrow the government gave the government the right to act. In the *Yates* decision in 1957, under a new Chief Justice, Earl Warren, the Court found that a purely abstract belief in the advocacy of force, which the Smith Act proscribed, was protected by the First Amendment and could not be the basis for a criminal proceeding. Moreover, the Court continued, "mere membership or holding of office in the Communist party" was not sufficient proof of specific intent to "incite" persons to overthrow the government.

That same year, in *Watkins* v. *United States,* which upheld a defendant who had admitted past Communist activities but had refused to disclose the names of Communist associates, the Court, in effect, warned congressional investigating committees that not every kind of question asked of a witness was constitutionally permissible. A citizen had the right to be fully informed of the purpose of the inquiry before he or she answered questions; Congress, the Court asserted, cannot "expose the private affairs of individuals without justification." The constitutional rights of citizens under congressional investigation, the court further declared, included freedom of speech, of political belief, and of association and protection against self-incrimination. Boldly the Warren Court defended the rights of the individual citizen against one of the most treasured powers of Congress: the power to secure facts for the writing of legislation.

In a decision in 1964 that declared unconstitutional an act of Congress denying passports to members of the American Communist party, the Court continued to protect the rights of all individuals. Indeed, a rare encouraging development to come out of the McCarthy period was the clarification and strengthening of all Americans' civil rights once the courts had an opportunity to review the antisubversive legislation and the excessive zeal of congressional committees which the Great Fear had spawned.

A striking measure of the extent of the Court's defense of individual rights was the series of decisions in the 1960s protecting the rights of persons accused of crimes. In *Gideon* v. *Wainwright* (1962) the Court not only overturned a twenty-year-old precedent but took an important step in providing equal justice for the poor. At his trial for burglary, Clarence Earl Gideon, a fifty-two-year-old, four-times-convicted ne'er-do-well, had asked for a court-appointed lawyer because he could not pay for one himself. The refusal of the trial court to provide a lawyer caused the Supreme Court to order a new trial on the grounds that without a lawyer Gideon could not receive a fair hearing, as required by the Fourteenth Amendment. (At his second trial, with a lawyer, Gideon was found innocent.) After the Gideon decision a number of states began to provide for public defenders or to appoint lawyers for defendants too poor to hire their own. In 1972 the Court extended the Gideon principle to all criminal cases, misdemeanors as well as felonies, thus assuring that no person would be denied counsel because of lack of money.

In a series of cases between 1963 and 1966 the Court went beyond Gideon in defense of the individual, ruling that the police must not in any way jeopardize an individual's right to the presumption of his or her innocence, even when in pursuit of a known criminal. In the most recent case, *Miranda* v. *Arizona* (1966), the Court ruled that no suspect could be questioned by the police without having his or her lawyer present. Although many law enforcement officials and others vehemently disagreed with the Court's approach, arguing that it would seriously handicap the work of the police, it was evident that the Court was striving to protect individual rights even in the face of a rising crime rate. Like those who probed to the realities of the social position of blacks, rather than stopping merely with their formal rights, the Court was insisting that justice for the poor and the weak on the one hand and for the well-to-do and the powerful on the other must be as nearly equal as possible. Like the protesting students and some of the novelists of the period, the Court sought to reduce the hypocrisy in the society.

The Court continued its concern for individual freedom by overturning in 1967 a Virginia law that had prohibited marriage between blacks and whites. A unanimous Court held that "freedom to marry" cannot be restricted on grounds of race alone. The decision was broad enough to strike down the antimiscegenation laws of the fifteen other states with restrictions on freedom of individual choice in marriage. The following year the Court upheld the right of illegitimate children to institute damage suits, asserting that such children "are humans, live and have their being," and therefore cannot be denied the protection of the Constitution. And in 1973, in a landmark decision that overturned laws in many states, the Burger Court ruled that no state may deny a woman's right to an abortion within the first three months of pregnancy.

The Court on the Side of the Cities. If the Court's decisions reflected the prevailing concern for the individual in a mass society, its decisions on legislative apportionment reflected the importance of the city in American life. Although population had been concentrating in cities for a generation, that social fact had not been mirrored in the distribution of seats in the state legislatures. The principal reason was that these legislatures were controlled by rural representatives, who refused to make any changes that would diminish their power. Protests by urban representatives were to no avail. Recognizing the impasse, the Supreme Court intervened in the case of *Baker* v. *Carr* (1962), which was as significant in the urban history of the United States as *Brown* v. *Board of Education* was in social history. The *Baker* case derived from Tennessee's refusal to reapportion its legislative seats in accordance with changes in the distribution of population since 1900, when the last redistricting had been made. Until *Baker* the Court had held that such an inequity was a political question beyond its jurisdiction. But in the *Baker* case the Court ruled that markedly unequal districts constituted an inequity for which the courts could rightly be expected to provide a remedy.

The Court did not stop there, however. In an almost equally revolutionary decision, *Reynolds* v. *Sims* (1964), the Court applied to the upper houses of the state legislatures the same principle it had asserted for the lower houses—that is, that districts in a given state must be of roughly equal population. In pithy justification of his position, Chief Justice Warren wrote, "Legislators represent people, not trees or acres." The implication was that even if the voters wished to give special representation to rural regions, the Constitution, as interpreted by the Supreme Court, prevented them from doing so. Since the *Sims* decision destroyed the last bastion of the declining rural interests in the states, it aroused great opposition. But a congressional attempt to pass a constitutional amendment which would overturn the decision of the Court failed in 1965. The urban majority was well represented in Congress, even if its power was not yet effective in the individual states. And already in a state like Georgia, where malapportionment had long given the rural interests predominance, the big city of Atlanta played a new and powerful role in the legislative and gubernatorial elections of 1963 and 1964. By 1971 more than half of the states had reapportioned their legislatures. In view of the needs of the cities, the more equitable representation had not come a moment too soon.

The Blighting of the Cities

The Explosion of the Suburbs. Since 1920 a majority of Americans had been living in towns or cities of 2500 population or more. By 1970 about 70 per cent of Americans lived there and the urban tide seemed irreversible; each census reported a further decline in the number of people living in rural areas. But the movement from country to city was not uniform, for after the Second World War Americans began to alter the kind of cities in which they lived. The flight to the suburbs, which had begun in the 1920s, became a mass exodus in the 1950s. The editors of *Fortune* magazine compared the movement in 1953 to the great immigration into the United States in the early twentieth century. About as many people—1.2 million—moved to the suburbs that year as entered the United States in 1907, the high-water mark of European immigration. The suburbs to which these restless apartment and tenement dwellers of the 1950s moved were most often sprawling developments, composed of thousands of one-family houses, often of the same design and price range. But these bulldozer-created suburbs did provide more space for the children, cleaner air, and less congestion than the industrial city.

What began in the 1950s as a move to the closest thing to "the country" for city workers became in the 1960s a part of the transformation of urban life. In place of the twofold division of rural and urban, American society by the 1970s was divided into three groupings: the central city or metropolitan area, the suburb, and the rural area. Between 1950 and 1970 the central cities of the nation—the old industrial and commercial centers—grew by 10 million people, but the suburbs surrounding them grew during the same years by 35 million. By 1970 there were more Americans living in suburbs than in central cities or rural areas. America had become suburban. Not surprisingly, therefore, the censuses of 1960 and 1970 showed marked declines in the population of the principal cities of the nation for the first time in history. Between 1950 and 1960 all but one (Los Angeles) of the six cities with populations over one million lost people. And between 1960 and 1970 sixty-one of the 153 cities with populations over 100,000 declined in size.

More important was the fact that the suburbs of the 1970s were of a new kind. No longer could they be considered merely "bedrooms" for people who worked in the central cities; they were now urban environments in their own right. They contained not only sprawling shopping centers, but large, modern factories and office complexes, and other sources of jobs. In 1970 it was calculated that the suburbs of the country provided over 10 million jobs, just a million fewer than the central cities of the nation. During the seventies, it seemed safe to predict, the suburbs would outdistance the metropolitan centers not only as the primary place of residence of Americans, but of work as well.

The new suburbs, which affluence encouraged and sustained, had a serious drawback. They permitted white Americans to leave the poor and the dark-skinned behind in the central cities. For the suburbs were overwhelmingly white as well as well-to-do. The central cities, on the other hand, were the homes increasingly of blacks, Puerto Ricans, Chicanos, Chinese, and the new immigrants from the Philippines, Portugal, and Italy. Although blacks, for example, made up about 11 per cent of the nation's population, in 1970 they constituted only 4.7 per cent of the suburban residents. In that way affluence facilitated and sustained social division and prejudice in American society.

The World the Automobile Made. It was primarily the automobile that made the flight to the suburbs possible and brought about the decline of the central cities. And it was the automobile that made it possible for the suburbs to become places of work as well as of residence. Almost three quarters of suburbanites in 1970 depended upon their personal cars to get to work, as compared with 58 per cent of city dwellers. The widespread ownership of automobiles was itself a measure of the affluence of Americans. Between 1940 and 1955 the number of cars in use doubled; by 1970 the number of cars on the roads was sufficient to put the nation on wheels simultaneously, with about two persons in each vehicle.

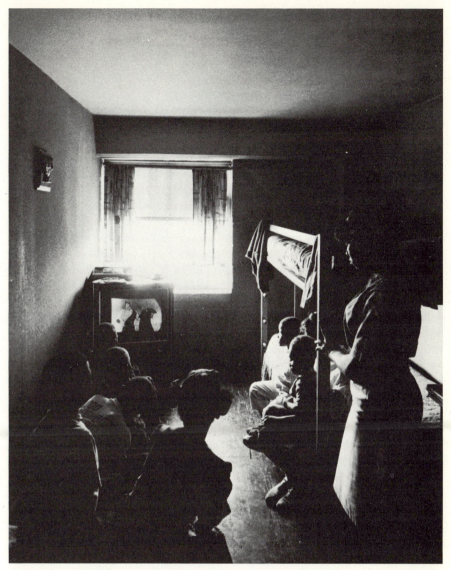

Urban renewal programs sought to replace dilapidated old tenements with good cheap housing for the poor. But the root causes of poverty, including discrimination and overcrowding, remained. *Photo: A. Lieberman*

The very prevalence of the car created almost as many problems as it solved. It may have made the escape from the central city possible and given mobility to the average American such as no monarch in the past could command, but it also choked the cities with traffic, covered the landscape with freeways and turnpikes, filled the air with noxious gases, and raised ugly banks of smog across the sky. The automobile may have freed many workers from the tyranny of commuter trains and trolley and subway lines, but it became itself a tyrant by demanding ever larger parking facilities and ever more highways and roads.

As traffic experts pointed out, the automobile was an inefficient means of moving large numbers of people: an automobile with a single driver took up nine times the space required to move a single person in a public conveyance. Yet the convenience of the individual car easily overrode the social efficiency of the commuter train. Since World War II over 150 public transit systems in the United States have been put out of business by the automobile. Thanks to the automobile and airplane together, by 1970 hardly anyone anymore traveled long distances by train. Between 1950 and 1970 the number of miles of railroad track operated for passenger traffic was cut by 70 per cent. Most American children in the 1970s had never ridden even once on a train, though before 1945 few children would have missed that thrill. In 1969, in order to keep some minimal long-distance train service in operation, the federal government set up the National Rail Passenger Corporation (Amtrak) to reorganize and run what remained of the passenger rail service. (Freight trackage, it should be noted, was still about what it had been in 1950.) In 1970 Congress passed the Urban Mass Transportation Assistance Act to help finance urban and interurban mass transit lines. One measure of the need as against the remedy offered was the fact that $400 million was appropriated under the act, but requests amounting to $2.2 billion came from cities and transit authorities. Another was that in 1974 Amtrak required a $200 million subsidy from Congress.

Although by the middle sixties the traffic congestion in the cities called for heroic measures, including a return to public transportation systems, the changes wrought by the automobile were difficult to counter or reverse. For example, as more workers drove to their jobs, more factories began locating in the suburbs without reference to the availability of public transportation. By spreading the population into the suburbs, both for residence and for work, the automobile reduced the concentration of population needed to justify financially a public transit system. In 1970, for example, 60 million Americans used their cars to get to work while only 2.3 million used trains and subways. Only government subsidy could provide fares low enough to meet the obvious social need and compete with the convenience of the automobile.

The world that the automobile created was jeopardized in 1973 when the price of petroleum throughout the world doubled overnight as a result of the Middle East war. Americans were suddenly made aware of how much their new way of life depended upon cheap gasoline. Yet given the many institutions—highways, parking lots, drive-in movies, shopping centers, not to mention suburban factories and offices—that were built around the broadly based ownership of the automobile, it was not likely that the car would play a significantly smaller role in the life of Americans in the foreseeable future. Besides, high as gasoline prices soared in America, they were still only half the level of prices in most of the countries of industrial Europe, where the automobile was only beginning its conquest.

A Multiplicity of Problems. The automobile was but one of the problems that beset the cities and suburbs of the country in the years of affluence. In a sense it was the increasing size of the cities that made their problems so difficult to grapple with. The Athens of Pericles was only the size of Yonkers, New York; Renaissance Florence was smaller than New Haven; Chicago is three times as large as imperial Rome. With over two thirds of the nation's population concentrated in cities and their suburbs, the sheer number of people to govern, the amount of wastes to remove each day, food to distribute, water to supply, crimes to prevent, fires to fight, and air to clean reached astronomical figures. In the years between 1940 and 1961, for example, the production of wastes alone almost tripled.

By the middle sixties the problem of the pollution of the air, water, and landscape had become a national issue. What good was it to be affluent, Americans asked, if the air was foul, the water slimy, and the landscape defaced? Once the concern principally of a relatively few conservationists and sportsmen, the desecration of the environment began to arouse the fears and anger of the average American. As a result, politicians took up the cause in the late 1960s. Both the states and the federal government enacted laws to protect the environment, particularly from the demands and effects of the automobile and the industrial factory, which were the principal offenders. In 1970, for example, Congress created the Environmental Protection Agency to recommend guidelines to industry and to oversee their implementation. Automobiles were required to have devices to purify their emissions, which helped create smog, and factories were required to cease dumping their wastes into rivers, streams, or the atmosphere. Although the laws were not always effective or even adequate to the task, the improvement in the atmosphere and rivers of the country was noticeable by the middle 1970s. If affluence with its emphasis upon economic growth could be blamed for much of the pollution, affluence also made it possible to pay for the

This photo of a steel plant near Pittsburgh graphically illustrates the pollution problem which accompanied increased industrialization. Environmental protection legislation helped make such scenes less common. *Photo: Courtesy of Pennsylvania State Department of Health*

cleaning up of water, air, and landscape. In the nineteenth century the befouling of the environment by industry was much worse, but then neither industry nor government was prepared to spend money to prevent it.

Even in the 1970s, however, the protection of the environment would not be an easy matter. For one thing, it was always cheaper for manufacturers to dispose of their industrial wastes in the nearest stream or into the air. Hence there would always be an economic conflict between producers' desires to lower their costs and the public's interest in an unspoiled natural environment. Nor were manufacturers the only natural opponents of environmental protection. As the public struggle over the building of the supersonic transport in the early 1970s demonstrated, protecting the environment could also cost workers their jobs. For in the case of the SST, the decision not to build the plane because of its adverse effects on the upper atmosphere doomed thousands of people in Seattle to unemployment.

There was also an inevitable conflict between power companies and environmentalists who feared the destruction of the natural wilderness or seacoast when new energy plants were constructed. Yet as the population grew, the economy expanded, and prosperity continued, demands for energy mounted, requiring a steady increase in production facilities. During the 1970s the conflict between those who wanted to expand energy sources and those who feared an adverse effect upon the natural environment came to the fore in the proposals to tap the newly discovered oil deposits in northern Alaska. Oil companies proposed building a pipeline from the north shore to the southern seacoast of Alaska, but this was vehemently opposed by environmentalists who thought the pipeline would destroy a large part of the animal life and vegetation of Alaska. Significantly, the issue was resolved during the oil crisis of 1973, when Congress took the issue out of the hands of the courts, where it had long been tied up by environmentalists seeking to prevent the construction of the pipeline. Fearful of an oil shortage in the near future, Congress ordered that the pipeline be built.

The cause of protecting the environment, which in theory everyone believed in, was no more immune from conflicts of values and interests than other reforms. In fact, given the conflict between the environment and economic growth, it appeared that in the future, as inflation gnawed away at the affluence of the economy, protection of the environment would be more, rather than less, difficult to accomplish.

Artistic Expression in an Affluent Mass Society

Affluence and anxiety were reflected in the artistic life of Americans in the postwar years, too. Some aspects, like painting, mirrored the new forces more than others, but all of the arts showed heightened concern with the identity of the individual in a new world of machines, wealth, and the threat of nuclear destruction.

Individualism in Painting. The years after 1945 opened a new era in painting, both in Europe and in America. The old styles had been profoundly interrupted, particularly in Europe, by the impact of six years of war and Hitlerian domination of the centers of Western art. In painting, as in music, where the medium is not language, communication and influence are international. Thus European artistic developments affected American art, and America, in turn, helped shape the new artistic forms of the postwar years in Europe.

Perhaps the most important influence shaping art immediately after the Second World War was the philosophy of existentialism, primarily as expounded by the French writer and philosopher Jean-Paul Sartre. Existentialism was a natural outgrowth of the destructiveness of the war and the German occupation; Sartre summed up its message in the slogan, "Existence comes before essence." By that he meant that men and women have to make their own lives without reference to tradition, religion, or other institutions. It was the ultimate expression of individualism, for each person was truly alone; it was an individualism more challenging, more demanding than any that had gone before. In artistic terms it meant that the artist would constantly search for originality, for freedom from artistic ancestors or precursors. This emphasis upon the individual was the central concern of the painting of the postwar era.

In American art after 1945 individualism was evident in another way. The prosperity of the postwar years tended to mute the social concerns that had influenced the painting of the 1930s. A few well-known, socially committed artists like Ben Shahn continued to concern themselves in the 1950s with social themes, representationally depicted. As Shahn said in connection with his painting *Miner's Wives,* he assumed "that most people are interested in the hopes, fears, and dreams and tragedies of other people, for those are the things that life is made of." But Shahn's social interests, like his representational style, were clearly a minority approach in the years after 1945. Instead abstract expressionism, as it came to be called, held the center of the artistic stage. Significantly this postwar art flourished in America, where affluence supported a large number of painters and where the emphasis upon the individual had always been strong. Simply because abstract works denied themselves the traditional symbols of visual communication, they fitted into the new individualism and freedom of the 1950s and 1960s. Painting became individually expressive rather than socially communicative. Indeed, as we shall see, communication was not the point at all.

Perhaps the best representative of the new American school of abstract expressionism was Jackson Pollock. He consciously broke with the social concerns of the 1930s, picking up where the great European abstractionists had left off when the war began. "Jackson Pollock broke the ice," said Willem de Kooning, himself an important abstract expressionist of the United States. Even in the 1940s Pollock had shunned the depiction of recognizable figures in his paintings. This complete rejection of representation came to dominate modern art. In the postwar world, more than at any previous period, art was a means of self-release for the artist and self-discovery for the observer. The work of art was keyed to the individual, whether artist or patron, not to society. The absence of the traditional symbols of visual communication made it unavoidably individualistic. Each painting was a distinctly individual statement by the artist, evoking an individual response from the viewer, thus removing any need even for titles. In fact, there often were none. At a time when men and women feared being lost in a increasingly homogenized mass society or being destroyed without warning in a nuclear war, the artistic accent was upon the originality and uniqueness of the individual.

When Pollock talked about his method of painting, the emphasis upon individualism was clear in his deliberate departure from convention and in his desire to be *in* the painting, thereby making it fully his. "My painting does not come from the easel," he pointed out. "I prefer to tack the unstretched canvas to the hard wall or the floor. . . . On the floor I am more at ease. I feel nearer, more a part of the painting, since I can walk around it, work from the four sides, and literally be *in* the painting. . . ."

Typical of Pollock's many paintings is *Blue Poles* (1953), which makes only a vague concession to representation in the eight slanting lines (poles?) that dominate the canvas. With silvery aluminum along with brilliant red, yellow, and orange, as well as cool blue, the huge painting overwhelms the viewer. To some critics the purpose of this and other works of abstract expressionism is to convey the intensity of the artist's personal reaction to an affluent and complex society composed of large organizations, where he is oppressed by the anxiety resulting from the threat of nuclear destruction. As one critic wrote, Pollack was "tortured with self-doubt and tormented by anxiety." But it is also worth remembering that abstract expressionism was not primarily a means of communication; any message had to come from the viewer. To Pollock, for example, "inner reality was the only reality."

The effort to involve the viewer in the work of art was even more pronounced by the so-called pop art that came into prominence in the 1960s in reaction against abstract expressionism. Unlike the earlier art of the period, pop art was highly representational, though in such a way as to shock and disconcert. Ready-made objects were affixed to the canvas, for example, or two quite dissimilar objects that never occurred together in real life were presented in juxtaposition on the canvas. As Claes Oldenburg (1929–   ), one of the prominent pop artists, said, he wanted people "to get accustomed to recognizing the power of objects, a didactic aim." Yet it is important to recognize that communication was not the aim here either, though individual response and effect clearly were. The intention was less subjective than in abstract expressionism—representation was used— and the viewer was forced to make some new associations with the environment.

One of the most important artists in the development of pop art was Robert Rauschenberg (1925–   ). Like Oldenburg, Rauschenberg's purpose was to un-focus spectators' minds, to make them more aware of themselves and their surroundings. In the beginning he tried "minimality," that is, painting in such a way that the hint to the viewer was minimal, as in his several all-white or all-black paintings. But more successful and certainly more typical of his art is a gigantic canvas called *Barge* (1962). Over thirty-two feet long and almost seven feet high, the whole surface of the work is crammed with disparate images, photographs, and objects in no discernible order and for no obvious purpose. The very size of the canvas involves the spectator in the painting, not unlike Pollack's description of his own personal involvement in his work.

If Robert Rauschenberg was the most significant of the American pop artists, Andy Warhol (1930–   ) was certainly the most controversial as well as the most famous. Warhol made his reputation by meticulously reproducing on his canvases common household items, such as Brillo boxes or Coca-Cola bottles. His canvas *Green Coca-Cola Bottles* (1962) shows dozens of bottles, standing side by side, in seven rows, one on top of the other. Some are lighter, some darker, as real bottles of Coke would be. There is undoubtedly some social comment here: on the tendency of a consumer economy to be more concerned with package than with content and on the importance of the machine. But there is also acceptance of these things, as there clearly would not have been in the work of artistic critics of capitalist society in the 1930s and before. The real social commentary in Warhol's art was to make fun of the excessive seriousness and pretension of abstract expressionism by showing that the public would buy anything, even pictures of Brillo boxes or Coca-Cola bottles.

Warhol's associate Paul Morrisey described pop art as "a return to the figure and a ridicule, a further ridicule, of what's called 'art,' or what you might call 'wall hangings.' " But, he went on, pop art was also serious, for "it was an honest thing. It was completely literal and it was extraordinarily direct." Warhol, he said, might be poking fun at pretentious art, but he was not making fun of society, "because society is people. . . . He wasn't ever criticizing society, I don't think at all. His notion was not to criticize. If he was critical of anything, it was forms; art forms, and film forms. He was always out to simplify, to make form a very simple thing."

Individualism in Sculpture. In some modern paintings the line between sculpture and painting was hard to locate since painters in the 1960s increasingly used three-dimensional objects as well as flat surfaces and paint. Collages, for example, were as much a part of the work of Robert Rauschenberg as the more traditional application of paint to canvas. But the movement away from representation that was so conscious in abstract expressionism in painting was also evident in sculpture. And in sculpture one could also see the connection between the ideas and development of the postwar period and artistic achievement. David Smith (1906–1965), for example, one of the most influential sculptors of the years after World War II, was a factoryworker before he became a sculptor. He brought his skills as a metalworker to his art, using large masses and long lines of steel and other metals in his creations, which were not representational. By refusing to disguise the durability and practicality of the steel he used, Smith reflected the honesty Warhol strove for and the counterculture insisted upon. Smith would have nothing to do with the interior world that so preoccupied the abstract expressionist painter. Where Pollock rejected the mechanistic, Smith gloried in it, thereby revealing himself as at once a product and a reflection of the advanced technological society in which he worked.

The sculpture of Louise Nevelson (1900–   ) also mirrored the attitudes and values of the 1960s, for her work was typically made up of different kinds of wooden objects fitted into open-faced boxes, arranged to form a wall or screen. Her sculpture often consisted simply of arranging objects, rather than creating them for the first time, as in traditional sculpture. Like the young people of the counterculture, Nevelson was more interested in the *relationships* of objects to one another than in the objects themselves. They could be obtained from anywhere—they might be discarded pieces of wood or even pieces of junk; it was the arrangement that constituted the artistic creation. In a sense Nevelson's sculpture, described by one critic as "the triumph of relationship over form," was a principal theme in the new sculpture of the 1960s.

The relationship between society and art was seen not only in the technological interest of David Smith's work or in Nevelson's concern with relationships. It could also be observed in the work of some younger sculptors who drew upon the new technology. In California particularly, where the plastics and space industries pioneered new materials and technical processes for handling and shaping plastics, artists began to experiment with techniques to create novel art materials and forms. Some of the artists, in fact, themselves become technicians, actually inventing original plastics or processes from which they created works of art. Bruce Beasley (1939–), for example, devised a method of casting acrylic in volume so he could sculpt it. Before his technical work, acrylic could be produced only in thin sheets.

Literature in an Age of Affluence and Anxiety. A connection between art and social developments was not as obvious in literature as in some kinds of painting or sculpture, but it was there. The ridiculing of pretension and hypocrisy that Warhol emphasized in his work could also be found in several of the popular and important novelists of the period. Kurt Vonnegut's zanily humorous novels that poked fun at pretension, war, and the modern world in general easily fit into the pattern. So did the novels of John Barth and Philip Roth. Barth's *Sotweed Factor* (1960) was at once an accurate reconstruction of seventeenth-century life and a spoof on serious historical novels, while Philip Roth in his quasiporno-graphic *Portnoy's Complaint* (1969) made wild fun of novels about Jewish life. Roth carried his remarkable talent for mimicry and satire into the political area in 1973 with *Our Gang,* a savage comment on Nixon and his entourage. Joseph Heller's *Catch-22* (1961) caught the mood of the young in the 1960s with its magnificently humorous attack upon the routine of the Army and its assertion of the futility of war. Its title passed into the language as a name for any kind of bureaucratic complexity that provided no escape but only a way of further enmeshing a person in a mass of rules and regulations. In that novel, as in many others of the 1960s, literature ranged itself on the side of the individual against the establishment and compulsive orderliness—just as many of the young people of the counterculture did.

From a somewhat different angle, the more traditional and serious writers of the 1950s and 1960s also concerned themselves with individuals caught in a world they did not make or want. Certainly the unsettled state of the post-1945 world encouraged individualistic introspection and self-analysis. The irony of the 1950s and 1960s was that as human beings became more powerful with their rockets, hydrogen bombs, and supersonic jets, individuals seemed to shrink in power. It was almost as if with each scientific gain in the ability to destroy, people felt less and less able to effect changes either in their own highly organized and complex society or in the world at large. Within the United States, as society itself became homogenized and artistic culture spread throughout all classes, the strug-gle to achieve individual identity became as insistent for the novelist as for the painter or sculptor.

Critic Ihab Hassan, writing on the literature of the 1950s, has characterized the protagonists of the novels of the period as being at once rebels and victims. The protagonists typically rebel against organization and society while at the same time they are victims of the state—the greatest concentration of power in modern society—and of technology. Because the protagonists are drawn too small in scale to be called heroes, the emphasis in the novel is upon their in-dividual search for identity. The purpose of many of the novels of the 1950s and 1960s was to find existential fulfillment—that is, freedom of self-identification.

The important thing was action, for in doing something—almost anything—individuals defined themselves; the action differentiated them from the mass, which was often inert and undifferentiated in a modern mass society and culture.

The existentialism of Sartre informed the literature of the postwar years, just as it helped shape abstract expressionism in painting. The novels of Albert Camus, who was a disciple and close friend of Sartre, particularly *The Stranger* (1946) and *The Plague* (1948), were widely read on college campuses and for a while in the 1950s Camus was an intellectual hero of many American college students. His book *The Rebel* (1954) became a handbook for many radicals in the 1960s. Camus summed up his conception of the existential position when he wrote, "I rebel—therefore we exist." Only in the assertion of self against society could an individual's humanity be recognized. Another critic, R. W. B. Lewis, saw the principal novelists of the period as being united on "the subject of self—of acquiring a clear sense of the self or of charging on against fearful odds to an integral self already in being." This concern for individual expression and self-realization was evident in the painting of the period, as we have seen, and also in the counterculture and the commitment of many students to activities on behalf of civil rights and protests against the Vietnam War.

This concern with individuality and identity can be observed in a number of major American novels of the postwar years. Among them should be mentioned James Jones' *From Here to Eternity* (1951), in which a private in the prewar Army fights to maintain his individuality, though he has little. Hence he is at once a victim and a rebel, though against the organization, not society. William Styron's powerful *Lie Down in Darkness* (1951) depicts the deteriorating relationship between a girl and her father in the stifling atmosphere of a small southern town; each searches for his and her own identity as well as for an enduring relationship with the other. In *The Confessions of Nat Turner* (1968) Styron grappled with the search for identity of a black rebel slave. Even clearer is the search for identity in two of the novels of Saul Bellow, one of the most significant writers of the postwar years. In *Henderson the Rain King* (1959) the question of identity is only lightly disguised by fantasy; in *Herzog* (1964) it is quite explicit and focused on an intellectual academic. Finally, mention must be made of J. D. Salinger's *Catcher in the Rye* (1951), which, in portraying the inner rebellion of an adolescent in his own language, not only chronicled the struggle of the hero, Holden Caulfield, for identification and self-awareness, but prefigured the kind of resistance to authority and to conventionality that the young of the 1960s would exhibit. It is not surprising that Salinger became one of the favorite writers of young people in the 1960s.

There are, of course, a number of writers in the postwar decades who cannot be fitted easily into the two themes of the search for identity and individuality in the midst of a mass culture. But that is to be expected when dealing with literally scores of important writers in a particularly rich period of American literature and life. Yet it is worth noticing at least one group of writers who represented a different aspect of the postwar decades. These were black writers, the two most important of whom were James Baldwin and Ralph Ellison. In the books of both there is a deep anger that reminds one of John Steinbeck's *Grapes of Wrath* or John Dos Passos' novels of the 1930s. For as we have seen, blacks lagged behind whites in their participation in the postwar prosperity. Ralph

Ellison's *Invisible Man* (1952) is probably the most highly regarded novel about the black experience in America. Because it straddles both North and South, it depicts black experience with a breadth that the writings of northern blacks like Eldridge Cleaver and Malcolm X lack. Surely the best known black writer of the 1950s and the 1960s was James Baldwin, a former protegé of the outstanding black novelist of the 1930s, Richard Wright, and like Wright, at least for a time, an expatriate in Paris. In his first novel, *Go Tell It on the Mountain* (1953), Baldwin wrote about the great black migration from the South to the urban slums of the North. As the black revolution boiled up in the 1950s, Baldwin revealed himself in a number of nonfiction books as an articulate and powerful spokesman for the black drive for equality. *Notes of a Native Son* (1955), *Nobody Knows My Name* (1961), and *The Fire Next Time* (1963) have become classic expressions of black outrage against white racism.

Baldwin and Ellison may not have fit into the pattern of the search for individuality and self-identity, but they naturally fell in with those who spoke out against hypocrisy and sham. After all, it was the struggle of blacks for equality and freedom in American society in the 1950s that did so much to spark the counterculture and the demands for recognition by young people, Chicanos, Indians, and women. Thus Baldwin spoke for more than blacks or writers when he wrote in 1962: "It is, alas, the truth that to be an American writer today means mounting an unending attack on all that Americans themselves hold sacred. . . . One must be willing, indeed, one must be anxious to locate, precisely, that American morality of which we boast." The obligation of the writer, Baldwin insisted—and most of his fellow writers, as well as many young people, would echo his remarks—is "to tell as much of the truth as one can bear and then a little more."

The End of an Era

Years of Change. The thirty years since the end of the Second World War have exhibited, as the preceding pages have implied, a bewildering array of transformations and surprises. Just think of the most obvious. Before 1945 television, with its enormous impact on culture and communication, was known to only a few advanced technologists. For most Americans in 1945 the rocket, now a source of dread for millions and a part of every national arsenal, was only a Fourth of July spectacular. The idea that men would orbit the earth, much less walk on the surface of the moon, was only a fantasy of science fiction. In the course of those thirty years, too, advances in science virtually eliminated from the lives of most Americans diseases that only recently had been classified as plagues without effective cures: infantile paralysis (poliomyelitis), pneumonia, and diphtheria, to mention only the most important.

Who in the 1930s could have predicted that within three decades the whole edifice of legal racial segregation, which generations of Americans had taken for granted, would be dismantled and black Americans would begin a long deferred participation in the mainstream of American life? Or who in 1945 could have foreseen the transformation of the United States from a continental republic, only intermittently involved in Europe's affairs, to a colossus of imperial power and scope, its armies stationed around the globe, its military and diplomatic commitments ramifying to a hundred countries, and its sons fighting two major wars on the Asian continent? Nor did anyone expect the rapid and complete collapse of the great colonial empires that had begun their rise half a millennium before, when America was being discovered by Europeans.

An End and a Beginning. These and other profound alterations in the lives of Americans are certainly striking. But it is not their novelty that is the principal conclusion to be drawn from the history of the past thirty years. Rather, what seems to be more significant is that the great forces and developments which gave shape and meaning to those years of affluence and anxiety seem now to have run their course. The 1970s, in short, constitute the close of the postwar era and the beginning of a new period in American and world history. The shift was symbolized in the announcement by the new Portuguese government in 1974 that its African colonies would be given their independence. Anticolonialism, as we have seen, was certainly a transforming force in the years after 1945. Of all the European colonial powers, Portugal was the last to surrender its empire. Thus Lisbon's decision in 1974 to grant independence to its colonies truly marked the end of an era; there simply were no more colonial empires left.

If the end of the Portuguese empire neatly symbolized the closing of an era, the alteration in the relationship between the United States and Communist Russia promised actually to change the lives of Americans. For the Cold War between the Soviet Union and the United States shaped more than international relations; it burdened the domestic lives of the American people. By the early 1970s it was clear that the Cold War was ending, if not over. The moderating of the long conflict between the United States and the Soviet Union also meant that NATO, once an alliance of central importance in the postwar years, was losing not only much of its sense of direction, but also a substantial part of its reason for existence, as the conflict between two members of the alliance—Greece and Turkey—over Cyprus in 1974 made painfully clear. A similar sense of purposelessness began to creep into the Common Market as well. In the early 1970s Europe's quest for unity and wealth, which had begun with the Marshall Plan, NATO, and the Common Market, began to falter. In 1974 European observers talked openly of the possibility that the Common Market might break up on the rocks of economic nationalism. Secretary of State Henry Kissinger himself warned of the danger in April 1973. "We are in a period of relaxation of tensions," he said. "But as the rigid divisions of the past two decades diminish, new assertions of national identity and national rivalry emerge."

As a shaper of the postwar world of Americans, the triumph of the Communists in China was second only to the power of the Soviet Union in Europe. It was largely because of the Communist triumph in China that Americans fought two wars in Asia and insisted upon a firm, if discreet, domination of conquered Japan. For two decades the hostility between the United States and Communist China and the subordination of Japan were staples of the Cold War in Asia. By the 1970s, however, the United States and China had entered upon a new and friendlier relationship, and Japan had emerged as the third most productive power in the world and the greatest industrial society in Asia.

The withdrawal of the United States from Vietnam was as important to Americans as to Asians; it promised to make their future quite different from the past. For one thing, the ending of American participation in the Vietnam War removed from American society a prime source of half a decade of national division and social violence. For another, it marked the first serious check since 1945 in the growth of American pretensions around the world. To appreciate the significance of the turning point one need only contrast the words of John F. Kennedy in 1961 with those of Richard Nixon ten years later. Americans, Kennedy said, would "pay any price, bear any burden, meet any hardship, support any friend, oppose any foe to assure the survival and the success of liberty." At the beginning of the 1970s, however, Nixon asserted that "Americans cannot—and will not—conceive *all* the plans, design *all* the programs, execute *all* the decisions, and undertake *all* the defenses of the free nations of the world." The shift did not mean, as some feared, a resurgence of the old isolationism, but it did mean that the United States in the 1970s would play a less aggressive and less active role than it had played during the preceding quarter of a century.

One concomitant of the expansion of American power and responsibility in the world since 1945, indeed, since 1940 at least, was the uninterrupted growth in the power and prestige of the presidency. Those American leaders who had been proud of American achievements in meeting the Depression of the 1930s and in helping defeat two powerful enemies during World War II saw in the presidency the prime agency for dealing most effectively with both domestic and international problems. And many things of which Americans could well be proud were achieved in the years after 1945 by Presidents who used and expanded the great powers of their office. But by the 1970s the dangers, if not the outright evils, of an imperial presidency, as one historian called it, had clearly outrun the advantages. Certainly the Vietnam War had exposed the international dangers that arose from a presidency free from congressional control, and the Watergate scandal had only too frighteningly revealed the threats to constitutional government posed by an imperial presidency. The movement to limit the President's role in foreign affairs and the forced resignation of President Nixon showed that the 1970s marked an end to an era in the history of the presidency, too.

Finally, by the 1970s it was also evident that the domestic and world economic climate was dramatically different from that of the 1950s and 1960s. For most of those years the principal concern of Americans and Europeans alike had been how to prevent economic depression and the recurrence of the mass unemployment that had been so intractable and widespread in the 1930s. By the mid-seventies the central issue in the United States, Europe, Japan—in fact, in the world—was inflation, not falling prices and mass unemployment. Inflation now endangered the affluence that since 1945 had been at once the boast of and the dominant influence on the lives of Americans. Moreover, the worldwide inflation confronted Americans in the 1970s with international as well as domestic conditions substantially different from those they had known over the preceding thirty years.

With the forces and circumstances that have shaped the years since 1945 largely played out, the shape of the late 1970s and after is only dimly discernible. It might indeed turn out to be the "generation of peace" for which President Richard Nixon strove, but clearly it could not be simply a continuation of the thirty years of affluence and anxiety that had gone before.

SUGGESTED READING

The great social changes and innovations of the thirty years since 1945 have been delineated in many books. One attempt to chart the domestic changes for most of the period is John Brooks, *Great Leap: The Past 25 Years in America* * (1966), a popular recital. A document revealing something of the variety inherent in American culture, as well as throwing light on the nature of the 1950s, is the massive but eminently readable Max Lerner, *America as a Civilization* * (1957). Less favorably disposed toward American society and a catalyst for much of the later social criticism is C. Wright Mills, *The Power Elite* * (1956). How a prominent social scientist viewed American society and social change in the 1950s can be gleaned from the influential David Reisman et al., *The Lonely Crowd* (1950).

The economic development of the United States and the nature of the economy have been analyzed in a number of books. Harold G. Vatter, *The United States Economy in the 1950's* * (1963) is excellent; a similar book for the 1960s is badly needed. Agricultural change is handled forthrightly and fully in Edward Higbee, *Farms and Farmers in an Urban Age* * (1963). An informative study of the technological revolution in agriculture is R. W. Hecht and E. G. McKibben, "Efficiency of Labor," in *Power to Produce: Yearbook of Agriculture* (1960). Robert Estall, *A Modern Geography of the United States* * (1972) is really about economic development. Herman P. Miller, *Rich Man, Poor Man* (1971) discusses in clear prose the distribution of income and related matters. A defense of economic growth is intelligently and persuasively made in the popularly written Peter Passell and Leonard Ross, *The Retreat from Riches: Affluence and Its Enemies* (1973).

Perhaps the two most influential books on the nature of poverty in the United States are John K. Galbraith, *The Affluent Society* * (1958), which emphasizes the hard-core character of poverty, and Michael Harrington, *The Other America* * (1962), which brought the issue of poverty to public consciousness. Gabriel Kolko, *Wealth and Power in America* * (rev. ed., 1964) is a statistical and critical study of the distribution of wealth in the United States.

Broader studies of the society of the 1950s and 1960s abound. John K. Galbraith, *The New Industrial State* * (1967) seeks to be realistic about the competitive character of American business, as does A. A. Berle, *Power Without Property* * (1959). The dangers that confront a highly organized and technological society are compellingly emphasized in Jacques Ellul, *The Technological Society* * (1964). A good survey of the problems confronting the cities in the sixties is Mitchell Gordon, *Sick Cities* * (1963); Jane Jacobs, *The Death and Life of Great American Cities* * (1961) is a provocative answer to those who think cities should resemble parks.

A fine study of the improvement in civil liberties gained through court decisions in the 1950s and 1960s is the authoritative Milton R. Konvitz, *Expanding Liberties: Freedom's Gains in Post-War America* * (1966). Anthony Lewis, *Gideon's Trumpet* * (1964) is an eminently readable account of the central civil liberties case of the period by the *New York Times'* legal correspondent. A good general study of the Court is the scholarly Paul L. Murphy, *The Constitution in Crisis Times, 1918–1969* (1972). Critical of the Warren Court is Philip B. Kurland, *Politics, the Constitution, and the Warren Court* (1970). Archibald Cox, *The Warren Court, Constitutional Decision as an Instrument of Reform* (1968) is analytical, but ultimately admiring.

* Available in a paperback edition.

The sixties spurred a number of books on its special intellectual and social character. Rather jaundiced about the decade, but eminently readable, is William L. O'Neill, *Coming Apart: An Informal History of America in the 1960's* (1971). Ronald Berman, *America in the Sixties* * (1968) is more concerned with formal ideas and systems of thought. An interesting, highly informal depiction of the 1960s is Joseph Peter, *Good Times: An Oral History of America in the Nineteen-Sixties* (1973).

The literature on youth and the counterculture is at once enormous and ephemeral. Lewis S. Feuer, *The Conflict of Generations* (1969) is an attempt to put the upheaval into a broad spatial and temporal context by one who is not sympathetic. Kenneth Keniston, *Young Radicals* * (1968) is more favorable, but less wide ranging. Kirkpatrick Sale, *SDS* (1973) is a thorough study of the most important radical youth organization of the 1960s. The intellectual character of the new youthful criticism is dissected with sympathy in Theodore Roszak, *The Making of a Counter Culture* * (1969). The best-selling Charles A. Reich, *The Greening of America* * (1971) should be read as a revealing document of the times rather than as a serious work of analysis.

The literature on the changing place of women is growing fast. The best general book is William Chafe, *The American Woman: 1920–1970* (1972). Cynthia Fuchs Epstein, *Woman's Place* * (1970) delineates the job situation in the 1960s from a sociological point of view; Juanita Kreps, *Sex in the Marketplace* * (1971) does it from the point of view of an economist. The indispensable document of the women's movement is Betty Friedan, *The Feminine Mystique* * (1963).

Books on Chicanos and American Indians are beginning to appear in profusion. A brief historical introduction is Matt S. Meier and Feliciano Rivera, *The Chicanos. A History of Mexican Americans* * (1972); more sociological is Joan Moore, *The Mexican American* * (1970). Two experts on Amerindians have brought together a number of significant short studies in Stuart Levine and Nancy O. Lurie, eds., *The American Indian Today* * (rev. ed., 1968).

There are several good studies of the literature and art of the postwar years. Ihab Hassan, *Radical Innocence: The Contemporary American Novel* * (1961) is excellent and Robert Bone, *The Negro Novel in America* * (rev. ed., 1965) treats an important new development in American literature. Developments in painting and sculpture are examined in a readable manner in Sam Hunter, *Modern American Painting and Sculpture* * (1959). A more recent and superior survey is Edward Lucie-Smith, *Late Modern: The Visual Arts Since 1945* * (1969). Two informative studies of Jackson Pollock are Frank O'Hara, *Jackson Pollock* (1959) and Bryan Robertson, ed., *Jackson Pollock* (1960).

INDEX

son, 105–7, 109, 110–15, 118, 134; and
Kennedy, 100; and labor, 13–14, 15–16, 82;
and McCarthyism, 32–36; and Medicare, 100,
107, 110–11; and Nixon, 149, 150, 152,
155–56, 158–62; and nuclear energy, 14, 26;
and price controls, 12–13; and Supreme Court,
151–52, 187–88, 189; and taxes, 12, 15, 17,
105, 118, 149, 150; and Tonkin Gulf resolu-
tion, 131, 134; and Truman, 15–17, 18, 19,
20–21, 24, 27, 34. *See also* Elections
Corporations, growth of, 166–67
Council of Foreign Ministers, 6, 8
Counterculture, 184–87
Cox, Archibald, 158, 159
Crime Control Act of 1970, 151
Cuba, 64–66, 119, 120, 122–25, 127
Cyprus, 201
Czechoslovakia, 26, 32

D

Dean, John, 156, *illus.* 157
Defense, Department of, 17, 54, 55, 56, 76, 94,
98–99, 121; expenditures for, 54, 55, 76, 89,
121, 167, 170; and nuclear weapons, 54, 56, 58,
80, 89, 121–22; and Sputnik, 88–91
De Gaulle, Charles, 64, 125
Deloria, Vine, Jr., 178
Democratic party, and business, 95; and civil
rights, 70, 80, 92, 108, 118, 154; and Eisenhower, 18, 69, 78, 79, 81, 82; and Kennedy,
80, 91; and labor, 15, 16, 73, 91, 108, 141, 155;
and Joseph McCarthy, 35, 36; and McGovern,
153–55; and Negroes, 20, 80, 93, 99, 110, 139;
and the South, 18, 20, 21, 73, 83, 91, 93, 109,
141, 142, 154, 155; and Truman, 17–18. *See
also* Dixiecrats; Elections
Dennis v. *United States,* 187
Depression (1930s), 1, 14, 19, 71, 75, 82, 105,
165, 175, 180, 183, 186, 202
Dewey, Thomas E., 18, 19, 20, 69, 74, 108
Dillon, Douglas, 81, 94
Dixiecrats (States Rights Democrats), 18, 20
Dixon-Yates contract, 77
Dominican Republic, 128
Dos Passos, John, 199
Douglas, Helen Gahagan, 143
Drugs, 185, 186
Dulles, John Foster, 43, 46, 54–55, 57–60, 62–63,
75–76, 79
Durkin, Martin, 75
Dutch East Indies. *See* Indonesia
Dylan, Bob, 183

E

Eagleton, Thomas, 153, 154
Economic Opportunity Act, 106
Economy, 10–14, 165–71, 179–80, 202; Asian
and African, 43; and Eisenhower, 54, 75–78,
81–82; European and the Marshall Plan,
23–28, 58; Germany, postwar, 5; Great Britain, postwar, 23, 26; Japan, 45, 202; and Johnson, 106, 108, 110, 112, 117, 118, 180; and

Kennedy, 97–100, 110, 180; and Nixon,
149–50, 160; Soviet Union, 3, 119; and Truman, 11–12, 13–14, 17, 19–22, 53. *See also*
Inflation; Poverty; Unemployment
Eden, Anthony, 55
Education, federal aid for, 15, 20, 77, 90–91, 100,
105, 106, 108, 111–12, 150, 169, 182
Egypt, 60–61, 80, 148
Ehrlichman, John, 152, 156, 157
Eisenhower, Dwight D., 69–70, 75, 94, 96, 99,
105, 108, *illus.* 68; and American Indians, 179;
and business, 76, 77, 98; and Castro, 65; and
civil rights, 84–86; and Congress, 72, 74,
78–79, 80–81, 82; and Democratic party, 18;
economic policies, 54, 75–78, 81–82; and Eisenhower Doctrine, 61; election victories,
72–73, 80–81; and foreign policy, 54–56, 59,
61, 62–63, 75–76, 79, 81; at Geneva conference, 59–60; and Hungary, 61; and Korean
War, 53, 72; and labor, 75, 82; and Joseph
McCarthy, 36; and national defense, 54–56,
58, 76, 78, 79; and NATO, 29, 69, 75; and
Nixon, 70, 71, 79, 81, 91; and Republican
party, 15, 18, 54, 69, 70, 74, 78, 79, 80–81; and
Suez crisis, 61; and TVA, 76, 77; and Vietnam,
58–59, 129, 131
Elections, (1946), 13, 14–15; (1948), 18–21, *map*
21; (1952), 69–73, *map* 73; (1954), 79; (1956),
79–81, *map* 81; (1958), 81; (1960), 91–94, *map*
93; (1962), 100; (1964), 107–10, *map* 109;
(1968), 139–42, *map* 142; (1970), 117, 149,
162; (1972), 153–55, 162, *map* 154; (1974), 162
Elementary and Secondary Education Act, 112
Ellison, Ralph, 199, 200
Ellsberg, Daniel, 158
Employment Act of 1946, 14
Environmental Protection Agency, 193
Equal Employment Opportunity Commission,
175
Equal Rights Amendment (ERA), 177
Ervin, Sam, 156
European Defense Community (EDC), 55
European Economic Community. *See* Common
Market
European Recovery Program (ERP). *See* Mar-
shall Plan
European Steel and Coal Community, 28
Evers, Medgar, 100
Existentialism, 195, 199

F

Fair Deal, 20–22, 77, 91, 118
Farmers, 13, 21, 22, 92, 170–72, 180; housing for,
97, 179; income, 171; voting, 19–20, 110. *See
also* Agriculture
Faubus, Orval, 85
Federal Bureau of Investigation (FBI), 34, 151,
157–58
Ford, Gerald, 151, 162
Formosa. *See* Taiwan
Forrestal, James F., 4, 17
France, 23, 26, 126; and Common Market, 97;
and Germany, 5, 8, 29, 55; and Indochina,

41–42, 58–59, 129, 131; and NATO, 28, 55; and Suez crisis, 60–61
Franklin, John Hope, 100
Freedom Riders, 99
Friedan, Betty, 176
Fuchs, Klaus, 34
Fulbright, William, 15, 36

G

Gavin, James, 56
Geneva Conference (1955), 59–60, 62, 79
Germany, 3, 4, 5, 6, 8, 25, 27, 29, 120, 166, 174; and Common Market, 97; and NATO, 55. *See also* Berlin
Gideon v. *Wainwright,* 188
Ginsberg, Allen, 182
Gold, Harry, 34
Goldwater, Barry, 81, 107–10, 132, 140, 155
Gonzalez, Henry, 178
Grand Alliance, dissolution of, 1–9
Gray, L. Patrick, 158
Great Britain, 4, 23, 24, 59, 174; and colonialism, 41, 42; economy, 23, 26, 166; and Germany, 5, 8, 29; and Iran, 7; and NATO, 28, 55; and Suez crisis, 60–61
Great Society, The, 107, 110, 118
Greece, 23, 24, 25, 28, 201
Griffin-Landrum Act (Labor-Management Reporting and Disclosure Act), 82, 174

H

Haggerty, James, 63
Haldeman, H. R., 152, 156, 157
Harding, Warren G., 79, 80, 109, 155, 158
Harriman, Averell, 4, 125
Hartley, Fred, 15, 16
Hassan, Ihab, 198
Heller, Joseph, 198
Higher Education Act, 112
Higher Education Facilities Act, 105, 111
Hiss, Alger, 33, 34, 70, 143
Ho Chi Minh, 129
Hodges, Luther, 94
Hoffa, James, 173
Hoover, Herbert, 14, 22, 33, 142, 165
Hopkins, Harry, 4, 22
House Committee on Un-American Activities, 33
Housing, 15, 20, 21, 77, 97, 106, 112, 168, 179, 186, *illus.* 164, 191; open, 114, 115–16
Housing Act of 1961, 97
Humphrey, George, 54, 75, 76
Humphrey, Hubert, 91, 92, 108, 140, 141, 142, 153
Hungary, 60–61, 80
Hutchins, Robert M., 91

I

Immigration and Nationality Act, 111
India, 41, 43, 59, 62, 63, 126
Indians, American, 139, 178–79, 200, *illus.* 178

Indochina, 41, 42, 58–59, 120, 129, 131. *See also* Cambodia, Laos, Vietnam
Indonesia, 41, 42, 59
Inflation, 10–13, 21, 82, 149, 150, 160, 162, 202; in Latin America, 127; in Vietnam, 146
Internal Security Act, 34
Iran, 7, 8, 63
Iraq, 61
Israel, 60, 61, 148, 160
Italy, 6, 8, 26, 97

J

Japan, 6, 8, 41, 44–45, 63, 146–47, 166, 171, 201, 202
Jenner, William, 74
Job Corps, 106
Johnson, Lady Bird, 133
Johnson, Lyndon B., 22, 91, 101, 105–7, 139, 143, 153, 179, *illus.* 104; and civil rights, 84, 99, 100, 105, 106, 108, 110, 113–15, 118; and Congress, 105–7, 109, 110–15, 118, 134; and Dominican Republic, 128; and economy, 106, 108, 110, 112, 117, 118, 180; and education, 106, 111–12, 118, 150; and foreign policy, 127, 128, 129, 133; and immigration laws, 111; and labor, 108; and 1964 election, 108–10; and 1968 election, 139, 141; and Vietnam, 118–19, 128–36, 141, 144; and welfare programs, 14, 106–7, 108, 110, 112, 118, 180
Jones, James, 199
Joplin, Janis, 185
Jordan, 41, 61, 148
Josephy, Alvin, 178

K

Kefauver, Estes, 70, 80
Kennan, George, 25
Kennedy, John F., 14, 59, 95–97, 107, 108, 139, 143, 149, 153, 180, *illus.* 95; and Alliance for Progress, 127; assassination, 100, 105; and Berlin crisis, 120–21; and business, 95, 97, 98–99; Catholicism, influence of, 80, 92–93, 96; and civil rights, 99–100, 113, 115; and Congress, 100; and Cuba, 65–66, 120, 122–25; economic policies of, 97–100, 110, 180; and foreign policy, 97–98, 100, 119–20, 125–26, 127, 202; and immigration laws, 111; and labor, 96, 98; and national defense, 121–22, 126; and 1960 election, 91–94; and Peace Corps, 127; and U-2 flights, 64; and Vietnam, 120, 129, 131
Kennedy, Robert, 93, 94, 99, 123, 125, 139, 140
Kerouac, Jack, 182
Key, V. O., 93
Khrushchev, Nikita, 48, 56–58, 62, 119, *illus.* 57; and Berlin crisis, 120–21; and Cuban missile crisis, 124–25; at Geneva Conference, 59–60; and U-2 incident, 63–64
Killian, James R., 89
King, Martin Luther, Jr., 84, 85, 93, 99, 114, 115, 116, 139, *illus.* 115
Kissinger, Henry, 143, 145, 148, 154, 160, 201
Kleindienst, Richard, 156

Stevenson, Adlai E., 66, 70, 72, 73, 79, 80, 91, 94, 126, *illus.* 71

Stimson, Henry L., 4

Strategic Arms Limitation (SALT), 147

Student Nonviolent Coordination Committee (SNCC), 116

Students for a Democratic Society (SDS), 183

Styron, William, 199

Suburbs, 114; growth in, 189–90; voting in, 110, 142, 162

Suez crisis, 60–61

Supreme Court, 21, 77, 78–79, 187–89; and Johnson, 113; and Nixon, 141, 151–52, 161; and racial segregation, 80, 82–83, 84, 85

Syria, 42, 61, 148

T

Taft, Robert A., 14, 21, 52, 75, 76, 77, 78; and neo-isolationism, 54, 70, 74; and Taft-Hartley Act, 15–16

Taft-Hartley Act, 15–16, 19, 20, 75, 82, 96, 174

Taiwan (Formosa), 44, 45, 46, 47, 54, 63, 146, 147

Taxes, 15, 53, 76, 81–82, 98, 105, 108, 118, 149, 150, 153, 154; excess profits, 12, 53; Revenue Act of 1945, 12; of 1948, 17; and revenue sharing, 150

Taylor, Maxwell, 56

Television, 181, 200; and Kennedy, 92, 97; and Joseph McCarthy, 36; and 1968 Democratic convention, 140; and Nixon, 70–71, 92, 141, 143, 156, 159, 161; and Vietnam, 134

Tennessee Valley Authority (TVA), 76, 77, 109, 170

Thailand, 59

Thurmond, Strom, 18

Tito, Marshal, 7

Tonkin Gulf resolution, 131, 134

Trade Expansion Act, 97, 98, 100

Transportation, 100, 190–92

Trujillo, Rafael, 128

Truman, Harry S., 1, 2, 9–10, 18, 22, 32, 45, 70, 74, 75, 96, 98, 99, 111, 147, *illus.* 1, 20; and armed forces, 17; and civil rights, 18, 20, 21, 22, 34, 100, 115; and Congress, 15–17, 18, 19, 20–21, 24, 27, 34; economic policies of, 11–12, 13–14, 17, 19, 20, 21, 22, 53; and Korean War, 46–47, 49, 50–53; and labor, 11, 13–14, 15–16, 20, 21; and MacArthur, 47, 49, 50–52; and 1948 election, 19–20, 21, 93; and Soviet Union, 3, 4–7, 26–27, 28; and Truman Doctrine, 23–25, 28

Turkey, 6, 7, 8, 23, 24, 25, 28, 122, 201

U

Unemployment, 10, 14, 22, 77, 97, 117–18, 149, 162, 165, 202

United Nations (U.N.), 4, 6, 7, 24–25, 29, 44, 74; and China, 45, 47, 48, 92; and Congo crisis, 43; and Cuba, 66; and Korean War, 46–53; and Suez crisis, 61

Urban League, 88

Urban Mass Transportation Assistance Act, 192

U-2 incident, 63–64, 66, 119

V

Valentine, Elmer, 185

Vandenberg, Arthur H., 24, 26, 29, 46, 74

Vaughn, Harry, 22

Vietcong, 131, 132, 134, 135, 144

Vietminh, 42, 58, 129, 131

Vietnam, 43, 109, 119, 129–36, 141, 143–46, 158, 167, 184, 201, *illus.* 132. *See also* Indochina

Vinson, Fred M., 9, 12, 70, 187

Volunteers in Service to America (VISTA), 106–7

Vonnegut, Kurt, 198

Voting Rights Act, 113

W

Wages, 12, 13, 21, 53, 98, 149, 179; minimum, 21, 97; in the South, 170; of women, 175–77

Wagner Act, 16

Wallace, George C., 114, 140, 141, 142, 154

Wallace, Henry A., 10, 18, 20

War Labor Disputes Act, 15

Warhol, Andy, 196–97

Warren, Earl, 18, 74, 82, 151, 187, 189

Watergate, 152, 154, 155–62, 202

Watkins v. *United States,* 187

Watts riot, 114

Weaver, Robert, 113

Wheeler-Howard Act, 179

Wilkins, Roy, 117

Williams, William Appelman, 2, 3

Wilson, Charles E., Wilson, Woodrow, 72, 105

Women, 73, 106, 150, 153, 175–77, 178, 200; and abortions, 151, 188; in Japan, 44; working, 151, 175, 177, 188, *illus.* 176

Wounded Knee, 179, *illus.* 178

Wright, Richard, 200

X

X, Malcolm, 116, 200

Y

Yalta, 2, 5

Yates v. *United States,* 187

Youth protest movements, 134–35, 140, 144, 182–87, *illus.* 135

Yugoslavia, 7, 8, 147